Behavioral Support

Second Edition

Teachers' Guides to Inclusive Practices

Behavioral Support

Second Edition

by

Rachel Janney, Ph.D.
Blacksburg, Virginia

and

Martha E. Snell, Ph.D.
Charlottesville, Virginia

·P·A·U·L·H·
BROOKES
PUBLISHING Co®

Baltimore • London • Sydney

Paul H. Brookes Publishing Co.
Post Office Box 10624
Baltimore, Maryland 21285-0624
USA

www.brookespublishing.com

Typeset by Spearhead Global, Inc., Bear, Delaware.
Manufactured in the United States of America by
Versa Press, Inc., East Peoria, Illinois.

All of the vignettes in this book are composites of the authors' actual
experiences. In all instances, names have been changed and identifying
details have been altered to protect confidentiality.

Library of Congress Cataloging-in-Publication Data

Janney, Rachel.
    Behavioral support / by Rachel Janney and Martha E. Snell.—2nd ed.
        p.   cm.—(Teachers' guides to inclusive practices)
    Includes bibliographical references and index.
    ISBN-13: 978-1-55766-911-7 (alk. paper)
    ISBN-10: 1-55766-911-2 (alk. paper)
    1. Behavior modification—Case studies. 2. Inclusive education—Case studies.
I. Snell, Martha E. II. Title.
    LB1060.2.J36 2008
    371.39′3—dc22   2007051143

British Library Cataloguing in Publication data are available from the British
Library.

2012   2011   2010   2009   2008

10   9   8   7   6   5   4   3   2   1

Contents

About the Authors

Rachel Janney, Ph.D., Inclusive School Works, Blacksburg, Virginia 24060

Dr. Rachel Janney is a consultant to school systems and developmental disabilities services agencies on issues related to inclusive education and behavioral support. She has worked with children and adults with disabilities in a number of capacities, including as a special education teacher, teacher educator, and researcher. She received her master's degree and later completed a postdoctoral fellowship in special education at Syracuse University and obtained her doctorate in psychological and cultural studies in education from the University of Nebraska–Lincoln. Between 1985 and 2007, Dr. Janney was a professor in the School of Teacher Education and Leadership at Radford University in Virginia, where she taught special education methods courses, supervised teachers in training, served as coordinator of the program in high-incidence disabilities, and was a director of the Training and Technical Assistance Center (T/TAC) for Professionals Serving Individuals with Disabilities. Dr. Janney is an independent consultant, providing inservice training and technical assistance to school systems and agencies seeking to improve their services and supports for children and youth with disabilities.

Martha E. Snell, Ph.D., Professor and Interim Associate Dean for Research, the Curry School of Education, University of Virginia, Room 236, Ruffner Hall, Charlottesville, Virginia 22903

Dr. Martha Snell has taught at the University of Virginia since 1973. Her focus is special education and, specifically, the preparation of teachers of students with intellectual disabilities and severe disabilities and young children with disabilities. Prior to completing her doctoral degree in special education at Michigan State University, Dr. Snell worked with children and adults with disabilities as a residential child care worker, a teacher, and a provider of technical assistance to school and residential programs. In addition to teaching courses at the undergraduate and graduate levels, she directs the graduate program in severe disabilities and coordinates the special education program. She is an active member of the American Association on Intellectual and Developmental Disabilities, TASH, and the National Joint Committee on the Communication Needs of Persons with Severe Disabilities.

Dr. Janney and Dr. Snell have conducted several research projects in inclusive schools and classrooms. These projects have studied the ways that special and general education teachers work together to design and implement adaptations and accommodations for students with disabilities placed in inclusive settings. Both authors are frequent presenters of workshops on topics related to successful inclusive education.

Acknowledgments

We have learned much about positive ways to support people with difficult behavior from our colleagues and friends. Included among those individuals to whom we wish to express our gratitude are Linda Bambara, Fredda Brown, Rob Horner, Herb Lovett, Luanna Meyer, and Ian Evans.

We also wish to acknowledge Kenna Colley, Johnna Elliott, and Cyndi Pitonyak for their valuable contributions to the case studies provided in this book, and for their untiring efforts to improve the lives of persons with disabilities who need positive behavior supports.

Special thanks and appreciation are owed to the faculty and staff at the school we have given the pseudonym Mountain View Elementary School, where students, families, teachers in training, and teacher educators have the privilege of experiencing authentic schoolwide positive behavior support within an inclusive community. This is a school where respect, caring, and concern for others are taught and learned and where best educational practices enable all students to achieve high standards.

Finally, we would like to acknowledge and thank our editors at Paul H. Brookes Publishing Co., Rebecca Lazo and Trish Byrnes, for their excellent guidance, editing, and persistence in helping us complete this book and others in the series.

*To all the educators, parents, and students who are working to create
and maintain inclusive school environments—places where all students
have membership, enjoy social relationships with peers, and have the
needed supports to learn what is important for them to be successful in life*

Introduction

Before the 1970s, many children with learning and behavior problems were removed from their families, local schools, and communities and placed in special schools or institutions. This book is designed primarily for use by teachers and other members of educational teams who are working together to educate these students and their peers in inclusive schools. Inclusive schools welcome all students and provide special education supports and services from a base within general education classrooms. One of the challenges of inclusive education is teaching students who sometimes behave in ways that can be difficult for parents, siblings, educators, and classmates to cope with and understand (Baker, Blacher, Crnic, & Edelbrock, 2002). Some students are disruptive and appear unable to control their feelings and behavior, whereas other students may try to hurt others or even themselves.

In addition to the serious behavior problems that some students may display, educators, parents, and other citizens have grown increasingly concerned about the existing and potential lack of safety and discipline in schools (National Center for Education Statistics, 2006). As more is learned about programs and strategies that improve schoolwide discipline, it has become evident that both individual students with behavior problems and the student body as a whole benefit most from proactive, positive, instructionally based approaches (Didden, Korzilius, van Oorsouw, & Sturmey, 2006).

This book describes and illustrates processes and tools that teachers, along with parents, administrators, educators, and school staff, can use to provide schoolwide, group, and individual interventions to address behavior problems in schools. The approach is most effective when classroom educators, administrators, school staff, and parents work collaboratively and in concert to create integrated systems for the school as a whole, for classrooms, and for individual students. The type of intervention applied will differ depending on the students addressed and the degree of specialization required, but schoolwide, classwide, and student-specific approaches to improving school discipline and student conduct are based on similar conceptions of behavior problems and behavior change and similar perspectives on the roles and responsibilities of teachers and schools in addressing them. The authors are careful to indicate which practices have been confirmed as effective by sound research and practice, which are based on "best guesses," and which are advocated based on values and philosophies. The purpose of this book is to help faculties and educational teams become better collaborative problem solvers; it is not meant to provide a "cookbook" approach to behavioral intervention. Although the principles and many of the practices described are useful in many educational settings, the examples and case studies provided come from our work in inclusive schools.

This book's organization and content reflect a three-tiered model for categorizing the systems of behavioral intervention used in schools that have adopted positive behavior supports (PBS; see Figure I). The model—originally based on the three-tiered model of prevention in public health—was adapted by Walker, Ramsey, and Gresham (2004) to classify the three tiers of intervention strategies required to provide a full continuum of behavioral supports in schools. The three tiers of interventions—primary, secondary, and

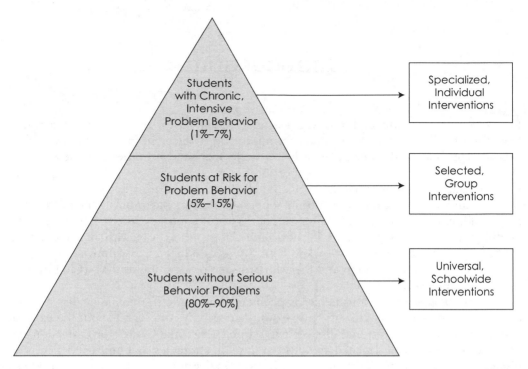

Figure I. Comprehensive systems of schoolwide positive behavior support. (From Walker, Ramsey, & Gresham, 2004; reprinted by permission of Wadsworth, a division of Thomson Learning.)

tertiary—are based on their intended prevention outcomes. According to this model, the goal of *primary prevention* is to prevent new cases of problem behavior, the goal of *secondary prevention* is to ameliorate current cases of problem behavior, and the goal of *tertiary prevention* is to reduce the intensity and complexity of current cases of problem behavior (Walker et al., 2004).

When applied to PBS in schools, primary prevention uses *universal interventions* that are part of a broad, schoolwide system of well-defined, consistent discipline policies, effective academic instruction, and social skills development. Universal interventions are effective in inhibiting the development of problem behavior for approximately 80% to 90% of students. Secondary prevention focuses on students (estimated at 5% to 15% of students) who exhibit risk behaviors such as poor school performance, affiliation with violent peer groups, and poor social skills. The *selected interventions* (e.g., adult mentors, self-management support, environmental supports such as careful scheduling) designed for these students often are delivered to small groups of students with similar emerging behavior problems.

The goal of tertiary prevention measures is to reduce the harm inflicted and experienced by the 1% to 7% of students who display chronic, severe problem behavior. These students require *specialized interventions* that are more individualized and intensive. They benefit from comprehensive PBS at school but will often need out-of-school services as well (Walker et al., 2004).

Chapter 1 describes the basic principles underlying the concept of PBS and its use in schools. Chapter 2 examines the development of a schoolwide systems approach to discipline and universal behavioral supports that help to create and sustain an environment in which behavior problems are prevented and/or more effectively ameliorated. Chapter 3 describes ways to provide selected interventions for groups of students whose behavior problems are not adequately improved through schoolwide interventions and/or who experience risk factors for developing more serious problem behavior.

Chapters 4 and 5 address the more specialized, individualized level of PBS required for students who exhibit the most severe problem behaviors. Chapter 4 outlines the process of gathering and analyzing functional behavioral assessment information to develop individualized behavioral support plans. Chapter 5 details intervention strategies and other supports that compose a behavioral support plan and ways to monitor and evaluate the plan's effectiveness.

Some of the chapters include "Student Snapshots," or case studies to illustrate how the chapter's topic has been used in schools. Where worksheets or other planning tools are described, examples of completed worksheets are included within the chapter. Blank worksheets for teachers to photocopy and use are provided in Appendix A at the end of the book.

This book, like others in the *Teachers' Guides to Inclusive Practices* series, is designed to be practical and user-friendly and to provide information about research-based practices that have been effectively applied in typical schools. The authors' primary intent is to provide teachers, along with the administrators, other educators, and parents with whom they work, with the foundational and applied knowledge needed to fill their vital role in planning, implementing, and evaluating PBS for the students in their schools and classrooms. Even when the guidance and assistance of outside experts is needed—such as for conducting the functional behavioral assessments described in Chapter 4—teachers should feel confident that they understand the purposes and general methods being used. And, when administrative support is required to put positive behavioral approaches into practice, teachers need to know how to advocate for the leadership, resources, and backing needed to enable them to fill their own roles effectively.

REFERENCES

Baker, B.L., Blacher, J., Crnic, K.A., & Edelbrock, C. (2002). Behavior problems and parenting stress in families of three-year-old children with and without developmental delays. *American Journal on Mental Retardation, 107*, 433–444.

Didden, R., Korzilius, H., van Oorsouw, W., & Sturmey, P. (2006). Behavioral treatment of challenging behaviors in individuals with mild mental retardation: Meta-analysis of single-subject research. *American Journal on Mental Retardation, 111*, 290–298.

National Center for Education Statistics. (2006). *The condition of education 2006*. Washington, DC: Author. Retrieved from http://nces.ed.gov/pubsearch/pubsinfo.asp?pubid=2006071

Walker, H.M., Ramsey, E., & Gresham, F.M. (2004). *Antisocial behavior in school: Evidence-based practices*. Belmont, CA: Wadsworth/Thomson Learning.

Behavioral Support

Second Edition

Chapter 1

Positive Behavior Support

USING POSITIVE BEHAVIOR SUPPORTS IN SCHOOL

Anyone who has been a teacher knows that there are always some students who have difficulty following the rules, getting along with others, controlling their emotions, or staying focused on the task at hand. Some students seem to get into trouble on purpose or seem to do things that make it difficult for others to want to spend time with them. Some even hurt themselves or others, or become involved in gangs and other subcultures that commit destructive and violent behavior. Why do some children behave in ways that can be so difficult to understand?

There are many different theories, models, and approaches to addressing behavior problems. An approach that is provided in this book to help students with behavior problems has been described as *positive behavior support* (PBS). This approach evolved in the 1980s as a movement away from traditional, mechanistic, and even aversive behavior management practices that were being applied to individuals with disabilities and toward behavior intervention grounded in person/student-centered values and socially valued outcomes (e.g., Donnellan, LaVigna, Negri-Shoultz, & Fassbender, 1988; Evans & Meyer, 1985; Horner et al., 1990; Lovett, 1985; Meyer & Evans, 1989). The movement sought to use the principles of behavior change that had been demonstrated through applied behavior analysis in contrived, isolated laboratories or segregated settings within effective yet practical interventions that could be implemented by educators in regular school settings (Carr et al., 2002). The movement also insisted that behavior-change practices for persons with disabilities must be respectful and individualized and result in quality-of-life improvements, not only in the reduction of targeted behavior

problems (Evans & Meyer, 1985; Horner et al., 1990).

A PBS approach emphasizes the use of collaborative teaming and problem-solving processes to create supports, programs, and other interventions that stress prevention and remediation of problem behaviors through the provision of effective educational programming and the creation of a supportive environment. The approach helps support students with behavior problems in a systematic, holistic way rather than by using a trial-and-error or fragmented approach. Although behavioral principles such as the role of consequences in shaping behavior are incorporated, positive behavior supports are not a set of rules and procedures for disciplining students with behavior problems. Instead, the emphasis of this approach is on preventing problem behaviors and teaching students alternative behaviors. The supports are based on a philosophy that places the development of positive relationships and successful participation in daily life at the heart of any effort to help people with difficult behaviors. A PBS approach recognizes individual choices and uses only interventions that are normalized and respectful (Turnbull et al., 2002).

Although PBS is a complex, multifaceted approach to behavior intervention and therefore difficult to study scientifically, the research base has grown dramatically over the past 20 years. PBS has thus been established as an effective approach that can be used by people close to the person with a problem behavior so that he or she can live and go to school in typical, inclusive settings (see Table 1.1). The use of PBS also has been incorporated into the Individuals with Disabilities Education Improvement Act of 2004 (PL 108-446), strengthening the support for practices such as conducting functional behavioral assessments (FBA)

Table 1.1. Effectiveness of positive behavior supports and future research needs

What the Research Says

Effectiveness of Positive Behavior Supports and Future Research Needs

Three major reviews of the published research on use of PBS with children and youth with disabilities have been published since 1999 (Carr et al., 1999; Horner, Carr, Strain, Todd, & Reed, 2002; Snell, Voorhees, & Chen, 2005). These reviews have supported the following findings about the effectiveness of PBS and the types of interventions used and that research is still needed to promote the most effective applications of PBS in schools and community settings.

Effectiveness of PBS

- PBS was successful in achieving at least an 80% reduction in targeted behavior problems for approximately two thirds of the behavioral outcomes that were studied. The behaviors studied most often were self-injury, aggression, and combinations (Carr et al., 1999; Horner et al., 2002).
- PBS was more effective when carried out by significant people in the individual's life (e.g., educators, families) than by people who did not have ongoing relationships with the individual (e.g., researchers, clinicians; Carr et al., 1999).
- PBS worked as effectively with individuals who have multiple disabilities as with individuals who have a single disability (Carr et al., 1999).
- The success of interventions nearly doubled when they were based on functional behavioral assessment (Carr et al., 1999).

Types of Interventions Used and Their Effectiveness

- The most frequently reported interventions were 1) positive reinforcement for appropriate behavior or use of an alternative skill (78%), 2) antecedent manipulations (65%), and 3) teaching replacement behaviors that match the function of the problem behavior (81% of studies of children with autism [Horner et al., 2002] and 49% of studies of individuals with disabilities [Snell, Voorhees, & Chen, 2005]).
- Multiple interventions tended to be more effective than single interventions. More than 75% of studies used multicomponent interventions, including antecedent manipulation, maximizing contingent access to rewarding events, minimizing the likelihood that problem behavior would be rewarded, and teaching socially appropriate behaviors that produced the same effects as the problem behavior (Carr et al., 1999; Horner et al., 2002).
- Antecedent manipulations, which change aspects of the environment (e.g., the people present, schedules, instructional activities) to reduce the likelihood of problem behavior or to increase the likelihood of positive behavior, were more effective than when the environment was not reorganized (Carr et al., 1999; Horner et al., 2002).
- Systems change procedures, including changing the structure or organization of the environment (e.g., changing personnel, providing supported employment or other enriching activities) or changing the behavior of people in the environment, increased the effectiveness of interventions. Only half of the outcomes reported, however, used these procedures (Horner et al., 2002).

Critical Features of PBS that Have Not Been Adequately Researched

- More research is needed to identify variables related to achieving comprehensive, long-term lifestyle changes, such as improvements in family life, work, and social relationships, and variables related to providing long-term support for individuals (Carr et al., 1999; Snell et al., 2005).
- The use of crisis management or emergency procedures has not been examined satisfactorily. There are questions about how well educators understand the distinction between the temporary solution afforded by emergency procedures and the proactive programming that is the heart of intervention to change extreme behavior (Snell et al., 2005).
- There is a need to further examine the social validation of PBS. Social validation of some sort was reported in only 22% of the research reviewed by Snell et al. (2005), and 3%–13% of that reviewed by Carr et al. (1999).
- Collaboration by researchers with parents or special educators has not been studied adequately. Only 25% of the research mentioned any sort of collaboration of the researchers with nonresearchers (Snell et al., 2005).
- More data are needed to document the factors affecting generalization and maintenance of positive behavior change (Horner et al., 2002).

(*Sources:* Carr et al., 1999; Horner, Carr, Strain, Todd, & Reed, 2002; Snell, Voorhees, & Chen, 2005.)

The Individuals with Disabilities Education Improvement Act (IDEA) of 2004 includes several requirements concerning school disciplinary procedures and strategies for addressing behavior problems of students with disabilities.

1. The use of positive behavior support (PBS) must be considered in two situations:
   a. During the development, review, and revision of an individualized education program (IEP) for a child whose behavior impedes his or her learning or the learning of others, the IEP team must "consider, if appropriate, strategies including positive behavior interventions and supports, and other strategies, to address that behavior."
   b. When a child with a disability violates a code of student conduct and is removed from his or her current placement more than 10 consecutive school days (unless the removal is due to certain specific reasons, such as behavior that resulted in bodily injury or other zero tolerance offenses), and if the local education agency, the parent, and relevant members of the IEP team determine that the conduct was a manifestation of the child's disability, the IEP team must conduct a functional behavioral assessment (FBA) and implement a behavioral intervention plan (BIP) for the child. If a BIP already has been developed, the team must review the BIP and modify it as necessary to address the behavior.

2. The IDEA 2004 does not specifically prohibit any particular behavior intervention strategies, but it does require that the behavior support plans developed for students who receive special education be based on an FBA process such as the one described in this book, and that PBS be considered.

Figure 1.1.   Individuals with Disabilities Education Improvement Act of 2004 and positive behavior support.

and developing individualized PBS plans based on FBA (see Figure 1.1).

Research is still needed to develop specific guidelines for the most efficient and effective ways to implement and evaluate PBS in schools. Research on punishment-based interventions, however, clearly shows their limited effectiveness on generalization and maintenance of behavior improvements (Strauss, 1994) and their ineffectiveness in reducing the antisocial behavior (e.g., aggression, vandalism) of students with emotional and behavior disorders (Mayer & Sulzer-Azaroff, 2002). Furthermore, punishment-based interventions run counter to the deep-seated values of equality and respect evident in our schools and society.

CORE FEATURES AND PRINCIPLES OF POSITIVE BEHAVIOR SUPPORT

The behavior-change methods that are incorporated within a school-based PBS approach are those that have demon-

strated effectiveness, are suitable for implementation by teachers and others in a school setting, and are based on values of equality and respect. Several distinct features and principles about the causes of behavior problems, the most appropriate and helpful ways to alter behavior, and the desired outcomes of behavioral intervention are at the foundation of a PBS orientation. PBS incorporates five core features and principles that distinguish it from other approaches to behavior intervention:

1. Behavior is learned and can change

2. Intervention is based on functional behavioral assessment

3. Comprehensive intervention emphasizes prevention and teaching

4. Interventions and outcomes are personally and socially valued

5. Intervention requires comprehensive, integrated supports

These features may be given slightly different names in various writings on PBS (Carr et al., 2002; Crone & Horner, 2003;

Turnbull et al., 2002), but the underlying concepts remain consistent. The features apply to each of the three levels of behavior intervention—primary, secondary, and tertiary—but are implemented differently depending on whether the intervention is schoolwide, for a smaller group of students, or for an individual student. Figure 1.2 contrasts the three levels of prevention with regard to the students addressed, the assessments required, and the type of intervention used.

Behavior Is Learned and Can Change

From a PBS perspective, the question "Why do people act in ways that are difficult to understand, disturbing to others, and even destructive to self, others, and property?" can be answered this way: A person's behavior is a function of the interaction between the person and the environment. According to this theory, which is sometimes referred to as an *ecological theory* of behavior, behavior problems are not just a reflection of some emotional or mental disturbance that dwells within the person. Although it is true that behavior is affected by individual biochemical, cognitive, physical, and psychosocial characteristics, behavior also is strongly affected by the environment in which one functions. Factors in the environment include the physical space, the people present, the social atmosphere, the events and activities, and the rules and norms affect the way people act. The environment can elicit as well as inhibit certain types of behavior. For example, most people behave quite differently at a football game and in a library. The atmosphere at a football stadium elicits enthusiastic cheering and conversation, whereas the atmosphere in a library discourages such loud activities. Because of the personal traits and feelings that each person brings to a situation, some people feel more at ease at a football game, whereas others feel more comfortable in a library. Personal factors, however, can interact differently with the environment at different points in time: A person who typically enjoys football games may leave early rather than remain at a game when she or he gets a migraine headache.

Along with the positive and useful things that children are taught by other people in the environment, many children have been unintentionally taught to use problem behaviors as a way to communicate their wants and needs—for example, the desire to remain at recess rather than go to math class, the need for help in reading a difficult reading assignment, the wish for someone to sit with them at lunch, or the desire to be left alone. The good news about this is that if problem behavior can be learned, it also can be changed through learning. Behavior problems cannot be simply removed, however; they must be replaced with other ways to achieve the same wants and needs. To reduce problem behavior, we must increase appropriate behavior.

Intervention Is Based on Functional Behavioral Assessment

A major principle underlying the PBS approach is that nearly all problem behavior serves a purpose. Knowing the purpose or function that a problem behavior serves for a student is basic to designing a support plan for that student. Behaviors such as tantrums, aggression, and self-injury may be disturbing to others, and we certainly want to help someone to stop engaging in such behaviors. People who exhibit these behaviors often do not have better ways to get their needs met. Also, the disturbing behaviors must be working for the person in some way— that is, they are being reinforced at least some of the time, or the person would probably stop using them.

Prevention levels	Students addressed	Required assessment	Type of intervention	Examples of interventions
Primary (80%–85%)	Those with mild or no problem behavior	Assessment of system (school, class, etc.) via office discipline referral data	Universal interventions devised by broader school staff	• Three to five schoolwide behavioral expectations taught as suited to different school settings • Continuum of rewards • Range of consequences • Violence-prevention skills training • Peer mediation programs
Secondary (5%–15%)	Those at risk for problem behavior	Simple functional assessment	Specialized group interventions devised by grade level or student teams	• Teach replacement skills • Prevention by rearranging the environment • Plan for responding to the problem behavior • Daily behavior card, check-in/check-out • Mentoring by an adult • Instruction in social skills
Tertiary (4%–9%)	Those with a chronic/serious (1%–2%) or dangerous (3%–7%) problem behavior	FBA or functional analysis	Specialized individual intervention addressing school, home, and community settings devised by individual teams	• Teach replacement skills • Prevention by rearranging the environment • Plan for responding to the problem behavior • Wraparound services • Student-centered planning

Figure 1.2. Theoretical model of the schoolwide positive behavior support (SWPBS) continuum of effective behavioral assessment and support. (Source: Snell, M.E. [2006]. What's the verdict: Are students with severe disabilities included in schoolwide positive behavior support? *Research & Practice for Persons with Severe Disabilities, 31*[1], 63.)

A plan for positive behavior intervention and support is based on a *functional behavioral assessment* (FBA) and, in some cases, a *functional analysis*. These assessment processes (which are described in detail in Chapter 4) are used to develop and test hypotheses about the ways the environment is triggering and then reinforcing problem behavior. Analyzing the patterns and relationships among the behavior, the conditions in the environment that precede it, and the ways the behavior is reinforced can reveal the purpose of the behavior.

It is helpful to think of problem behaviors as having one or both of two broad purposes: 1) obtaining something or 2) escaping or avoiding something. Most often, problem behavior serves a social-communicative function: It serves as a way to influence people and the external world. Less often, problem behavior is controlled by internal factors such as having too little or too much internal stimulation.

The social-communicative purposes or functions of behavior problems are

- Obtaining attention, nurturance, comfort, or help

- Obtaining something tangible or preferred activity

- Escaping or avoiding tasks or activities

- Escaping or avoiding attention or other social interaction

The internally controlled or automatically reinforcing functions of behavior (both of which can serve to self-regulate internal stimulation) are

- Obtaining internal stimulation such as deep pressure, visual stimulation, or endorphin release

- Escaping/avoiding internal stimulation such as itching, pain, or hunger (O'Neill et al., 1997)

A key to effective PBS is understanding what the person is obtaining or avoiding by using the problem behavior. This is not to say that the person is necessarily using the behavior intentionally to achieve these purposes; however, research has shown that these are the consequences that commonly maintain problem behavior (Horner & Carr, 1997). Therefore, intervention for socially mediated behaviors includes prevention of situations that predict the problem and teaching alternative social-communicative behaviors to serve the same purpose. Intervention for internally controlled problem behavior requires changing the cause of the stimulation (e.g., physical pain, sensitivity) and teaching the person skills to obtain or escape stimulation in less problematic ways. In addition to altering the antecedents and teaching replacement behaviors, the adults implementing the intervention plan must ensure that their responses make the new, appropriate behavior work better than the old, problem behavior.

The following student snapshots describe children and young adults the authors have known. Their behaviors help illustrate the varied purposes of problem behaviors.

Student Snapshots

Jenny is 6 years old and in the first grade. She has a significant cognitive disability and mild cerebral palsy. She speaks only a few words and has no other conventional communication system. When Jenny wants more juice at snack time or does not want to put the blocks away when it is time to clean up after center time, she points to the thing she wants and shrieks. Her teachers and the classroom instructional assistant often feel that there is virtually nothing that Jenny likes to do except eat snacks and look at books. It is quite clear that Jenny is saying "I want juice" or "I want the blocks" when

she shrieks and cries. Her shrieking serves to get something tangible.

Brian is a second grader who has a difficult time coping with frustration. The situations that are frustrating for Brian at school include independent practice activities that take more than 5–10 minutes to complete and activities such as learning centers that require students to make choices about the order in which they will complete a series of tasks. Brian can communicate quite well when he is calm and engaged in an activity; however, when he becomes frustrated, he is not able to explain how he feels or to ask for help. Instead, he destroys materials, hits other children, and tries to leave the room. These behaviors seem to be a way for him to say, "This is too hard! I can't do this!" Brian's behaviors serve the function of escape or avoidance of a difficult task.

Jason is a fourth grader with autism. He uses a few words and signs and has basic reading, writing, and math skills; however, he is not adept at communicating his feelings. When Jason is in a place where there are a lot of people, noise, and confusion, he sits and rocks back and forth. He appears to use this behavior as a way to shut out the noise and confusion, the same way that other people might put their hands over their ears and close their eyes. These behaviors enable Jason to escape internal stimulation that is aversive to him.

Alicia is a tenth grader who is classified as having a behavior disorder and a obsessive-compulsive disorder for which she takes medication. She has good general knowledge and basic skills and can communicate quite well with the adults in her life; however, Alicia lacks skills for initiating social interactions and making friends with her peers. When she wants to interact with peers, she may approach them and make a rude or off-color comment as she laughs loudly, or she may become physically aggressive. Although these behaviors do not help Alicia to make friends, she usually gets a dramatic reaction from her peers. Alicia seems to crave attention so much that she wants any type of peer attention, whether it is positive or negative.

Coping with the behaviors displayed by some students is a difficult task for teachers and parents; the goal is to teach these students other ways of expressing themselves and getting their wants and needs met. Unless teachers and parents understand the purpose or purposes that a problem behavior serves, however, they will not be able to help the student accomplish that purpose in other ways. Once teachers and parents understand the consequences that are maintaining the behavior and how the behavior works for the student, they are in a better position to develop a plan for change that will help the student learn and use more appropriate behaviors that will serve the same purpose (Durand, 1988; Evans & Meyer, 1985).

FBA involves gathering data through indirect (e.g., interview, self-reflection) and direct observations of baseline and intervention conditions and analyzing those data for patterns of behavior. Functional analysis, which involves purposefully manipulating the behavior in order to test hypotheses about its function, may or may not be necessary in every case. (Figure 1.2 summarizes the required assessments for each level of intervention.) One of the most important findings of research on PBS is that when systematically collected information about the student's behavior problems and the environmental variables associated with them is used as the basis for behavioral support interventions, the likelihood of success increases significantly (Carr, Horner, et al., 1999; Didden, Korzilius, van Oorsouw, & Sturmey, 2006; Scotti, Evans, Meyer, & Walker, 1991).

Comprehensive Intervention Emphasizes Prevention and Teaching

The fundamental practices used in PBS focus not on manipulating consequences to manage or suppress problem behavior but on preventing problem behavior by improving the environment and teaching new skills that give students ways to communicate and meet their needs without having to resort to difficult behaviors.

A PBS approach puts emphasis on

- Using the strategies that educators and parents have available to them to change the environment to prevent problem behavior and to promote positive behavior

- Teaching students the new skills they need to be more effective as individuals and as members of their families, schools, and communities

It is the responsibility of educators and other adults whose role is to help students grow and develop to take the first steps to improve behavior. Intervention typically begins with teachers and other adults who have created the setting in which the student is required to function. Educators cannot control a student's history or personality, but they can create and control many of the conditions that will help support success and inhibit failure. Improving the fit between the person and the environment by creating an environment for success is a fundamental intervention strategy when using PBS.

Multiple intervention components are used to achieve the sorts of meaningful outcomes that are the goal of a plan for PBS. A recent review of individualized PBS intervention programs found that almost 80% of the studies applied more than one type of intervention and up to five interventions (Snell, Voorhees, & Chen, 2006). When educational teams provide PBS for students, they use a much broader approach to behavior intervention than the contingency management or reinforcement procedures typically seen in a behavior management approach. The supports that teachers and other adults provide for students are multiple and may include

- Individualized education program (IEP) accommodations (e.g., a place to go to calm down, additional adult supervision during transitions, extended time for completing assignments)

- Curricular adaptations (e.g., a simplified curriculum or one that emphasizes functional skills)

- Instruction in communication skills

- Instruction in social skills or self-management techniques

- Changes to the classroom environment (e.g., preferential seating, a quiet place to study or read)

- Opportunities to make choices

- Instruction in the use of classroom schedules

- Creative scheduling (e.g., placement in classes with particular peers, placement in heterogeneous classes, alternating easy and difficult subjects or courses)

- Support of peer buddies, partners, or tutors

Interventions and Outcomes Are Personally and Socially Valued

In the broadest terms, the goal of a three-tiered schoolwide PBS system is prevention of behavior problems both currently and in the future. Other objectives include enhancements of social skills and overall social competence, development of personal responsibility, and academic success. The goals of specialized PBS for students with the most severe behavior challenges are not limited to reducing behaviors of concern within specific settings, although such changes compose one desired outcome. A PBS approach takes a much broader view of the possible outcomes of behavioral intervention and supports (see Figure 1.3).

Goals of PBS also include helping students to 1) develop new communication, social, and self-control skills; 2) form more positive relationships with classmates, teachers, and other community members; and 3) take more active and autonomous roles in their classrooms,

Student behavior change	• Decreased problem behaviors, sustained over time • Improved communication skills • Increased social and self-management skills
Student quality of life	• Greater participation in activities at home, in school, and in the community • Increased and improved peer interactions and relationships • More opportunities for autonomy • Improved health
Individual staff change	• Improved teaching strategies • Improved communication skills • Increased problem-solving ability
Organizational effectiveness	• Improved team effectiveness • Increased interactive problem solving • Improved systems for prevention of behavior problems

Figure 1.3. Multiple outcomes of positive behavior supports. (From Meyer, L., & Janney, R. [1989]. User-friendly measures of meaningful outcomes: Evaluating behavioral interventions. *Journal of the Association for Persons with Severe Handicaps, 14*[4], 264–270; and Mount, B., & Zwernik, K. [1989]. *It's never too early, it's never too late: A booklet about Personal Futures Planning* [Report No. 421-88-109]. St. Paul: Minnesota Governor's Planning Council on Developmental Disabilities; adapted by permission.)

schools, and communities. These outcomes may be preceded by, accompanied by, and/or followed by improvements in academic achievement. In addition to the positive outcomes for the individual student, PBS can result in improved family quality of life, as indicated by measures such as improved family interaction (e.g., enjoyment of spending time together), increased feelings of safety at home, work, and school and in the neighborhood (cf. Smith-Bird & Turnbull, 2005).

The practices described and illustrated in this book were selected based on their proven effectiveness in reducing problem behavior; increasing socially acceptable behavior; and generalizing and maintaining those behavioral changes through means that are respectful, normalized, and suited to the student's age, culture, and gender (Carr et al., 1999; Horner, Carr, Strain, Todd, & Reed, 2002; Snell et al., 2005). Along with other criteria, PBS interventions are judged by the extent to which they achieve good *contextual fit*, meaning that

• Teachers, parents, and others assisting with implementation have the *skills* to implement the plan

• The procedures are consistent with teachers', parents', and students' *values* and beliefs about how students should be treated

• Parents and teachers view the plan as potentially *effective and efficient* because the procedures are feasible and can be implemented within typical routines and activities

• Adequate *resources* are available to implement the plan (e.g., staff time, material resources)

• *Administrative support* is provided to ensure that the plan is managed and monitored effectively (Albin, Lucyshyn, Horner, & Flannery, 1996)

In short, interventions must be acceptable to the student and his or her PBS team, not too difficult to implement, and yield results relatively quickly. Plans need to include strategies based on the FBA and chosen specifically to suit the context and the team members who will apply them. Otherwise, interventions will not be implemented by school team members willingly and competently (Walker, Ramsey, & Gresham, 2004).

Intervention Requires Comprehensive, Integrated Supports

A clear finding from research on problem behavior in schools is that multiple systems of support are required to create and sustain safe schools with a positive climate, high levels of academic achievement, and plans for the prevention of problem behavior (Carr et al., 1999). A continuum of least-to-most special or universal-to-individualized supports is needed, including universal interventions for all students, selected interventions for some students, and specialized PBS for a few students. Designing and implementing PBS plans that are based on FBA and that involve systematically putting into place multiple interventions and supports require more than the care and concern of one staff member or a small team of people. The use of effective PBS for students with the most serious behavior problems requires systems and processes to ensure *high-fidelity implementation*. These systems and processes include collaborative teaming with family, student involvement, in-service training and other staff development activities, staff time, leadership, consultative services, and evaluation.

In the case of students with severe, long-standing emotional and behavior disorders, supports may need to extend outside of school and to involve multiple agencies and individuals other than those on the student's IEP team. The needs of students with severe emotional and behavior disorders for services and supports outside the school setting also are addressed through wraparound systems of care that address both the student's and the family's needs and strengths. In these cases, student-centered planning may be the process used to develop strategies for improving the student's quality of life (Scott & Eber, 2003).

POSITIVE BEHAVIOR SUPPORT TEAMS

Addressing any level of antisocial, disruptive, or destructive behavior calls for a team effort. Whether the problem is minor misbehavior that occurs frequently schoolwide or the severe, chronic behavior problems of a few students, a team effort involving parents, teachers, psychologists, administrators, and other knowledgeable people is needed. A team approach brings together different ideas, knowledge, and skills. Educators know how to teach and manage classrooms, parents know their child best, and psychologists have expertise in behavior-change principles. Used alone, these different skills may not be enough for a successful approach to a student's problem behavior; however, when these different skills are used together, with teamwork, each person's skills are more powerful.

Schools that implement effective PBS systems use various team configurations. Creating three teams, one to facilitate each level of intervention (i.e., universal, selected/group, and specialized or student specific) is one possible approach. A more manageable approach, however, may be to institute two permanent teams: 1) a schoolwide PBS planning team that coordinates the comprehensive schoolwide effort and 2) a student-focused PBS team that facilitates both group and individual student interventions. While some members of the student-focused PBS team take the lead responsibility for planning and facilitating selected group interventions, others focus more on facilitating the work of individual students' support teams (Freeman et al., 2006).

The schoolwide planning team should include members who provide broad representation of faculty, staff, parents, and administrators, as well as individuals with expertise in PBS. The schoolwide planning team is most familiar with the data that can indicate the prevalence and distribution of office disciplinary referrals and other student data that are reported at the administrative level. The PBS team that facilitates interventions for groups of students or individual students also must include faculty and staff, parents or guardians, an administrator, and members with FBA/PBS expertise. The team may also include ad hoc members with expertise in particular programs or strategies being implemented (e.g., social skills, conflict management, augmentative communication). Decisions about providing selected group and specialized supports for students should be made using a protocol that has been designed by both the schoolwide planning team and the student-focused PBS team and agreed to by the faculty and staff in general.

When a student with severe behavioral difficulties receives special education services, which is likely to be the case, the student's behavioral support team essentially consists of the core members of the student's IEP team: the student's special education and general education teachers; the parent(s); a school psychologist, a testing specialist, or a behavior specialist; an administrator; and, as relevant and necessary, an instructional assistant and/or related services providers. Siblings and peers often are productive team members, although their participation may be appropriate only at particular meetings. In addition to being required by IDEA and principles of best practice in behavioral support, the involvement of family members and other people who have an ongoing relationship with the student leads to more effective interventions and supports (Carr et al., 1999). Families have important knowledge about their children's lives and are deeply affected by behavior problems and supports (Dunlap, Newton, Fox, Benito, & Vaughn, 2001).

Supplementary team members or consultants from outside the school may be needed to round out the team's expert-

ise, particularly in the area of collecting and interpreting FBA data and conducting functional analyses (Horner, Albin, Sprague, & Todd, 2000). In some places, consultants from the school district administrative offices, a university, or a technical assistance center may be available to assist in developing behavioral support plans.

Team Member Roles and Training

As for any efficient and effective educational team, the roles and responsibilities of team members must be clear. All team members do not need the same level of knowledge and expertise in behavioral assessment and intervention, but all should be responsible for learning the fundamentals of FBA and the collaborative problem-solving process needed to create positive behavior supports. Administrators may not necessarily attend every team meeting, but they should ensure that team members have access to adequate in-service training and consultative support and should be fully informed and supportive of each team's work.

Support teams for individual students need a team coordinator to coordinate the FBA process and the development and monitoring of interventions. This person might be a school psychologist, special education teacher, consulting teacher, or behavioral consultant. Typically, the coordinator is responsible for organizing team meetings and ensuring that all team members are informed about team decisions and serves as liaison between school and out-of-school team members.

As noted previously, there will be cases in which a student's school-based support team members need outside assistance in conducting the assessment and designing a PBS plan. Students with significant cognitive, behavioral, and/or emotional disabilities who have had severe, long-standing behavior problems can have needs so complex that the expertise of a behavioral consultant is needed. Many school support teams, however, find that as they gain skill and experience in using this process, they are able to address many problems with limited outside expertise.

Team Approach to Decision Making

Developing and implementing a school-wide, group, or individual behavioral support program requires a commitment to regular team meetings and ongoing communication among team members and others involved in or affected by the program. Many teachers have had frustrating experiences with meetings and group decision making. Teams can spend too much time sharing stories and never arrive at any decision. Teams sometimes can be dominated by a self-appointed leader who controls the discussion and does not give others a chance to contribute. The authors have found a number of helpful strategies for making team meetings and the team decision-making process both cooperative and efficient:

1. Begin and end the meeting on time.

2. Develop an agenda either before each meeting or at the beginning of the meeting. Begin each meeting by setting time limits for each agenda item.

3. Adopt or develop a team meeting form to use for writing down the agenda and the decisions made by the team. A sample Team Meeting Agenda and Minutes form is shown in Figure 1.4. A blank copy of this form is provided in Appendix A of this book. Completing the Team Meeting Agenda and Minutes form on pressure-sensitive paper enables each team member to leave the meet-

ing with a copy of the minutes. Or, if all team members have access to computers, an electronic template can be created so that minutes can be entered during the meeting and the completed form can be distributed electronically.

4. At each team meeting, ask team members to adopt specific roles. In groups with fewer than four members, each person may need to fill more than one role. In groups with more than four members, some members may not have a particular assigned role at each meeting. In order to distribute accountability among team members and to ensure that the team's decisions reflect everyone's contributions, consider rotating roles at different meetings. Some roles that many teams have found necessary are

   Facilitator: Keeps the meeting moving, making certain that each agenda item is addressed and that the team stays focused on the tasks at hand

   Recorder: Records team decisions and makes certain that all team members receive a copy of the minutes

   Timekeeper: Keeps team members aware of time spent and time remaining in the meeting; makes certain that the team sticks to time limits agreed on for the meeting

   Observer: Gives team members feedback on the group process (e.g., "It seems like we are evaluating ideas when we should be brainstorming," "We need to remember to listen to one another's ideas more carefully")

5. When making decisions about how to address identified problems, use an explicit series of problem-solving steps:

Team Meeting Agenda and Minutes

Student/team __Jason's PBS Team__   **Date** ____3/3/07_____

People present	Role for today	Absentees
Jared, special education teacher	Facilitator	Ashley, aide
Carly, Jason's mother	Timekeeper	Rob, Jason's father
Mara, school psychologist	Recorder	
Rita, fourth-grade teacher		

Purpose of meeting   __Biweekly review of PBS team (fourth week of implementation)_____

Agenda items	Decision or action to be taken	Who and when?
1. Review/discuss behavior data: Are improvements acceptable? Are revisions needed?	• Pushing others decreased by 25% so far; rate is on track for the goal we had set. • Would Jason like to keep a graph of his own? Ask him and help set it up. • Jared needs help with data collection of peer interaction/ replacement behaviors. • Revise visual schedule; he wants the pictures taken off. Also wants a new "finished" folder.	• Everyone keep up the good work! • Jared by 3/10/07 • Mara on 3/5/07 @ 1:00 recess • Jared and his student teacher by 3/7/07
2. Specialty teachers have received written copy of PBS plan but have not been briefed in person.	Specialty teachers will be at schoolwide PBS training next week; ask to meet with them for 20 minutes after the training.	Jared and Ashley by 3/10/07
3. Safety Plan: How often has it been used? Does it need work? Is it being used consistently? Concerns about need to train instructional aides to catch triggers, interrupt as soon as possible, not repeat commands as he escalates.	Meet with aides to review the safety plan and the Incident Records they have written.	Mara will take Jared's bus duty on 3/9/07 so that Jared can meet with aides.

Agenda items for next meeting   **Date:** __3/17/07__   **Time:** _3:10 P.M.–3:30 P.M._

1. Review and discuss progress data; revise plan as necessary.

2. Discuss/brainstorm about possible recreational/leisure activities for after school and Saturdays.

3. Investigate additional relaxation training and techniques. Mara will bring resources.

4.

Figure 1.4.   Completed Team Meeting Agenda and Minutes form for Jason.

- Clearly identify the problems or issues that need to be addressed.

- Brainstorm possible solutions. This is the time for a free flow of ideas, even those ideas that may sound silly at first. Refrain from evaluation at this point.

- Evaluate the pros and cons of each idea. Cross off ideas that the team members agree are not the best. The team's goal is to reach an agreement about the best idea to try.

- Organize the best ideas into an action plan.

6. Establish accountability. The ideas that the team decides to implement will require some action. For example, who will take the photographs for Jason's picture schedule? Who will call Jason's previous teacher to get more information about the behavioral intervention plan that was in place last year? Be sure to record who agrees to do specific tasks and when they will complete them. It is important that everyone pitches in and helps, and team members should not only accept responsibilities but also gently hold other team members accountable. Many plans have failed not because they were bad ideas but because they were never actually used. Another way to reinforce accountability is to begin each meeting by reviewing the tasks that were assigned to each team member at the previous meeting. Please refer to another book in this series for more detail on collaborative teaming (Snell & Janney, 2005).

Chapter 2

Schoolwide Positive Behavior Support

Every school must make the creation of a safe and supportive learning community one of its highest priorities. Each component of this phrase—safe, supportive, learning, community—is critical. Schools may be safe and orderly, but if they fail to build a supportive community and press for high academic expectations, students learn little. Similarly, schools may be warm and supportive, but if they have low expectations for their students, little learning takes place.

Learning First Alliance (2001, p. 1)

As described in Chapter 1, positive behavior supports (PBS) no longer address only the serious behavior problems of students with severe disabilities. PBS is now conceived as a continuum of supports that vary in intensity, complexity, and the number of students targeted. The *universal* interventions and prevention programs that are the subject of this chapter are used with all students in the school: when delivered proactively and consistently, they generally are adequate to prevent antisocial behavior for 80% to 90% of a school population (Walker et al., 2004). Over the past decade, the schoolwide processes, structures, and practices designed to prevent behavior problems at the broadest and most universal level have come to be known as schoolwide positive behavior support (SWPBS; Sugai & Horner, 2002). These interventions are designed to create a safe, healthy learning environment where behavior problems are prevented and students learn the self-discipline that is necessary for a true learning community to flourish.

To be maximally effective, the universal interventions implemented within the SWPBS process must be part of a *comprehensive* system of behavioral supports that also involves selected practices for students at risk for behavioral problems and individualized, intensive supports for the few students with chronic and/or dangerous behavior problems. All three levels of behavior support focus on both academic achievement and social competence; use research-validated and evidence-based practices that are appropriate for use in schools; rely on data-based decision making; and employ a systems approach that includes working groups to guide the program, administrative supports, operating routines such as an action plan process, and professional development (Sugai & Horner, 2002, p. 31). SWPBS, as primary prevention systems, have the important goal of improving the school's overall behavioral climate and limiting the number of students who require more individualized, specialized (and labor-intensive) supports.

RATIONALE
FOR SCHOOLWIDE
POSITIVE BEHAVIOR SUPPORT

Discipline problems, use of drugs, and violence have been among the general public's and teachers' top concerns about schools in their communities for many years (Rose & Gallup, 2006, p. 43). Before the advent of PBS approaches, and continuing today in many schools, school discipline programs tended to be reactive and exclusionary, focusing on the use of negative consequences for misconduct. Since the emergence of *zero-tolerance* policies in the early 1990s, more rigid and extreme applications of suspension and expulsion policies have been mandated, often resulting in the application of the same negative consequences for all offenses, from firearms, drugs, alcohol, and fighting to threats and swearing (Skiba, 2000).

There are a number of reasons why reactive, exclusionary, zero-tolerance approaches to school discipline are ill-advised. Although youth violence has increased dramatically since the early 1980s, relatively little of that violence occurs in schools. Serious violations such as drugs, weapons, and gang activity occur much less frequently in schools than minor disruptive behaviors (Heaviside, Rowand, Williams, & Farris, 1998).

Expelling the relatively small number of students who do commit serious, violent offenses in school does not rid schools of the more frequent problems of disruptive behaviors or incivility. Furthermore, for students with the most severe, chronic antisocial behavior, the use of punishment and disciplinary removal (suspension or expulsion) does not work and is even likely to result in a greater intensity and frequency of antisocial behavior (e.g., aggression, vandalism) and a greater likelihood of dropping out of school (Mayer, 1995; Mayer, Butterworth, Nafpaktitis, & Sulzer-Azaroff, 1983). An additional drawback to the use of punishment and exclusion is revealed in their negative effects on students' social and emotional states, the relationships between the students and the adults in a school, and the culture of the school (Shores, Gunter, & Jack, 1993; Thorson, 1996).

By contrast, for more than 40 years there has been evidence of the success of positive and prevention-oriented approaches to disruptive, violent, and other antisocial behavior in schools (e.g., Sugai & Horner, 2002). Research on schoolwide disciplinary practices associated with PBS (e.g., actively teaching behavioral expectations and social skills, rewarding appropriate behavior, increasing supervision in problem-prone locations) provides convincing evidence of the success these strategies can have in reducing disruptive and antisocial behavior and creating a positive social climate (see Figure 2.1).

What the Research Says

Research Evidence for Schoolwide Positive Behavior Supports

Much of the research related to schoolwide positive behavior supports has examined the effectiveness of schoolwide discipline systems that are consistent with a positive behavior supports orientation. Such systems emphasize prevention, actively teaching behavioral expectations and social skills, and rewarding appropriate behavior.

Schoolwide Unified Discipline Approach

Safe, responsive, effective schools have schoolwide discipline systems that are well defined; clearly communicated to all students, families, teachers, and other school personnel; and consistently implemented. An effective, unified schoolwide discipline approach typically includes six features: 1) a purpose statement that relates the goal and rationale for the discipline system; 2) three to five clearly defined, positively phrased schoolwide expectations for appropriate behavior, along with observable examples of expected behaviors; 3) procedures for actively teaching, monitoring, prompting, and correcting those expectations and behaviors; 4) a variety of ways to acknowledge appropriate, expected behavior; 5) a consistently used continuum of consequences for correcting rule violations; and 6) procedures for record keeping and decision making (Sugai & Horner, 2002).

Research showing that discipline systems incorporating these features significantly reduce disruptive and antisocial behavior and create a positive social climate is quite compelling (Colvin, Sugai, Good, & Lee, 1997; Lewis, Sugai, & Colvin, 1998; Luiselli, Putnam, & Sunderland, 2002; Mayer, 1995; Mayer, Butterworth, & Nafpaktitis, 1983; Nakasato, 2000; Nelson, Martella, & Galand, 1998; Nelson, Martella, & Marchand-Martella, 2002; Oswald, Safran, & Johanson, 2005; Sulzer-Azaroff & Mayer, 1994; Taylor-Greene & Kartub, 2000).

The discipline systems examined in this research incorporated practices such as actively teaching expected behaviors to students; using positive practice, precorrection, verbal praise and individual and group reinforcement systems; actively supervising problem-prone contexts and environments; and establishing a consistently used continuum of consequences for infractions. Some studies measured the effects of schoolwide discipline systems on the incidence of vandalism, assaults, substance use, and other disruptive and antisocial behavior such as hitting, yelling, or arguing. For example,

- Oswald, Safran, and Johanson (2005) saw a 42% reduction in problem hallway behaviors in a middle school after 5 weeks.

Figure 2.1.　Research evidence for schoolwide positive behavior supports.　　　*(continued)*

Figure 2.1.   *(continued)*

> •   Mayer, Butterworth, & Nafpaktitis's (1983) study of vandalism in elementary and junior high schools showed that vandalism costs in participating schools decreased significantly over control schools, with treatment schools averaging a 79% reduction.
>
> Other research has measured reductions in the number of office disciplinary referrals and other administrative disciplinary actions. For example:
>
> •   The rate of office referrals was reduced by 47% after 1 year and 68% in 5 years in the middle school described by Taylor-Greene and Kartub (2005).
> •   Seven elementary schools that implemented schoolwide programs for preventing problem behavior significantly reduced their rates of suspensions, emergency removals, and office referrals in contrast with 28 comparison schools (Nelson, Martella, & Marchand-Martella, 2002).

Positive, prevention-oriented school discipline programs are increasingly advocated by educators, psychologists, parents, university educators, and others who are familiar with the research supporting their effectiveness in increasing behavioral and academic success. Support also comes from reports on violence-prevention programs that have been written for the U.S. Department of Education (2001) and the U.S. Department of Justice (Gottfredson, 1997). These reports have recommended addressing school violence and other antisocial behavior at the primary level of prevention, using universal interventions that are proactive, that include multiple components, and that involve families, students, and the community.

UNIVERSAL INTERVENTIONS FOR EFFECTIVE SWPBS

Effective SWPBS efforts typically entail four components: 1) a safe and responsive school climate, 2) a unified approach to school discipline, 3) active development of students' problem-solving and conflict-resolution skills, and 4) effective academic instruction (Sugai & Horner, 2002). As well as incorporating those four key elements, SWPBS also must use strategies that are *feasible* (Scott & Martinek, 2006). Teachers and other team members must find the SWPBS plan both reason-

able and practical enough to put into place accurately. The total action plan for the school should reflect the simplest and least intrusive set of planning, implementation, and evaluation strategies that will achieve the desired improvements in behavior and academic achievement. In addition, school teams should implement one intervention at a time rather than trying to do everything at once.

The following sections will address three of the four components of effective schoolwide PBS: a safe and responsive school climate, a unified approach to school discipline, and active development of students' social and conflict-resolution skills. The topic of effective academic instruction has been discussed more fully elsewhere, but it should be noted that effective behavior management and effective instructional methods and approaches most often complement one another in generating positive effects on students' academic and social development.

A Safe and Responsive School Climate

Creating and sustaining a positive school climate requires taking active steps to shape and sustain a community where everyone belongs and is valued. Teaching children to be responsible, caring individuals who are adept at forming and maintaining social relationships and who demonstrate good character can seem like a daunting responsibility to teachers and administrators who also are responsible for their students' academic success. However, when students' academic experiences occur in classrooms and schools where they feel safe, valued, and cared for, academic achievement is facilitated (Zins, Weissberg, Walberg, & Wang, 2004). In addition, the social-emotional skills that enable students to be self-directed, make responsible decisions, communicate effectively, and work well with others are not only essential to success in school but to future success in the workplace, the home, and the community (Elias et al., 1997). The goal of education in the United States is traditionally said to be the development of responsible citizens (Langdon, 1997), which requires that students learn to be self-directed, caring, and reflective.

Schools with a positive social and behavioral climate typically evidence these indicators: perceptions by students, teachers, staff, and parents that the school is safe; high attendance rates; minimal general student misbehavior; low rates of juvenile delinquency and behavior disorders; student academic success and social adjustment; and orderly classrooms and public spaces (Irvin, Tobin, Sprague, Sugai, & Vincent, 2004). Accordingly, the rate of behavioral incidents warranting office disciplinary referrals is low. School improvement activities that focus specifically on climate-enhancement (e.g., school fairs, volunteer programs) are complemented by those focused on improving the schoolwide discipline program and teaching social and conflict-resolution skills; these efforts all seem to be reflected in a more positive school climate and decreases in office disciplinary referrals (Irvin et al., 2004).

The Child Development Project (Educators for Social Responsibility, 2006) is a noteworthy example of a comprehensive school-improvement program based on the interconnectedness of positive school climate, appropriate student behavior, and high academic achievement. Over a 3-year period, 12 elementary schools in six different school districts used a combination of components including a student-centered approach to classroom management, increased student collaboration in the classroom, and parent involvement in order to create a "caring community of learners" (Solomon, Battistich, Watson, Schaps, & Lewis, 2000). In the five schools that reliably implemented the program, students made significant gains in their personal, social, and ethical attitudes and values. The analysis authors used to examine these results showed that the program produced positive effects to the degree that it was successful in establishing a caring community in the school (Solomon et al., 2000).

A number of helpful resources on improving school culture and climate are listed in Appendix B.

Schoolwide Unified Discipline Approach

Safe, responsive, and effective schools have schoolwide discipline systems that are well defined; clearly communicated to all students, families, teachers, and other school personnel; and consistently implemented. An effective schoolwide discipline approach typically includes six features:

1. A purpose statement that relates the goal and rationale for the discipline system

2. Three to five clearly defined, positively phrased schoolwide expectations for appropriate behavior, along with observable examples of expected behaviors

3. Procedures for actively teaching, monitoring, prompting, and correcting those expectations and behaviors

4. A variety of ways to acknowledge appropriate, expected behavior

5. A consistently used continuum of consequences for correcting rule violations

6. Procedures for record keeping and decision making (Sugai & Horner, 2002; Sulzer-Azaroff & Mayer, 1994)

Each of these elements—presented as six steps to follow when creating an effective schoolwide discipline system—is briefly described and illustrated in the following section. A series of figures in this section will illustrate aspects of the schoolwide discipline plan used by an elementary school known to the authors. To protect the school's anonymity, we have changed its name in this book to Mountain View Elementary School. This discipline plan incorporates the components and steps described here.

Step 1: Generate a purpose statement that relates the goal and rationale for the discipline system. Most schools have a mission or purpose statement, but that statement may not be used for ongoing guidance in fostering a positive school climate. The statement should be positively phrased, focus on all staff and students, and relate the desired outcomes of social and academic success for all students. For example, *"Hometown Elementary School is a community of learners. We are all here to learn and grow together and to become good citizens."*

Step 2: Define positively phrased expectations for appropriate behavior, along with observable examples. A schoolwide discipline system begins with three to five simple, positive phrases that guide behavioral expectations for the entire school. These essential expectations for behavior emphasize key values on which the school social and behavioral climate is based. Often, schools give a name to

their expectations, which might be based on the school name or the mascot—for example, a school whose mascot is the honeybee named its expectations the *"Three Bs: Be respectful, Be responsible, Be safe"* (Taylor-Greene & Kartub, 2000). In another school these student expectations were called the "High Fives":

1. Be Respectful

2. Be Responsible

3. Follow Directions

4. Keep Hands and Feet to Self

5. Be There—Be Ready (Taylor-Greene & Kartub, 2000)

One function of the key expectations for behavior is that they contribute to the sharing of a common language among staff and students so that they can easily communicate about their school's social-behavioral climate. The key expectations should be seen in many places and spoken or heard often. For instance, posters picturing the school mascot and the expectations for behavior can be posted in classrooms and around the school. A school pledge that incorporates the school expectations could be recited each morning. In a school that has adopted the *"Three Bs,"* for example, the pledge might be: *"As a Hometown Elementary School student, I will be respectful: I will honor all people and their ideas. I will be responsible: I will use my time wisely and do all tasks that are assigned to me. I will be safe: I will keep myself and others from harm."*

The general expectations for behavior must be described as *observable examples of behaviors* that can be identified by all staff and students. Students cannot learn the approved behaviors if the adults cannot define and demonstrate them. The definitions must preclude those behavior problems that are of the greatest concern and identify alternative, suitable behaviors for various settings in the school. One purpose of a functional behavior assessment (FBA) at the schoolwide level is to identify common behavior problems that are of greatest concern and their predictable relationships with antecedents in the environment such as places, times, student groupings, and the context (e.g., the degree of structure and adult supervision provided; Scott & Caron, 2005). For example, the lunchroom, hallway transitions, playground or gym, and bus area often are likely to set the stage for behavior problems when they are crowded and unsupervised and/or when helpful physical arrangements and routines have not been established. The consequences of

problem behavior also can be detected through an FBA. For example, pushing, running, or verbally harassing peers may work to gain the attention of peers or adults or to be first in line at lunch. The FBA information is used to help design routines and arrangements to assist in preventing problem behavior and increasing the likelihood of desired behavior (Scott & Caron, 2005).

Figure 2.2 shows Mountain View Elementary School's mission statement, its three major expectations for behavior, and the specific behaviors that define those expectations for the school settings

Mountain View Elementary School is a community of learners. We are all here to learn, grow, and become good citizens.			
	Respect self	**Respect others**	**Respect property**
Hallways		Walk quietly Stay in self space Stay right	
Cafeteria		Stay seated Stay in self space Use inside voices	
Playground		Be safe Take turns and share Stay in safe area Report problems	
Bathrooms		Keep clean Report problems Flush toilet and wash hands	
Bus Room Busses		Stay seated Stay in self space Use inside voices Stay packed	
Assemblies		Listen quietly Stay in self space Stay seated	

Figure 2.2. Key behavior expectations for different school settings. (*Source: Mountain View Elementary School Staff Handbook* [2005–2006].)

that predictably set the stage for problem behavior.

Step 3: Design procedures for actively teaching, monitoring, prompting, and correcting expectations and behaviors. Initially, all teachers in the school directly teach the specific behaviors that evidence each general expectation through a direct instruction sequence: 1) introduce the skill (e.g., "Be Respectful") and give the rationale for being respectful or have students generate reasons why it is important to be respectful; 2) provide clear examples of the respectful behavior and the non-respectful behavior and ask the students for examples and non-examples (these can be listed on a T-chart and posted in the classroom); 3) the teacher and another adult demonstrate the behaviors, pointing out critical features; 4) students practice the behaviors in role-play situations and are given immediate feedback; 5) teachers

cue and prompt the use of appropriate behavior both in and outside the classroom; 6) all adults supervise target environments (e.g., hallways, restrooms) and provide positive or corrective feedback. Instruction might begin in the classroom but then should proceed to the specific settings in which the behaviors will be required. If skills are only taught in the classroom and not followed by prompts, active supervision, and contingencies, the levels of problem behavior in target environments in the school may not decrease (e.g., Lewis, Sugai, & Colvin, 1998).

Figures 2.3 and 2.4 illustrate strategies used at Mountain View Elementary School to teach, monitor, prompt, and correct students' behavior. Figure 2.3 shows a sample lesson plan for teaching "hallway expectations." Figure 2.4 provides the plan devised to improve behavior in the cafeteria; the plan clarifies the

---

Sample Lesson Plan for Hallway Expectations

1. Discuss the schoolwide expectations for the hallway:

    Walk quietly   Stay in self space   Stay right

    With the children: Ask the children to tell what they think respectful hallway behavior looks like/sounds like/feels like. Contrast with a similar discussion of what disrespectful behavior in hallways looks like/sounds like/feels like.

2. Present several scenarios and ask the children to identify the respectful aspects of each (focusing on the positive examples rather than the negatives).
3. Just before going into the hallway, review the expectations of respectful behavior (either as teacher prompts or having selected children reiterate).
4. Actively teach (not just verbal teaching—go out in the hallways), practice, monitor, and reward (use Buck-a-Roos) appropriate behaviors.

Kid Activities

1. Role play: Groups of children demonstrate what respectful hallway behavior looks like, either in an organized line (walking as a class with the teacher) or walking individually without the teacher (e.g., taking a note to the office). Have children demonstrate the wrong way to walk in the hallways (in an organized line or not). Concentrate on average behaviors (e.g., trying to pass others in line, pushing, walking next to a friend so they can talk, touching artwork, kicking walls).
2. Students write stories or draw pictures that indicate both the respectful ways to move about in the hallways and the inappropriate ways to move about.
3. Practice! Go somewhere as a class; students discuss with peers the respectful behaviors they have practiced.

Figure 2.3.   Sample lesson plan for teaching expected behaviors. (*Source: Mountain View Elementary School Staff Handbook* [2005–2006].)

Cafeteria Procedures and Routines

- Teachers will walk students into the cafeteria threshold (doorway) of the serving line.
- When students enter the serving line, they will be quiet except for talking with the servers.
- Students will be reminded by teachers and posted signs to get all of their lunch supplies (forks, spoons, milk, ketchup, napkins, and so forth) while going through the line.
- Students will proceed to the tables and sit down and eat.
- Students will raise their hands to request help from an adult.
- If students ask to go to the bathroom, the instructional assistant will respond, "Can you wait until after lunch—it will be over in __ minutes?" If the student says, "No," the student will be given permission to go to the bathroom. Teachers need to provide time for students to use the bathroom before lunch.
- Students will be reminded throughout lunch to follow the cafeteria expectations:

  Stay seated
  Use inside voices
  Stay in self space

- Students will bus their trays when an instructional assistant calls their table.
- Students will return to their tables to wait for their teachers and talk quietly.
- When teachers arrive to pick up their students from the tables, students will line up and leave the cafeteria quietly.

Figure 2.4. Cafeteria procedures and routines. (*Source: Mountain View Elementary School Staff Handbook* [2005–2006].)

routines and procedures that teachers, cafeteria aides, and students are to follow.

Step 4: Develop a variety of ways to acknowledge appropriate, expected behaviors. A schoolwide reward system should include an array of ways to acknowledge expected behaviors: tangible and social, predictable and unpredictable, frequent and infrequent (Sugai & Horner, 2002). Often, a school will use a token or ticket system and a range of activities or goods that students may trade for their reward tickets. Each classroom teacher uses these rewards with his or her own students, but all teachers and other staff members also may bestow reward tickets on any student in the school for engaging in behaviors that demonstrate the schoolwide behavioral expectations (Scott & Caron, 2005). Some examples of acknowledgement or reinforcement systems follow:

- The reinforcement system used in the middle school whose High Fives expectations were listed previously incorporated a High Five coupon, which could be redeemed for products or entry into school activities. Activities included raffles, open gym, classroom visits, and Gold Card night (Taylor-Greene & Kartub, 2000).

- At another middle school, public recognition was given to students who successfully demonstrated one of the school's universal behavioral expectations (which were dubbed the "Five Steps to Success"). For example, students who were successful in demonstrating "being safe" behaviors in the hallways were acknowledged as "Certified Hallway Walkers" via a school announcement over the public address system (Turnbull et al., 2002). A schoolwide ticket or *positive referral* system was also developed to reinforce desired behavior. Teachers and other school staff would issue a positive referral ticket when they "caught" a student displaying behaviors related to the Five Steps to Success. Students would then place these tickets in boxes, which were separated by grade level, in the school office. Each day, the vice principal pulled a ticket from each box and, using the school's intercom system, called out the student's name and the universal expectation the student had followed. The winning students were called to the office, where the vice principal took their pictures, escorted them to a display case where they selected a prize, and then mounted their pictures with a statement of what expectations they had followed (Turnbull et al., 2002).

- In an elementary school, a token system was used to acknowledge students who demonstrated the key behavioral expectations; acknowledgements included chance tickets, monthly awards assembly, and a self-manager program for students with an 80% or better compliance rate. Group reinforcers also were awarded for the entire class when cafeteria and playground expectations were met (Lewis, Sugai, & Colvin, 1998).

Mountain View Elementary's ticket system is described in Figure 2.5. The system utilized tickets that could be bestowed by any teacher or staff member in the school whenever students were witnessed enact-

ing the schoolwide behavioral expectations. Also shown in Figure 2.5 is a list of the *opportunities* (the term the school community preferred over *rewards*) offered to students. One thing that stands out about the opportunities available to students in this school is the value given to social interactions. Whereas in some schools eating lunch with a teacher or the principal would be viewed as a negative consequence, it was viewed as a privilege in this school.

Step 5: Establish a consistently used continuum of consequences for correcting rule violations. The schoolwide discipline plan must 1) provide clear definitions of behaviors that are to be corrected, 2) give guidance in preventing and interrupting behavior problems so that they do not escalate, and 3) specify which consequences are administered by teachers or by school administrators (Horner et al., 2004). The behavior–consequence relationships must be as clear as possible. At the lower level of the continuum of consequences are on-the-spot corrections delivered by teachers for minor misbehaviors (e.g., a brief incident of teasing or running in the hall). Somewhat more serious violations (e.g., a heated verbal exchange between students that

---

Guidelines for Using Buck-a-Roos

"Buck-a-Roos" are tickets that students will earn for demonstrating behaviors in our school that are consistent with our teachings and expectations: respect self, respect others, and respect property. Students will save Buck-a-Roos they earn throughout the school and exchange them later for special opportunities.

Buck-a-Roos are a means for recognizing positive behaviors being used by our students. This is not a deficit-based system. Buck-a-Roos are never taken away from students to punish misbehavior. They are given only to reward positive behavior. It is critically important for us to use positive language and praise along with the Buck-a-Roos to reward students meeting our school expectations. We do not use them in a negative fashion—such as [threatening] not to give them out.

Things to remember:
- Have around 10 choices
- Mix choices throughout the year
- Set some opportunities high, some low
- High= person/schedule change involved (e.g., eat lunch with special person)

Figure 2.5.   Guidelines for using a ticket system to acknowledge appropriate behavior. (*Source: Mountain View Elementary School Staff Handbook* [2005–2006].)

stops when a teacher intervenes) are still handled by a teacher or teachers and might include mild consequences such as loss of free time or a disciplinary technique such as "Think Time" (Nelson & Carr, 1999). The Think Time strategy is designed to give students time to regain control, reflect on their behavior and the expectation that they "forgot," and make a plan for how to be more successful in the future. Still more serious offenses (e.g., physical aggression, a heated verbal exchange with cursing) would warrant office disciplinary referrals. It is especially important that the office disciplinary referral system include clear definitions of the applicable behaviors and the procedures teachers are to follow when making a referral.

The instructions on the use of office forms and procedures at Mountain View Elementary School are provided in Figure 2.6. An example of a completed office disciplinary referral form is included in the school's staff handbook, as is sample copy of the letter sent to parents/guardians to inform them if their child receives a disciplinary referral.

Step 6: Establish procedures for record keeping and decision making. It is essential for record-keeping and decision-making procedures to be established and used

consistently. As is true for the rest of the schoolwide discipline plan, the procedures must be as efficient and user-friendly as possible, or they will not be used regularly and there will not be sufficient reliable information to show whether the school's behavioral climate is moving in the right direction. The schoolwide leadership team should communicate the results of record keeping and data analysis regularly to staff. Data should be presented in ways that allow the team and other school staff to analyze patterns across students, locations, times, types of behavior, and consequences (Horner et al., 2004). As well as analyzing student data for individual, classroom, and grade-level rates and types of infractions, trends in disciplinary referral data may indicate when teachers and staff need booster training with respect to issues such as supervision of particular locations in the school or consistency in determining which behavior problems warrant office referrals (Taylor-Greene & Kartub, 2000).

Active Development of Skills for Solving Social and Behavior Problems

"Cooperative school and classroom environments foster open and honest communication, accurate perceptions of the

---

Office Forms and Procedures

There are three office forms:

1. Health/general concern (green form)
2. Celebration (gold form)
3. Discipline referral (blue form): Use this form to send students to see an administrator for an office offense. Be sure to complete the entire form, explain the incident in detail at the bottom of the form, and use one form for each student. *Needs to be kept on file for records. Thank you!*

A student should not be sent to the office without a form in hand.

Students are only to be in the office for health/general concerns or for discipline—no "chill time."

Teachers are encouraged to use a team or buddy teacher for minor offenses (chill time) or use the "Think Time" plan (Nelson & Carr, 1999).

Figure 2.6. Office forms and procedures. (*Source: Mountain View Elementary School Staff Handbook* [2005–2006].)

intentions and feelings of others, trust, and orientation of maximizing positive outcomes for both parties" (Johnson & Johnson, 1996, p. 497). Schools that embrace PBS not only teach students the skills they need to meet the school's basic expectations for behavior but also teach students how to manage their own behavior and deal positively with the social challenges that arise in schools and elsewhere. Conflict resolution and peer mediation programs are two approaches to teaching students skills for social problem solving.

Conflict resolution programs are curriculum-based programs designed to teach social skills, empathy training, bias awareness, and anger-management skills that give students the tools to use alternatives to violent conflict resolution. Johnson and Johnson (1996) reviewed 15 studies of the types of conflicts in which students engage in schools. Physical violence that results in serious injury is infrequent, although, of course, still of concern. The most common conflicts between and among students were gossip, physical fights, dating/relationship issues, rumors, harassments and arguments, and name calling and insults. Without explicit training, students largely tend to use conflict strategies such as withdrawal or suppression of the conflict, intimidation and force, and/or win-lose negotiations (Johnson & Johnson, 1996). In contrast to untrained students, students trained in conflict resolution face the problem, engage in problem solving, and use *integrative* or *win-win* negotiations (Johnson & Johnson, 1996).

Peer mediation programs use trained student mediators to resolve a conflict that has already developed (Johnson & Johnson, 1996). Students can be referred by other students, teachers, or administrators, or they may come voluntarily to their peer mediators to work to create solutions that are acceptable to everyone involved. Both conflict resolution and peer mediation programs can use a cadre of trained students or involve training the total student body. Effective implementation of a peer mediation program can be quite complex because it requires 1) training the peer mediators and the school team guiding the program, 2) establishing a referral protocol, 3) scheduling the mediations so that academics are minimally disrupted, and 4) monitoring the program continually (Johnson & Johnson, 1996). Conflict resolution and peer mediation programs can improve students' ability to resolve conflicts through negotiation and discussion, decrease discipline problems, and improve students' attitudes toward school (Aber, Brown, & Henrich, 1999; Daunic, Smith, Robinson, Miller, & Landry, 2000). Students are able to learn the procedures for negotiation and peer mediation, retain that knowledge over time, and transfer the procedures to nonclassroom and nonschool environments (Johnson & Johnson, 1996). These programs also have been useful in supporting the development of students' self-direction, self-esteem, sense of personal control, and other aspects of their psychosocial health. As a result, rates of student–student conflict, physical violence, office referrals, and suspension have been found to decrease (Johnson, Johnson, & Dudley, 1992).

A number of schoolwide problem solving or conflict resolution programs (e.g., Greenberg, Kusche, & Mihalic, 1998; Johnson & Johnson, 1995; Schrumpf, Crawford, & Usadel, 1991) and other violence-prevention programs (e.g., Flannery et al., 2003; Grossman et al., 1997) have been recognized by governmental, educational, and professional organizations as *model, effective,* or *promising* programs. Programs with these designations have documented effectiveness in helping schools prevent violence, improve students' problem-solving skills, create positive solutions to students' emotional and behavioral difficulties, and enhance students' achievement. The social and emotional learning programs listed in Figure 2.7 met the following criteria: documented effectiveness, based on sound theory, easily integrated into existing school practices, and sufficient technical assistance or other resources available to support effective implementation (Osher, Dwyer, & Jackson, 2004). Most of these programs require professional develop-ment (e.g., workshops, institutes, and follow-up coaching) from specialized trainers and purchase of training and implementation materials. Appendix B lists several resources that provide additional information about these and other research-validated and promising programs for universal social and behavioral interventions in schools.

Two of the programs included in Figure 2.7 are more comprehensive pro-

Program, relevant ages, author(s), source for more information	Brief program description	Expert evaluator designations*, key research
Project ACHIEVE (pre-K–8; some use in high schools) (Knoff & Batsche, 1995) Sopris West Educational Services 4093 Specialty Place Longmont, CO 80504	A comprehensive school improvement program to strengthen resilience and self-management skills. Focuses on social skills, conflict resolution, self-management, academic progress, positive school climate, and safe school practices. Uses a collaborative team approach to problem solve ways to support individual students with challenging behavior, early intervention services for at-risk students, and decision making based on data.	• SAMHSA* Model program • CSAP Model program • CASEL* Select program (Dwyer & Osher, 2000)
Bullying Prevention Program (K–8) (Olweus, 2000) Center for the Study and Prevention of Violence (CSPV) University of Colorado at Boulder Box 442 Boulder, CO 80309 http://www.colorado.edu/cspv/	A program designed to reduce the opportunities and reward structures for bullying and to reward positive, prosocial behavior. Uses anonymous bullying questionnaire to assess bullying at the school. A Bullying Prevention Coordinating Committee coordinates the effort. Interventions include increased supervision at "hot spots" for bullying; firm limits on unacceptable behavior; and consistently applied nonhostile, nonphysical negative consequences for violations.	• CSPV* Blueprints Model program • SAMHSA Model program
Caring School Community (Child Development Project [CDP]) (K–12) Developmental Studies Center 2000 Embarcadero Suite 305 Oakland, CA 94606-5300 Phone: 800/666-7270 http://www.devstu.org	A comprehensive school improvement program that focuses on good citizenship, school bonding, academic success, and social-emotional learning. The purpose is to build a caring school community and to foster academic, social, and ethical development. Four program components: class meetings, cross-age buddies or peer mentoring, inclusive schoolwide activities, and home or family involvement activities. Includes optional cross-curricular components.	• CASEL Select program • SDDFS* Promising program • SAMHSA Model program

(continued)

Figure 2.7. Universal programs with documented effectiveness in promoting student achievement and preventing behavioral and emotional problems.

Figure 2.7.   *(continued)*

Program, relevant ages, author(s), source for more information	Brief program description	Expert evaluator designations*, key research

I Can Problem Solve (ICPS)
(pre-K–8)
(Shure, 1992)
Research Press
  Dept. 27W
  P.O. Box 9177
  Champaign, IL 61826
  http://www.research-press.com
	Focuses on interpersonal problem solving to prevent antisocial behaviors (e.g., physical and verbal aggression, impatience, social withdrawal) and to help children learn to generate nonviolent solutions to everyday problems. Provides extensive guided practice in using constructive conflict-resolution skills (e.g., recognizing and labeling emotions in oneself, considering the other's perspective, generating alternative solutions before acting). Especially good for at-risk children in urban settings.	• CASEL Select program
		• SAMHSA Promising program
		(Shure, 1992)

PeacePartners
(K–8)
PeacePartners
  P.O. Box 12158
  Tucson, Arizona
  http://www.peace-builders.com (requires site license to access online materials)
	Changes school characteristics that trigger aggressive, hostile behavior. Focuses on developing positive adult and child models of caring, positive behavior; directly teaching nonviolent attitudes, values, and beliefs; and providing incentives for students to display these attitudes and behaviors at school.	• CASEL Safe and Sound program
		• SAMHSA Promising program
		(Flannery et al., 2003)

Promoting Alternative Thinking Strategies (PATHS)
(K–5)
(Greenberg, Kusche, & Mihalic, 1998)
Center for the Study and Prevention of Violence
  University of Colorado at Boulder
  Box 442
  Boulder, CO 80309
  http://www.colorado.edu/cspv/
	Designed to promote social and emotional competence, including the expression, understanding, and regulation of emotions. Focuses on development of self-control, frustration tolerance, anger management, emotional understanding through affective, behavioral, and cognitive strategies. Proven as useful with students who have language or cognitive delays. Taught throughout the school year.
	Can be used as a universal or targeted intervention approach.
		• CASEL Select program
		• CSPV Blueprints Model program

Resolving Conflict Creatively Program (RCCP)
(K–8)
Educators for Social Responsibility
  23 Garden Street
  Cambridge, MA 02138
  http://www.esrnational.org
	Primary aims are to help students develop the social and emotional skills needed to reduce violence and prejudice, form caring relationships, and become good citizens. Provides a comprehensive strategy for preventing violence and other risk behaviors and creating caring and peaceable learning communities. Focuses on managing anger, analyzing conflict situations, examining bias and stereotyping, and enhancing communications and negotiation skills. Includes classroom-based social and emotional skills lessons, extensive staff development component, parent workshops, and a peer-mediation program.	• CASEL Select program
		• SAMHSA Effective program
		(Aber, Jones, Brown, Chaudry, & Samples, 1998)

Program, relevant ages, author(s), source for more information	Brief program description	Expert evaluator designations*, key research
Responsive Classroom© (K–5) Northeast Foundation for Children 85 Avenue A, Ste. 204 P.O. Box 718 Turners Falls, MA 01376 http://www.responsive-classroom.org	Designed to create classrooms that are responsive to children's physical, emotional, social, and intellectual needs through developmentally appropriate experiential education. Teaches competencies in self-awareness, self-management, relationship management (especially cooperation and negotiation), decision making, and social awareness (especially appreciating human differences). Does not use structured lessons but is based on six essential components: 1) classroom organization; 2) morning meeting; 3) rules based on respect for self and others and logical consequences of violating these rules; 4) academic choice; 5) guided discovery; and 6) family communication strategies.	CASEL Select program (Elliott, 1995; Rimm-Kaufman, 2006)
Second Step (pre-K–9) Committee for Children 568 First Ave. S. Suite 600 Seattle, WA 98104-2804 http://www.cfchildren.org	Designed to reduce aggression and promote social competence. Targets the skills and behaviors of empathy, impulse control, problem solving, and anger management. Instruction emphasizes taking responsibility for actions, being honest, recognizing feelings, and communicating in respectful and assertive ways to solve problems. Students learn strategies to manage anger, fear, and stress, as well as refusal techniques.	• CASEL Select program • SAMHSA Model program • SDDFS Exemplary program (Grossman et al., 1997)
Teaching Students to Be Peacemakers (K–12) (Johnson & Johnson, 1995) Interaction Book Company 7208 Cornelia Drive Edina, MN 55435 http://www.co-operation.org/	Aims to develop social-emotional competence to reduce antisocial, aggressive, and violent behavior. Students learn skills for problem-solving negotiations and how to mediate peers' conflicts. Skill lessons involve role-playing with two peers per lesson serving as mediators so that all students have equal opportunities to be leaders. Each spring, booster sessions prepare students for the next grade, where weekly follow-up lessons are delivered.	SAMHSA Model program

* **CASEL:** Collaborative for Academic, Social, and Emotional Learning (2003); designates programs as Select or Safe and Sound.

* **CSPV:** Center for the Study and Prevention of Violence; designates programs as Blueprints Model or Blueprints Promising (Mihalic, Fagan, Irwin, Ballard, & Elliott, 2004).

* **SAMHSA:** Substance Abuse and Mental Health Services Administration, U.S. Department of Health and Human Services; designates programs as Model, Effective, and Promising. See SAMSA's National Registry of Evidence-Based Programs and Practices. Available from http://nrepp.samhsa.gov/

* **SDDFS:** Safe, Disciplined, and Drug-Free Schools Initiative, U.S. Department of Education; designates programs as Model and Promising (U.S. Department of Education Safe, Disciplined, and Drug-Free School Expert Panel, 2001).

grams that go beyond the development of social problem solving skills to address a broader spectrum of social, self-management, and conflict resolution skills. The Resolving Conflict Creatively Program (RCCP; Educators for Social Responsibility, 2006) and Teaching Students to Be Peacemakers (Johnson & Johnson, 1995) both include broad efforts to affect school climate and allow schools to use an integrated curriculum approach that builds program content into core subject area instruction.

Teaching Students to Be Peacemakers (Johnson & Johnson, 1995) includes instruction in problem-solving, negotiation, and mediation strategies. Peacemakers is a K–12 program that begins by creating a cooperative school climate and then teaches all students in the classroom or school the steps of the negotiation and mediation processes (see Figure 2.8). Once all students understand these processes, particular students are selected to serve as official mediators to whom their peers can turn if they have been unable to resolve a conflict themselves. The peer-mediation aspect of the Peacemakers program can be implemented with a cadre of peer mediators, an entire class, or a student body. Figure 2.8 outlines the six steps of the Peacemakers program.

The RCCP, available at the Educators for Social Responsibility web site listed in Appendix B, is a comprehensive, multi-year program in social and emotional learning for children in grades K–8. The broad aim of the program, which originated in New York City and now serves more than 400 schools among 16 school districts in the United States, is to help create caring and peaceable communities of learning that increase school success for all children. Children who participate in RCCP are taught self-management, cooperation, and problem-solving skills and participate in a schoolwide peer-mediation program. A 2-year study of RCCP showed that when students received a high number of lessons from the curriculum (about 25 lessons per school year), they showed reductions in aggression and prejudice and improvements in communication, anger-management, and conflict-resolution skills (Aber, Brown, & Henrich, 1999). The RCCP model relies on extensive teacher training and coaching in implementing curriculum-based skill instruction, classroom management, peer mediation, and parent involvement.

The Teaching Students to Be Peacemakers Program Six Steps

1. ***Create a cooperative context.*** The Peacemakers program requires students to see themselves and their peers as interdependent. If they view themselves as trying to "win" or "beat out" their peers, conflicts will not be resolved peacefully.

2. ***Teach students to recognize when a conflict is and is not occurring.*** Conflicts may involve laughter and learning as well as anger, hostility, and violence.

3. ***Teach students concrete and specific procedures for negotiating agreements.*** Students need demonstrations and practice of specific behavioral steps, not simply to be told to "Be nice!" or "Solve your problems cooperatively!"

4. ***Teach students to use concrete and specific mediation procedures.*** Students need demonstrations of negotiation procedures and adequate practice to make the procedures automatic. Approximately 30 half-hour lessons are recommended.

5. ***Implement the peer mediation program.*** Initially working in pairs, students identified as mediators assist their peers in negotiating more effectively. The role of mediator should be rotated so that every student has an opportunity to mediate.

6. ***Continue weekly training in negotiation and mediation procedures from first through twelfth grades.*** Becoming truly competent in peaceful conflict resolution takes time. Students need repeated practice in using their skills.

Figure 2.8. Teaching Students to Be Peacemakers. (From Johnson, D.W., & Johnson, R.T. [1995]. *Teaching students to be peacemakers.* Edina, MN: Interaction Book Company; adapted by permission.)

SYSTEMS-CHANGE PROCESS FOR ESTABLISHING AND SUSTAINING SWPBS

The change from a reactive, punitive, and uncoordinated approach to school discipline to a proactive, preventive, unified approach can require from relatively minor to dramatic major changes in a school's culture and climate, in the attitudes and skills of teachers and staff, and in administrative practices. Without a systems-change process for establishing and sustaining a SWPBS initiative, the success of both schoolwide and individual student-focused efforts will be limited. A *systems approach* is based on an articulated and vital mission statement and incorporates committees or work groups to coordinate and guide the program, administrative support (e.g., involvement, decision-making guidance, resources), operating routines for action planning and communications, and professional development (Sugai & Horner, 2002, p. 31).

Sugai and Horner, directors of the Center on Positive Behavioral Interventions and Supports at the University of Oregon, have articulated four major steps in a process for initiating and sustaining SWPBS. These four steps are briefly summarized here:

STEP 1
ESTABLISH A LEADERSHIP TEAM

The SWPBS team or working group should include the principal, teachers who represent their colleagues (e.g., representatives from grade level or departmental teams), support personnel such as school psychologists, and parents. To avoid the problems of inefficiency and frustration that can occur when a school has too many committees and teams, this team should play a leadership role in the school regarding behavior (another team typically serves as the referral team for students needing selected or individualized PBS). The team's responsibilities include 1) developing ways to communicate with school staff about the team's work, 2) conducting needs assessments, 3) developing action plans, 4) establishing measurable progress indicators, and 5) planning staff development activities. The schoolwide team, which typically meets monthly, will likely need training and technical assistance in both the content of SWPBS and the processes and structures necessary to implement it.

STEP 2
SECURE SCHOOLWIDE AGREEMENTS AND SUPPORTS

For the initiative to be successful, the staff as a whole must (largely) agree that 1) this is a priority for staff development (as indicated by its being one of the top three school improvement goals [Horner et al., 2004]); 2) it is a long-term (3 to 5 year) commitment of staff time, energy, and fiscal resources; and 3) the approach must be preventive and instructional. In addition to the needs assessment and information-sharing activities that must occur at this step, resources must be garnered to secure the in-service training activities and materials that will be needed.

STEP 3
DEVELOP DATA-BASED ACTION PLAN

Next, the SWPBS team reviews data to assess the school's current disciplinary practices and make decisions regarding which practices should be improved, maintained, deleted, or added. The types of data required include attendance and tardy patterns; office discipline referrals; detention, suspension, and expulsion rates; and behavioral incidence data. Office discipline referral data are most useful in developing action plans if they include not only the number of referrals per school year but also the average number of referrals per day, the annual referral rate per student attending, the referral rates by problem behaviors and location, and the proportions of students with 1 or more, 5 or more, and 10 or more referrals (Sugai, Sprague, Horner, & Walker, 2000).

An action plan also should reflect assessments (e.g., surveys, checklists) of the extent to which behavioral support strategies and practices are in place. Horner and his colleagues have developed the School-Wide Evaluation Tool (SET; Sugai, Lewis-Palmer, Todd, & Horner, 2001, as cited in Horner et al., 2004) as a research instrument to assess the extent to which SWPBS practices are in place before and after school staff receive in-service training and technical assistance. They found the SET to be a reliable way to measure the implementation of PBS practices and suggested that the SET also could be used by school districts to guide planning and evaluation of their systems of universal PBS.

Another helpful assessment measure is the California School Climate and Safety Survey: Elementary/Secondary (see Osher et al., 2004, p. 247), which asks students to report their direct experiences with violent and antisocial behavior, their feelings about school and themselves as students, and their beliefs about the school discipline system.

The SWPBS team examines the discipline data and other needs assessment information to develop an action plan to guide the implementation of a SWPBS approach. An effective action plan typically includes the following components: 1) measurable outcomes, goals, and objectives; 2) specific activities that lead to the accomplishment of objectives; 3)

activities to address staff development and training needs; and 4) activities to garner resources and supports.

Data on office disciplinary referrals can provide a valid measure of overall progress toward improving student behavior and school climate. In addition, patterns detected by analyzing disciplinary referrals can assist the team in judging the extent to which the action plan should emphasize universal, schoolwide, or targeted interventions for smaller groups of students, as well as interventions for individual students with extreme social-behavioral needs (Sugai et al., 2000). In general, the need to establish or to reform universal, schoolwide behavior support systems is indicated if the total number of referrals per year per student is high, the average number of referrals per day is high, and/or the proportion of students with at least one referral is high. Reform of selected support systems (the topic of Chapter 3) for students at risk for more serious behavior problems may be indicated if the percentage of students with at least one referral is low, but the percentage of students with 1–10 referrals is relatively high. Individualized, targeted student behavior supports (which are addressed in Chapters 4 and 5) are indicated if there are students who received 10 or more referrals during the year and/or if the 5% of students with the most office referrals account for a high proportion of all referrals (Sugai et al., 2000).

STEP 4
ARRANGE FOR ACCURATE IMPLEMENTATION

 An action plan may fall short of achieving the desired effect on school behavior problems for various reasons. Even if intervention components with proven effectiveness are incorporated, for example, inaccurate or uncommitted implementation of the plan can result in disappointing outcomes. Sugai and Horner (2002) recommended that "action plans not be put into full implementation until more than 80% of the staff support these agreements" (p. 40). Implementing the plan as designed requires ongoing administrative and team leadership, professional development and training to build and maintain faculty and staff skills, continued staff commitment, and recognition and appreciation for implementation efforts and successes (Sugai & Horner, 2002).

STEP 5

CONDUCT FORMATIVE DATA-BASED MONITORING

 Ongoing data collection on student attendance, tardiness, suspensions, expulsions, and behavioral incidents resulting in office disciplinary referrals should be analyzed to determine successful strategies or those that need improvement. Of course, it is important to be sure that the data being gathered are valid and reliable, which requires having efficient ways to process data (Sugai & Horner, 2002). Schoolwide Information System (SWIS™), a web-based software system for recording, organizing, and reporting office disciplinary referrals, can summarize data for individual students, groups of students who share particular characteristics (e.g., gender, special education status, grade level), or the entire student body (May et al., 2002).

Use of a schoolwide data collection system may require even greater levels of in-service training and technical assistance than other aspects of the SWPBS initiative. Forty-two school teams, who had received intensive PBS training and follow-up coaching for one year, reported "entering data into the database" as the issue with which they needed the most coaching assistance; the second most difficult issue reported was data analysis and decision making (Scott & Hunter, 2001).

CONCLUSION

SWPBS systems do not fully meet the social-behavioral or mental health needs of all students. They have been proven effective, however, in preventing the development or worsening of behavior problems in the vast majority of students in a school. Like any significant school improvement effort, effective SWPBS requires accurate, durable implementation of doable practices (Sugai & Horner, 2002). The following elements of effective school change efforts must be in place:

• Teams that create a common vision and keep that vision in focus throughout the process

• Strong administrative leaders

• Staff buy-in and understanding of, and support for, school improvement

• A long-term perspective that provides for unanticipated challenges and delayed dividends

• Capacity-building efforts that include extensive training and support

• The efficient use of human and material resources and a culture and structure that help all members of the school community succeed (Osher et al., 2004, p. 7)

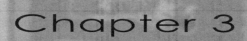
Chapter 3

Selected Interventions for
Students at Risk for Behavior Problems

Universal positive behavior support (PBS) and interventions such as those described in Chapter 2 can successfully prevent behavior problems and facilitate academic success for the majority of students in schools. Some students, however, will continue to display patterns of difficult behavior. A subset of these students have behavior problems that, although troubling for parents and teachers, do not warrant the specialized, intensive level of intervention required by students with the most severe, chronic behavior problems. Nevertheless, students who demonstrate emerging behavior problems and/or who experience other risk factors that make more serious behavior problems likely in the future, clearly need additional supports to achieve successful social-behavioral and academic outcomes. Therefore, when schools establish integrated, comprehensive systems of PBS, they augment universal interventions with *selected interventions* for this group of students (estimated at 5% to 15% of a school population). In the three-tiered model of prevention of behavior problems, this is the secondary level of prevention; it is designed to remediate students' behavior problems or prevent them from worsening. This middle level of PBS is less well defined and researched than the other two levels of intervention: universal and individualized (Snell, 2006), although the specific intervention practices and strategies (e.g., social skills instruction, academic interventions such as peer tutoring, the use of self-management strategies) are well tested.

Students who are candidates for selected, often group-based, interventions (other terms used to describe this type of intervention include *specialized group systems* [Sugai & Horner, 2002], *targeted supports* [Freeman et al., 2006)], and *strategic interventions* [Simmons, Kuykendall, King, Cornachione, & Kame'enui, 2000]) may have emerging conduct or psychoemo-

tional disorders or experience family, community, and/or school factors that place them at risk for more serious behavior and academic difficulties. Research has shown that students who, at an early age, exhibit risk behaviors including poor school adjustment, noncompliance, and antisocial behavior are highly likely to progress to more serious disruptive and aggressive behavior (Loeber, Green, Lahey, Frick, & McBurnett, 2000). Antisocial behavior patterns in young children can be quite durable and resistant to intervention and can place children at severe risk for many negative outcomes including delinquency, school dropout, drug and alcohol abuse, and relationship difficulties (Walker et al., 2004). In fact, children who by about the end of the third grade are still using immature, coercive behavioral strategies to achieve their social goals are highly likely to display some degree of antisocial behavior throughout their lives (Loeber & Farrington, 1998, as cited in Walker et al., 2004). Therefore, *it is imperative that interventions for these students be provided early, be targeted to the students' specific areas of need, and be based on research or other sound evidence.*

The needs of students who experience risk indicators can be pressing and immediate at times—for example, when the student experiences an event at home or at school such as an argument with a peer, fails to make the track team, or is the victim of bullying that creates anxiety, disappointment, or fear. In contrast with more specialized interventions, however, selected interventions should be relatively easy to use and, whenever possible, designed for small groups of students. Therefore, to be successful, selected interventions must be easily accessed through a flexible but systematic process, implemented with low effort by teachers and other relevant personnel, and consistent with schoolwide expectations.

The remainder of this chapter explores ways to identify and provide supports for these students in the middle ground between students with no unusual social or behavioral needs and those with significant needs for behavioral support. Selected interventions may include

- Environmental supports such as scheduling changes or careful seating arrangements

- Adult or peer mentors

- Participation in existing academic support programs such as homework clubs, tutoring, or study skills programs

- Reteaching and more strongly reinforcing the schoolwide disciplinary system

- Social skills interventions, including reinforcement of schoolwide programs or additional small-group instruction

- Additional supports such as frequent monitoring via a check-in/check-out system

IDENTIFYING STUDENTS FOR SELECTED INTERVENTIONS

As described in the discussion of collaborative teaming in Chapter 1, a primary model for organizing a system of secondary prevention uses the schoolwide PBS (SWPBS) team to assist in identifying students who should receive additional supports. This team examines administrative behavioral data and coordinates any schoolwide screening efforts that are conducted to identify students with at-risk behaviors and experiences. A second PBS team typically is more directly involved in providing leadership and coordination for the planning, implementation, and follow-up for selected and specialized interventions. This team may have

evolved from an existing Student Support Team, Child Study Team, Teacher Assistance Team, or other prereferral intervention team. The Student-Focused PBS Team (as we shall refer to it here) establishes a regular meeting schedule (often biweekly), with specific team meetings also being attended by teachers or other personnel who work directly with the focal students. Selected PBS requires less expertise in applied behavioral analysis and behavior intervention than the specialized, individualized PBS, which is the topic of Chapter 5. If a new group intervention program is to be adopted, however, consultants with expertise in that program may be needed to train school personnel and to assist with initial implementation of the intervention.

One way to identify students who need selected interventions is to examine schoolwide disciplinary data that have been used to evaluate primary prevention efforts. Data on office disciplinary referrals can be examined to reveal students who may require selected supports in addition to the universal supports provided for all students. For example, students with one office disciplinary referral in a school year are not likely candidates for greater support. Students with between 2 and 10 office disciplinary referrals, however, should be further assessed to determine the student factors (e.g., missing or weak self-control, peer group modeling of antisocial behavior) and the school factors (e.g., poor instructional match, failure of adults to teach and consistently follow through on the schoolwide discipline system) that may have influenced this poor outcome. In some schools, students with 2 to 10 office referrals are considered for selected behavioral interventions, while students with more than 10 referrals would be considered candidates for more specialized, intensive interventions (Sugai et al., 2000).

Office disciplinary referrals should not serve as the only measure used to screen for students at risk for greater behavior difficulties. First, although noncompliance and antisocial behavior patterns are among the best predictors of later behavior problems (Loeber et al., 2000), school disciplinary referrals do not necessarily predict later delinquency and are not always a reliable indicator of increasingly disordered behavior in the future (Nelson, Gonzalez, Epstein, & Benner, 2003). Second, students with a "quiet" problem behavior may be missed. Disciplinary referrals typically are issued for disruptive, externalizing behavior, not for internalizing behavior difficulties such as depression, phobias, or social avoidance, which also can be seriously debilitating (Walker & Severson, 1990).

In order to study the issue of using office disciplinary referrals to screen for behavior problems, Walker and his colleagues (Walker, Cheney, Stage, & Blum, 2005) had teachers in three elementary schools use the Systematic Screening for Behavioral Disorders (SSBD; Walker & Severson, 1990) to identify students who were most at risk for behavior disorders. The number of office disciplinary referrals received by these target students was tracked across the school year. The same students also were evaluated using the Social Skills Rating System (SSRS; Gresham & Elliot, 1990), which gives scores on two scales: a Social Skills Scale and a Problem Behavior Scale. The researchers found no significant correlation between students' ratings on the Social Skills Scale and number of office disciplinary referrals (ODR). Scores on the Problem Behavior Scale, however, did correlate significantly with the number of ODRs. Furthermore, students whose problem behaviors were externalizing received the majority of ODRs in each school, and all of the students who received two or more disciplinary referrals exhibited externalizing behavior problems. The results of this

research point to the need to augment office disciplinary referral data with more systematic schoolwide screening for behavior and social skill problems, so that both externalizing and internalizing behavior difficulties are detected (Walker et al., 2005).

A third limitation of using only office disciplinary referral data to choose candidates for selected behavioral interventions is this: Waiting for students to fail socially or academically, rather than being proactive and prevention-oriented, is inconsistent with a PBS approach. As noted previously, antisocial behavior patterns and conduct disorders are likely to be very difficult to change and are stable over time; *the longer the behavior problem has existed, the more resistant it will be to intervention* (Walker et al., 2005). Therefore, it is important for teachers to be aware of at-risk factors and indicators of emotional and behavior problems and to advocate for the use of preventive support strategies. Figure 3.1 lists some of the at-risk indicators for antisocial behavior and emotional/behavioral problems, as well as some of the protective factors that may exist or be fostered to mitigate the impact of risk factors.

The following student snapshot illustrates the case of a student who has experienced a number of significant risk factors but also has the benefit of protective factors that make future academic and psychosocial success more probable.

Student Snapshot

 Josh, who just entered the sixth grade, has twice been evaluated and found ineligible for special education services for either his learning difficulties or his obsessive-compulsive tendencies. In addition to his academic and psychological risk factors, Josh had lived in a series of foster homes until he was adopted at age 8;

Child factors	Family factors	School context and community–culture factors
Risk factors		
• Prematurity, prenatal, or birth injury • Chronic illness • Poor problem solving • Poor social skills • Low self-esteem • No friends • Mood swings • Bully or bully victim • Frequent absences • Inappropriate affect • Shyness, alienation • Obsessive-compulsive behaviors • Long periods of isolation • Sleep disturbances or nightmares • Lack of empathy or compassion • Gang attachments • Poor academic performance • Conflicts with authority figures • Physically aggressive • Damages property • Use of obscene language • Hyperactive/impulsive behavior	• Teenage mothers • Single parents • Psychiatric disorder, especially depression in mother • Substance abuse • Criminality • Antisocial models • Family violence • Marital discord • Disorganization • Social isolation • Long-term parental unemployment • Living in poverty • Placed in foster care • Poor supervision and monitoring of child • Harsh or inconsistent discipline style • Rejection of child • Child is neglected or physically, socially, or emotionally abused • Lack of warmth and affection • Low involvement in child's activities	• School failure • Normative beliefs about aggression • Deviant peer group • Bullying • Peer rejection; cliques • Inadequate behavior management • Obliviousness to cultural differences; stereotyping • Socioeconomic disadvantage • Population density and housing conditions • Urban area • Neighborhood violence and crime • Cultural norms concerning violence as acceptable response to frustration • Lack of support services • Social or cultural discrimination
Protective factors		
• Social skills, social competence • Above average intelligence • Attachment to family • Empathy • Problem-solving ability • Optimism • School achievement • Easy temperament • Internal locus of control • Moral beliefs and values • Self-related cognitions • Good coping style	• Supportive, caring parents • Family harmony • More than 2 years between siblings • Responsibility for chores or required helpfulness • Secure and stable family • Supportive relationship with other adult • Small family size • Strong family norms and morality	• Positive school climate • Prosocial peer group • Responsibility and required helpfulness • Sense of belonging/bonding • Opportunities for success and recognition of achievement • School norms against violence • Access to support services • Community networking • Attachment to community • Participation in church or other community group • Community/cultural norms against violence

Figure 3.1. Risk and protective factors associated with behavioral and/or emotional problems. (From Walker, H.M., Ramsey, E., & Gresham, F.M. [2004]. *Antisocial behavior in school: Evidence-based practices* [2nd ed., pp. 91–92]. Pacific Grove, CA: Brooks/Cole Publishing; adapted by permission. Henley, M. [2006]. *Classroom management: A proactive approach* [p. 261]. Upper Saddle River, NJ: Pearson Education; adapted by permission.)

he had experienced a history of inconsistent discipline practice and, in one case, emotional abuse. In elementary school, Josh had been subjected to social discontinuity due to changing schools several times. Josh's adoptive parents, however, are supportive and caring and have a stable family life. Josh has one foster brother in high school who willingly helps Josh with his homework and takes Josh to sporting events. Josh attends religious services with his parents and brother and has received some counseling for his obsessive-compulsive tendencies. Josh's new middle school prides itself on its positive school climate and high rate of parent and community involvement. The school has a well-established, effective schoolwide discipline program, a peer mentoring program that connects sixth graders with an older peer mentor, and an active conflict resolution program.

Identification of students for selected interventions requires consideration of multiple factors: administrative disciplinary data, students' social-behavioral and academic profiles, and the risk and protective factors that students experience. In addition, many experts in the fields of PBS and behavior disorders recommend that prekindergarten settings and elementary schools implement systematic, schoolwide screening for early identification of emotional and behavior problems (e.g., Forness, 1990; O'Shaughnessy, Lane, Gresham, & Beebe-Frankenberger, 2003; Walker & Severson, 1990; Walker, Severson, & Feil, 1995). The following is a list of guidelines for appropriate screening and identification of students with antisocial behavior patterns who may be candidates for intervention:

1. Use a *proactive* rather than a *reactive* process to screen and identify students at risk for antisocial behavior.

2. Whenever possible, use a multiagent (teacher, parent, observer) and multisetting (classroom, playground, home setting) screening–identification approach to gain the broadest possible perspective on the dimensions of target students' at-risk status.

3. Screen and identify students experiencing risk factors as early as possible in their school careers—ideally at the preschool and kindergarten levels.

4. Use teacher nominations and rankings or ratings in the early stages of screening and supplement them later in the process, if possible, by direct observations, school records, peer or parent ratings, and other sources as appropriate (Walker et al., 2004, p. 59).

Figure 3.2 provides descriptions of three systematic screening programs with excellent psychometric properties. These programs are relatively easy to administer (with modest amounts of training), reliably predict behavior disorders in children, and aid in targeting specific social-behavioral goals for instruction. Results from these well-tested schoolwide screening programs provide important information about the type and degree of social skill deficits that students display. The information gleaned should be used in concert with teachers' knowledge of students' classroom behavior, evidence of students' risk or protective factors, and administrative data about office disciplinary referrals, tardies, and absences. And, of course, families' knowledge of the student and his or her behavior at home also gives important input for decision making about intervention.

In spite of its benefits, schoolwide screening for behavior problems warrants careful use and cautious interpretation of the results. Schoolwide behavioral screening tools are mostly designed to serve as curriculum-based or criterion-referenced assessments to guide the choice of social skill goals for intervention (Walker et al., 2004). It is critical to avoid the potential for stereotyping, ability grouping, and labeling that can be suggested by the

Student Risk Screening Scale. Teachers use the Student Risk Screening Scale (SRSS) for screening of elementary students for early antisocial behavior (Drummond, 1993). It is easily used and highly reliable in identifying behavioral indicators that lead to conduct disorders and later delinquency if students do not receive appropriate intervention (Loeber, 1991). The easy-to-administer and cost-effective instrument uses a seven-item scale that gives both the frequency and importance of problem behaviors and therefore aids in targeting specific instructional goals. The seven items are stealing; lying, cheating, sneaking; behavior problems; peer rejection; low academic achievement; negative attitude; and aggressive behavior. Teachers rate students on a scale of 0–3 (0 = never, 1 = occasionally, 2 = sometimes, and 3 = frequently) for each item. The total of the seven ratings is used as an indicator of the student's level of risk: high risk (9–21), moderate risk (4–8), or low risk (0–3). High-risk students should then be evaluated more carefully to see if intervention is needed.

Systematic Screening for Behavior Disorders. The Systematic Screening for Behavior Disorders (SSBD) process is used with children in Grades 1 through 6 (Walker & Severson, 1990). The SSBD, which is cost-effective, group-administered, and highly valid and reliable, detects both externalizing and internalizing behaviors. The device uses three sequential assessments known as "gates": Gate 1 uses teacher nominations, Gate 2 uses a teacher rating scale, and Gate 3 employs direct observation of children in the classroom and on the playground. The direct observations conducted in Gate 3 should be conducted by a trained professional (e.g., school psychologist, social worker, behavior specialist); the observations yield measures of the student's academic engaged time during independent seatwork periods in the classroom and the student's social behavior during recess. Walker and Severson recommended that children who are above normative criteria at Gate 3 be referred for a more comprehensive diagnostic assessment. Researchers have found, however, that students who pass through Gate 2 can be considered "at least at moderate risk" for developing further emotional or behavioral problems (McKinney, Montague, & Hocutt, 1998); their academic and behavioral performance should be carefully monitored if group supports are not provided immediately.

Early Screening Project. The Early Screening Project (ESP) is similar to the SSBD but is for use with children ages 3–5 (Walker, Severson, & Feil, 1995). Like the SSBD, it is group-administered and is designed to detect children who are at risk for either externalizing or internalizing behavior problems. It also is easily administered, highly valid and reliable, and is nationally normed. Similar to the SSBD, it uses three successive gates, except that a parent rating scale is incorporated into Gate 3.

Figure 3.2. Reliable instruments for screening of behavior problems/disorders.

identification of groups of students sharing family and socioeconomic risk factors (e.g., Oakes, 1985).

School Snapshot

The first-grade team at Hometown Elementary School—four classroom teachers and a special education teacher—were concerned about the number of students who had not reached their age- and grade-level benchmarks on the statewide assessment of children's phonological awareness and language skills. A number of these same children were having difficulty following school and classroom rules and were not successfully interacting with their peers either in the classroom or on the playground. The first-grade team consulted the school's

Student-Focused PBS team about the possibility of using a systematic screening process to determine more specifically the social and behavioral needs of their students. The PBS team researched some screening programs and suggested the SRSS (see Figure 3.2 for a description). The first-grade team nominated approximately 22 students (about 25% of the school's first graders) for screening based on their knowledge of the students' behavior, social skills, and academic performance. The SRSS scores placed 10 of those students in the "moderate-risk" range and 4 in the "high-risk" range. Eight of the students nominated for screening received scores in the "low-risk" range. The first-grade team then met with the Student-Focused PBS team to discuss selected interventions that might be used with the 10 students whose scores put them in the moderate-risk range. The four students in the high-risk range were scheduled to be observed by a member of the PBS team in preparation for a discussion about whether their problem behaviors warranted a complete functional behavioral assessment.

FUNCTIONAL BEHAVIORAL ASSESSMENT FOR SELECTED INTERVENTIONS

Functional behavioral assessment (FBA) at the secondary level of prevention is less specialized and complex than those conducted for students with the most serious behavior problems (Crone & Horner, 2003). At present, there is no database to show the difference between FBA for secondary and tertiary prevention, nor to indicate the differences between the levels of expertise required (Snell, 2006; refer to Figure 1.3 for a comparison of the features that characterize the three levels of prevention). The general consensus in the field of PBS, however, is that a "simple" or "brief" FBA should 1) be conducted by existing school personnel; 2) be based primarily on indirect data such as school records, administrative disciplinary data, and questionnaires (completed through interviews or self-report by teachers, staff, and/or parents, and by students); and 3) not be difficult to execute. The complete FBA theory and process is detailed in Chapter 4, and therefore only a concise outline of the brief version is presented here.

The purpose of the brief FBA is to identify 1) the approximate frequency of the behavior(s), 2) the antecedents predicting that the behavior will or will not occur (including both near events or triggers and setting events that may have occurred at a more distant time), and 3) the consequences that follow the behavior and somehow make it effective in achieving a particular purpose. For students needing selected interventions, the purpose or function of problem behav-

iors is likely to be socially mediated (rather than self-regulatory or sensory). Thus, the combination of data about the antecedents and consequences of the problem behavior will be used to hypothesize whether the behavior serves to 1) obtain attention or other forms of social interaction from a peer or an adult, 2) obtain something tangible or participate in an activity, 3) avoid social interaction with a peer or an adult, or 4) avoid something or some activity.

The three steps for conducting a brief FBA and a field-tested instrument to guide school teams in the process are described next.

The first step is to identify the specific behavior(s) of concern, which might include swearing at other students or teachers, sleeping in class, being tardy frequently, disrupting class with negative comments about other students' personal characteristics or academic performance, threatening other students with physical harm, or not completing work. Also consider how often the behavior(s) in question occurs. For example, how many tardies or absences occur each week or month? What is the rate of not completing in-class assignments or homework? How many instances of teasing or ridiculing peers occur each week?

The second step is to gather information about the antecedents and consequences of the behavior:

- *Antecedents:* Consider who is present, what activities are occurring, and when and where the problem tends to occur. For example, does the behavior occur more frequently in English class? In the hallways? In the restroom? When a certain clique of peers congregates in the cafeteria? In classes that require a lot of reading or writing? After a long weekend? When asked to work independently? At school and at home immediately before grade reports are distributed?

- *Consequences:* Consider what happens after the problem behavior occurs. Does the teacher lecture the student(s) about behavior in front of the class? Do peers laugh? Do peers remove themselves from the situation? Does the teacher send the student to the hallway to calm down?

The Functional Assessment Checklist for Teachers and Staff (FACTS) is a simple tool that is designed to gather this information in a brief (15 to 20 minutes) meeting of teachers, staff, and parents (Crone & Horner, 2003). There is some research support for the reliability of the FACTS in helping teams to reach hypotheses about the functions of problem behavior that lead to the design of effective interventions (Lewis-Palmer, 1998, as cited in Horner et al., 2000). Figure 3.3 provides a blank sample of the FACTS. To gain insight into behavior problems and intervention preferences from the student himself or herself, the Student-Directed Functional Assessment Interview (SDFAI) can be administered by interview, with the assistance of family members if necessary (O'Neill et al., 1997).

The third step is to use the FBA information to build a summary statement or hypothesis about the predictors of the behavior and the consequences that are enabling the behavior to work for the student. This summary statement or hypothesis is used in selecting specific interventions for individual students or small groups with similar needs. The following Student Snapshot describes use of the FACTS to conduct a brief FBA of the social and academic difficulties being presented by Josh, a sixth grader with several risk factors in his background.

Student Snapshot

 Josh's parents and some of his sixth-grade teachers were concerned about his social isolation from peers and his weak grades in English and social studies. Josh's guidance counselor, his English teacher, his social studies teacher, his parents, and a representative from the school's Student-Focused PBS team met after school one day to complete the FACTS. (Josh chose to complete a self-assessment with his guidance counselor at another time.) Their consensus was that "work completion" in English and social studies was the specific behavior of concern, and that the predictors of the behavior were in-class assignments that required reading. The consequence that typically followed Josh's failure to complete his in-class assignments was to complete the work at home. At home, Josh's foster brother and/or his parents helped Josh with his homework, assisting him with his reading as necessary. Josh had no difficulty with comprehending the material in his textbooks but was not able to read the textbooks independently. After examining this information, Josh's parents and teachers realized that the consequence for not completing reading-based assignments in class was to avoid them temporarily until he could receive the assistance he needed at home. Josh's parents discussed this hypothesis with Josh later that evening. Josh said, "It's too embarrassing to ask for help in class. At home, nobody makes fun of me because I can't read."

CHOOSING AND IMPLEMENTING SELECTED INTERVENTIONS

Selected, or group-focused, interventions can target social, self-management, and/or academic skills. Like individualized PBS, selected interventions can change behavior through 1) prevention strategies to alter triggering antecedents and setting events; 2) teaching new, desirable behaviors; and 3) making sure that

---

Functional Assessment Checklist for Teachers & Staff (FACTS)

Student_____   Date_____

Grade_____   Staff Reporting_____

Student Profile: *Please use the space below to identify the student's strengths. Some possible strengths include academic interests, social skills, hobbies, sports, etc.* _____
_____
_____

Directions: *To gain a better understanding of the nature and scope of the problem behavior(s), please check the most relevant item(s). Then use the CONSIDERATION space at the bottom of each section to provide a brief description of the problem behaviors, predictors, and consequences.*

Problem behavior(s): Behaviors of concern that have been occurring:

___ Tardy	___ Fighting/physical aggression	___ Insubordination/ disrespectful	___ Vandalism
___ Inattentive			___ Other _____
___ Sleeping	___ Verbally harasses others	___ Work completion	
___ Inappropriate language	___ Disrupts class activities	___ Theft	

CONSIDERATIONS: *What behavior typically occurs first and how does it escalate? What does behavior look like?* _____
_____
_____

Predictor(s) and Setting Event(s): Person(s), place(s), or time(s) where behavior of concern is most likely to occur.

Location	Person(s)	Time	Academic Concerns	Setting Event(s)
___ In class	___ Peer(s)	___ Before school	___ All classes	___ Use of medication
___ Hall	___ Teacher(s)	___ Morning	___ Reading	___ Physical health
___ Cafeteria	___ Staff	___ Lunch	___ Math	
___ Bus		___ Homeroom	___ Spec. ed. eligible	___ Illegal drug use
___ Other _____		___ Afternoon	___ Other _____	___ Conflict at home
				___ Other _____

CONSIDERATIONS: *A specific activity that is difficult for the student? Does behavior occur alone or with peer group?*
_____
_____

Consequence(s): What typically happens after behavior of concern occurs?

Obtain Attention	Escape/Avoid Demand or Situation	Current Strategies
___ Peer attention	___ Escape difficult activity	___ Change seating
___ Adult attention	___ Adult attention	___ Contact parents
___ Activity	___ Negative peer interaction	___ Send to office
___ Other _____	___ Other _____	___ Other _____

CONSIDERATIONS: *What strategies have been effective? After an incident, what does the student obtain (e.g., attention) or avoid (e.g., difficult task)?*
_____
_____

Summary of Behavior(s)

Directions: Please use the items selected above and information you've written in CONSIDERATIONS to complete section below.

Predictor(s) & Setting Event(s)	Behavior(s) of Concern	Consequences

Figure 3.3. Functional Assessment Checklist for Teachers & Staff (FACTS). (From O'Neil, R.E., Horner, R.H., Albin, R.W., Sprague, Jr., Storey, K., & Newton, J.S. [1997]. *Functional assessment and program development for problem behavior: A practical handbook* [2nd ed.]. Reprinted with permission of Wadsworth, a division of Thomson Learning: www.thomsonrights.com; fax: 800-730-2215.)

the students' appropriate behaviors are reinforced and problem behaviors are not. The new skills that students should be taught include specific social and communication skills to replace problem behaviors as well as the academic and self-management skills needed to aid their overall social and personal adjustment and their academic performance.

Secondary prevention efforts are, by definition, less resource-intensive than tertiary prevention systems for the most serious behavior problems. When choosing selected interventions, it is legitimate to evaluate the balance between the costs and benefits of the intervention. For example, adopting a new program for students at risk and their families would require in-service training and consultative assistance and would be time-consuming to implement. Therefore, a new program should be adopted only if a group of students will benefit, strong administrative support exists, professional development training and other resources are available, and the program will likely be continued in the future.

Interventions at this level should

- Be as low cost and low effort as will yield acceptable results

- Be no more intrusive, specialized, or adaptive than necessary

- Be proven effective by research and practice

- Match the function of the problem behavior(s)

- Be designed with family and student involvement

- Demonstrate good contextual fit

- Be monitored and assessed for progress

The following sections describe some possible selected interventions, from broad-based practices that are easy and efficient for teachers and other school personnel

to put into place to those that are somewhat more difficult and time-consuming to implement. The strategies are organized into the following five categories:

1. Effective instructional practices

2. Effective school and classroom behavior management

3. Existing programs and supports

4. Group or individual supports and adaptations (e.g., environmental supports)

5. Newly adopted social-behavioral intervention programs/packages

Effective Instructional Practices

It can never hurt to begin a behavioral intervention process by examining the match between the student's learning needs and the instruction being provided. Educators have long known that effective teaching is associated not only with academic success but also with reduced rates of disruption and other problem behavior (Lee, Sugai, & Horner, 1999; Sulzer-Azaroff & Mayer, 1991). The teaching practices and classroom management strategies that enhance students' academic success are well documented and include, for example, well-organized classrooms where teachers have established and taught classroom rules and procedures; engaging lessons at appropriate levels of difficulty; a high rate of active participation by all students, which is facilitated by the use of small groups and hands-on learning activities; and the use of visuals and conceptual organizers (Berliner, 1986; Brophy & Good, 1986; Kounin, 1970; Marzano, Marzano, & Pickering, 2003; Marzano, Pickering, & Pollock, 2001; Rosenshine, 1983).

Peer tutoring and cooperative learning are two peer-mediated instructional models that have been extensively and successfully used in inclusive classrooms, including those with students having cognitive disabilities and emotional or behavior problems (Hunt, Staub, Alwell, & Goetz, 1994). Cooperative learning has been linked to a number of positive social and academic outcomes for students with and without disabilities, including enhanced academic achievement and expanded and improved affective skills (e.g., Johnson & Johnson, 1989; Slavin, 1991; Slavin, Madden, & Leavey, 1984). Chapter 5 in the companion book *Teachers' Guides to Inclusive Practices: Social Relationships and Peer Support, Second Edition* (Janney & Snell, 2006) provides in-depth information about using cooperative learning groups as a strategy for inclusion.

Some of these generally effective instructional practices and processes may need to be strengthened and/or made more strategic for students with emerging behavior problems. Depending on the results of the FBA, selected interventions for some students might include the following:

- Increase the use of small-group instruction, both teacher directed and peer mediated.

- Use interest inventories to gain a better understanding of students' motivations.

- Give students choices between two or three options instead of no choices or open-ended choices; for example, if math worksheets are predictive of disruptive behavior, give a choice of three different worksheets, all of which address the same skills but use varying formats or visual organization.

- Provide more structure when using cooperative learning and peer tutoring (e.g., make sure the focal student is assigned a role in which she or he will be successful, avoid peer interaction difficulties by carefully choosing the group members).

Effective School and Classroom Discipline

Effective schoolwide discipline systems are prevention oriented; they consider environmental influences on students' behavior, emphasize self-discipline over external control of behavior, and incorporate hierarchies of rewards and negative consequences for positive and negative behavior. Students at risk for behavior problems, however, may need more support in learning how to self-regulate, how to participate in group processes, and how to make good choices. Before making any individualized adaptations or creating new interventions, teachers should assess their application of the schoolwide discipline system to ensure that they are teaching the behavioral expectations and consistently following through on positive and negative consequences. Students who are exposed to multiple risk factors are "particularly susceptible to the lack of a schoolwide foundation; therefore, intensive interventions for these students work best in schools that have a solid schoolwide foundation" (Osher et al., 2004, p. 65).

Teachers may need to reflect on their relationships with students with problem behavior. Strong evidence exists to support the importance of teachers' rapport with students as a necessary setting event for social and academic growth. Ideal teachers are often described as evidencing two complementary dispositions: 1) warmth or cooperation and 2) leadership or dominance in their relationships with students (Marzano et al., 2003). Yet students whose behavior is disruptive, antisocial, or disrespectful can be trying for teachers and lead them to respond impulsively, sarcastically, or even aggressively.

Teachers must also bear in mind that some students' behavior difficulties will not be remediated by even the most effective universal interventions or the best of teacher intentions. Therefore, teachers may need to adapt certain features of the schoolwide strategies and arrangements, including classroom or school routines, reward systems, and the amount of modeling, cueing, and supervision provided.

Student Snapshot

 An FBA of second-grader Mariah's disruptive behaviors—which included taunting classmates and refusing to follow her teacher's directions— revealed that the behaviors tended to occur most at times when other students received recognition for doing their classroom jobs, but much less on days when Mariah was assigned a classroom job and received positive attention for doing her job. Mr. Jarvis, Mariah's teacher, hypothesized that Mariah was finding ways to receive attention from the teacher and her peers. Although the classroom job routines had already been established, Mr. Jarvis made some adjustments that gave Mariah and several other students more opportunities to fill small roles in the classroom. He made sure to give these students positive attention for completing their jobs. Even a job as small as handing out materials, reading aloud the name of tomorrow's line leader, or carrying something for a teacher had a positive impact on Mariah's and the other students' behavior.

Some selected supports that can make schoolwide or classroom discipline systems and procedures more effective for students include the following:

- Provide environmental supports such as careful seating or additional supervision in situations that predict problems.

- Reteach school and classroom rules for behavior, provide more frequent modeling and cueing, and increase the frequency of reinforcement for meeting expectations.

- Reteach, remind, and reinforce classroom routines and procedures for transitions, group and individual work, homework, signaling for teacher attention, use of restroom, and so forth. In addition, analyze whether there are aspects of these routines and procedures that should be adjusted— either for the entire class or for one or more particular students.

- Remember to cue positive behavior by reminding the students of what *to do* rather than what *not to do* ("You can throw that paper in the trash" rather than "Do not throw that paper on the floor"), and to deliver effective encouragement and praise by calling attention to the specific behavior that was displayed and emphasizing the student's own effort and pride.

- If reward tickets are given on a random or intermittent basis when a teacher catches a student demonstrating a school expectation, give the students extra social recognition and enthusiasm as the ticket is bestowed ("You showed respect and kindness when you held the door for Mr. Branson. What a good school citizen you are!").

- Provide additional supervision—in positive ways. Use "with-it-ness," proximity control, and other surface management techniques to prevent slight disruptions from escalating (Kounin, 1970; Long & Newman, 1996).

- Give the students additional ways to make contributions or fill valued roles (e.g., taking notes to the office, reading to a younger student, researching an answer to a student's question you could not answer, taking down bulletin board displays).

- Provide additional prompting and reinforcement of the social skills being taught to the entire class.

Existing Programs and Supports

Some programs and supports may already be available in the school for use as selected interventions. These interventions are slightly more time-consuming to use than simply reinforcing or making slight adaptations to effective instructional and behavior management practices, but they are still relatively low cost and manageable. The following is an array of possible interventions and supports that could be accessed selectively for individuals or groups of students:

- Homework clubs
- After- or before-school social, physical health, or academic programs (e.g., running clubs, intramural sports, computer clubs)
- Counseling programs
- Adult mentoring programs
- Peer mentoring programs
- Tutoring by volunteers or older students

Group or Individual Supports and Adaptations

In this somewhat more intensive category of selected interventions, consider virtually any of the intervention strategies that could be used in individualized PBS plans (individualized PBS is examined in Chapter 5), but select only a few that are relatively easy to administer and will have an immediately noticeable impact. Some of these supports or adaptations are antecedent alterations and some involve teaching and reinforcing new or weak social, communication, and self-control skills.

One intervention in this category is the "check-in/check-out" system, an intervention specifically designed for students needing secondary interventions. The check-in/check-out system is designed to provide added structure for the student, to improve communication between school and home, and to increase the adult social recognition available to participating students. Taylor-Greene (2002) described one middle school's version of this support system. Students are nominated for the Behavior Education Plan (BEP) team (a school team similar to what we have referred to in this chapter as the Student-Focused PBS Team) based on having received five or more office disciplinary referrals, or through nomination by teacher, student, or family. The student and parents meet with the BEP team to develop a written contract for improving the student's behavior. As part of this contract, students are to "check in" at the school counseling center each morning to pick up a daily BEP form. The student gives each teacher the BEP form at the start of each class; at the end of class, the teacher evaluates whether the student met, partially met, or did not meet the "High Fives," or schoolwide rules for behavior. At the end of the day, the student "checks out" at the counseling center and obtains social recognition and a small edible treat if the BEP form has been completed. Students take a daily report home for their parents' signature (Taylor-Greene, 2002).

Fifty-four percent of the students in Taylor-Greene's middle school met their BEP goal (Taylor-Greene, 2002). In their evaluation of this check-in/check-out system, however, March and Horner (2002) discovered that the effectiveness of the system varied according to the function of the students' behavior problems. The intervention was far more effective for students whose behavior problems were motivated by peer or adult attention than for students whose behaviors were motivated by escape. Furthermore, a considerable number of students demonstrated an increase in problem behavior after entering the program; the majority of those students evidenced behavior problems that served an escape function. The results of this study point once again to the importance of tailoring interventions to an FBA so that reward systems do not further reinforce the original problem behavior (March & Horner, 2002).

The following list suggests a number of other possible selected supports and adaptations:

- Use careful scheduling in order to place a student with a particular teacher or peer group.

- Send home daily notes or report cards to parents; keep them as positive as possible, making sure that the student is capable of meeting the goal that has been set.

- Provide small-group booster sessions in social skills, problem solving, and conflict-negotiation strategies that are being taught in the students' classrooms; either review previous lessons or rehearse for an upcoming lesson.

- Supplement classwide social skill instruction with small-group instruction on *additional* social and self-management skills identified through an FBA; prompt and reinforce use of those skills throughout the day.

- Add self-monitoring and self-reinforcement strategies to the classroom discipline system and/or the use of social skills that have been taught (Chapter 5 provides guidance regarding the use of self-management systems).

- Have the students assist teachers with role playing during social skills lessons for younger students to give them additional practice in performing social skills, along with valued roles and responsibilities.

- Provide brief but strategic and intensive one-to-one instruction (e.g., two 5-minute sessions per day) that focuses on remediation of specific skills or supplemental literacy intervention.

- Implement facilitative strategies or formal programs for building supportive peer relationships, especially for students with more severe disabilities.

A number of these approaches and programs are described in a companion book in this series, *Teachers' Guides to Inclusive Practices: Social Relationships and Peer Support, Second Edition* (Janney & Snell, 2006).

New Programs or Intervention Packages

Although the research base for selected interventions for problem behavior is sparse in contrast with that for universal and individualized interventions (partly because it is difficult to define precisely what a selected intervention is), research has been conducted on several "packages" of interventions and on some proprietary/commercial programs that were designed to be used with groups or sets of students having particular social and behavioral needs. Three of these are outlined in this section. These are the most resource- and time-intensive of the strategies presented in this chapter. They have been proven effective in improving behavior and academic performance for not only individual students but also for small groups and entire classes. If a school is seriously intent on preventing new cases of serious behavior difficulties, and if the program fits with the school's overall improvement plans and other contextual factors, these programs are worth consideration as interventions for students who are at risk.

First Step to Success

The First Step to Success program (Walker et al., 1997) consists of three interconnected modules that provide a comprehensive and very successful intervention package for preventing antisocial behavior patterns in young children who experience risk factors for poor behavioral and academic outcomes (Golly, Stiller, & Walker, 1998; Walker, Golly, McLane, & Kimmich, 2005; Walker et al., 1998). The three components include universal screening and early detection, school intervention, and family support and parent training. Brief descriptions of the three modules follow:

1. *Universal screening and early detection.* The screening component consists of systematic screening of K–3 classrooms to detect behaviorally at-risk students and students with signs of antisocial behavior. There are four different screening options that vary in cost and complexity.

2. *School intervention.* The school component uses the CLASS (Contingencies for Learning Academic and Social Skills) Program for Acting-Out Children, which teaches adaptive behavior for school success and developing friendships. The intervention involves close monitoring of classroom behavior, a rich schedule of points and praise for academic engagement and following class rules, and home–school communication about the student's performance at school.

3. *Family support and parent training.* This component uses a 6-week in-home parent training program called Homebase, which focuses on showing parents how to teach their children skills such as cooperating, problem solving, and playing well with other children. The lessons complement the CLASS program.

The second component of First Step to Success is based on 5 years of develop-

ment and testing, and the third component is based on 30 years of research. The program was cited by Joseph and Strain (2003) as having a high level of evidence of success. The large-scale replication of the program in Oregon (Walker, Golly, et al., 2005), which received 2 years' funding from the state legislature, yielded results consistent with the initial trials conducted by the program's authors, including significant improvements in rates of adaptive behavior, aggression, and maladaptive behavior by target students and positive consumer satisfaction. A number of limitations, however, resulted from logistical difficulties, problems with data collection, and the need for behavioral coaches to implement and evaluate the project. In the real world, the fidelity and overall quality of implementation varied from excellent to quite poor (Walker, Golly, et al., 2005).

RECESS: Reprogramming the Environmental Contingencies for Effective Social Skills

RECESS is a program for reducing aggressive behavior (e.g., bullying, teasing, harassing) of children in kindergarten through third grade—which is, with respect to child development, the optimal time for effective intervention (Walker, Hops, & Greenwood, 1993). This comprehensive (and rather complex) behavior management program emphasizes a "reduce-and-replace" strategy for decreasing problem behavior and teaching prosocial forms of peer-related behavior. The program's focus on first reducing aggressive and other negative responses toward peers and then increasing positive responses is based on observational research showing that aggressive children display negative responses toward peers (i.e., verbal or physical aggression) at a rate that is about eight times that of their typical peers; however, these same aggressive children display approximately the same rate of positive social responses as their peers.

The four major components of the RECESS program are

1. Systematic training in cooperative social behavior using scripts, discussion, and role playing for students who are aggressive and their classmates

2. A response cost system involving sanctions (point loss and time-out) for negative and aggressive behavior, breaking rules, teasing, and bullying; points are allotted at the beginning of recess and then taken away if the student exhibits aggressive behavior toward peers, with bonus points awarded for extra kind or cooperative behavior toward peers or handling a problem well

3. A high rate of praise by the consultant, teachers, and other adults when the focal student(s) exhibits positive, cooperative social interactions

4. Group contingencies (rewards and privileges) that are used at school while individual contingencies are applied at home

The program is gradually extended from recess to the classroom and includes maintenance strategies. The RECESS program was developed, tested, and revised over 5 years and has had a powerful effect on the social behavior of aggressive children in grades K–3 (Walker et al., 1993). Like other programs designed to improve children's social behavior, it must be implemented correctly in order to have the desired effects. Although the program has been effective with hundreds of students, its drawbacks are that it does require a program consultant and a significant commitment of time and effort (Walker et al., 2004).

Social, Behavioral, and Academic Prevention Strategies Tested in Urban Elementary Schools

Kamps and colleagues evaluated a prevention program that was implemented for 28 students in multiple classrooms in three urban elementary schools (Kamps, Kravits, Stoize, & Swaggart, 1999). The participating students were selected either because they had been classified as having an emotional or behavioral disorder (EBD) or because they obtained a score on the SSBD (described in Figure 3.2) in the range of "serious maladaptive behavior" and "persistent difficulty in class participation and learning" and therefore were identified as at risk for more serious emotional or behavior problems.

The intervention package included social, behavioral, and academic interventions that were delivered as "universal" interventions for entire classroom groups; however, data were collected only for at-risk students and students with diagnosed emotional or behavior disorders. The three intervention components were as follows:

1. *Classroom management system.* The contingency management system included a reward/reinforcement system using points awarded for task completion and appropriate behavior, and a levels system with a hierarchy of reprimands and consequences for inappropriate behavior (warning, loss of recess time, time-out or office referral, call to parent, parent conference).

2. *Social skills instruction.* Social skills instruction used a combination of lessons from McGinnis and Goldstein's (1997b) *Skillstreaming the Elementary School Child.* The ASSIST Program (Affective/Social Skills: Instructional Strategies and Techniques; Huggins,

1995), and Violence Prevention: Second Step (Fitzgerald & Edstrom, 2006). Targeted skills included basic classroom survival skills, positive peer interaction and friendship skills, and problem-solving strategies.

3. *Peer tutoring.* Classwide peer tutoring, which was developed at Juniper Gardens Children's Project (Greenwood, Delquandri, & Carta, 1997), was used for reciprocal peer tutoring in reading.

After one year of implementation, targeted students showed significant improvement in contrast with a control group on rates of on-task behavior, out-of-seat behavior, following directions, disruptive behavior, aggression, and positive recess interaction and play. Significant differences were not obtained on negative verbal behaviors in the classroom and levels of negative interactions at recess (Kamps et al., 1999).

EVALUATING SELECTED INTERVENTIONS

Monitoring the use of the planned intervention and changes in students' problem behaviors should be as great a concern to teachers and other members of school PBS teams as any other aspect of the behavior support system. The check-in/check-out system described earlier sounds like an excellent way to provide increased support, supervision, and rewards for students; however, it may have actually worsened the behavior of some students (March & Horner, 2002).

The evaluation measure used should be the same measure that was used to identify students who should receive selected interventions. If referrals to the Student-Focused PBS team are based on number of office disciplinary referrals, then the number and reasons for those referrals should be tracked. If ratings on a social-behavioral screening system were used to detect students needing intervention, then the same rating system should be used again after the intervention is in place to evaluate the effects.

The evaluation of selected interventions should address both individual student progress and trends within the school. It is important to evaluate the secondary prevention system and not only its effects on an individual student.

CONCLUSION

Students who are at high risk for developing behavior problems and those who show emerging behavior problems need a higher intensity of support than many of their peers. Best practice suggests, and intervention research shows, that further prevention efforts are imperative to the future mental health and well-being of students whose behavior difficulties cannot be remediated through universal, schoolwide interventions. In this chapter, the elements, strategies, and processes that can be used to identify and deliver selected behavioral interventions for this group of students have been briefly discussed. Further research is needed to help us understand how to be more prescriptive in matching students with interventions and to identify the sorts of training and expertise that teachers need to design and deliver this level of PBS.

Chapter 4

Individualized Positive Behavior Support
Conducting a Functional Behavioral Assessment

Chapters 4 and 5 describe the four steps of a process that educational teams can use to develop positive behavior supports (PBS) for individual students. Chapter 4 presents Steps 1 and 2, which require defining the behavior(s) of concern and conducting a functional behavioral assessment (FBA). Chapter 5 concentrates on Steps 3 and 4, which entail designing, implementing, and evaluating a PBS plan.

The students considered in Chapters 4 and 5 are those whose problem behaviors are *seriously disruptive or destructive*. These students—who most often are classified as having emotional or behavioral disorders, cognitive disabilities, or severe disabilities—have behavior problems that do not improve adequately in response to schoolwide behavior supports or selected interventions created for groups of students. The number of students with behavior challenges of this magnitude is relatively small (often estimated at 5%). Proper assessment and effective intervention are likely to require in-service training for school staff and, in the most challenging cases, the guidance of experienced behavior specialists. More people are involved in designing and providing the specialized interventions needed by these students, so the importance of effective communication, coordination, and collaborative teaming also increases.

Research strongly supports the value of FBA as the basis for developing effective individualized behavioral supports. Significant improvements have resulted from PBS interventions for diverse participants (adults and children; persons with autism, mental retardation, emotional/behavioral disorders, and other disabilities) with a variety of targeted behavior problems, with aggression/destruction, disruption/tantrums, self-injury, and stereotypic behavior being the most likely behavior targets in published research (Horner et al., 2002). Analyses of the research on PBS have found PBS to be effective in reducing targeted problem behaviors by an average of 80% in approximately two thirds of cases. When one uses a 90% reduction in problem behavior as the criterion, about one-half of the outcomes of PBS intervention are successful. When the type of function (i.e., *communicative* in contrast with *sensory*) is considered, the success rate drops to about 60% for improvements in behaviors that serve sensory functions (Carr et al., 1999; Didden, Korzilius, van Oorsouw, & Sturmey, 2006; Horner et al., 2002; Marquis et al., 2000). One thing that is especially important to note about the research results on PBS, however, is that when the intervention was based on an FBA, the success rates almost doubled (Carr et al., 1999). The few research studies that have contrasted *function-based* and *non–function-based* interventions on rates of problem behavior for individual students have found the function-based interventions to be far more successful (Ingram, Lewis-Palmer, & Sugai, 2005; Newcomer & Lewis, 2004).

In this chapter, the process of conducting an FBA in schools is detailed. The specific examples in this book that illustrate the process involve students with individualized education programs (IEPs) who exhibit serious behavior problems and who are based in inclusive, general education classes. The examples come from students known to the authors or our colleagues in K–12 schools, although some demographic information, such as age or gender, has been changed and some examples are composite cases. In some of these cases, the authors served as consultants and assisted school teams in learning the functional behavioral assessment process so that they could then implement it more independently in the future.

WHAT IS FUNCTIONAL BEHAVIORAL ASSESSMENT?

Functional behavioral assessment (also called functional assessment) is a process for gathering and analyzing information to uncover the purpose of a student's behavior problems and the relationships between those behaviors and the physical and social context. The FBA process is used to make behavior support plans more effective and efficient.

Two types of methods are used for collecting FBA information:

1. *Indirect (informant) methods* include records reviews, questionnaires, and checklists. Indirect methods rely on existing records and interviews with knowledgeable persons.

2. *Direct methods* require observation of the student in relevant places and situations. Direct methods are used to obtain information at the specific time the behavior occurs.

When sufficient relevant information has been gathered, an FBA should reveal 1) a well-defined *behavior* (or behaviors) of concern, along with baseline data on the frequency and duration of the behavior(s); 2) the *antecedents* that predict when the behavior occurs and does not occur (antecedents include *triggers* that immediately precede the behavior and *setting events,* more distant antecedents that increase the likelihood of problem behavior); 3) the *consequences* that maintain the problem behavior by enabling the person to obtain something or avoid something; and 4) one or more verified *hypotheses* as to why the problem behavior happens based on the information about antecedents and consequences.

The Behavior. First, the target behavior(s) is defined in observable and measurable terms, and a baseline assessment of the rate and/or duration of the behavior is conducted. It is crucial to gather baseline data about how frequently and/or how long a problem behavior occurs so that you can know for certain whether the plan you develop is helping. Sometimes the plan helps you feel like you are doing something to improve the situation, but it has few actual effects on the problem behavior itself.

Antecedents. Information about what is going on when the behavior occurs—or does not occur—helps reveal how the environment is related to the behavior. For example, if the behavior tends to occur more often when the student is asked to do paper-and-pencil tasks than when doing hands-on, functional tasks, then the function of the behavior *may* be to avoid those difficult or nonpreferred tasks. If the behavior occurs more often when the student is left alone than when she or he is working with an adult or with other students, then the purpose of the behavior *may* be to get attention. If you can discover what antecedent variables (e.g., events, people, places, objects, physical conditions) are *triggers* for the behavior, you can change some of those stimuli (at least temporarily) and sometimes prevent problems from occurring. (In scientific research, the specific variables are called *discriminative stimuli;* these are the cues that set the stage for the behavior.)

In addition to the effects of specific triggers on behavior, behavior can also be influenced by *setting events.* Setting events are biological, social, or physical incidents or circumstances that are more distant from the behavior but make it more likely that a specific cue will trigger the behavior. This is similar to the phenomenon of "having a bad day" or "getting up on the wrong side of the bed." Once a certain negative event happens, its after-effects taint the rest of the day.

When gathering information about antecedents, look for answers to "who, what, when, and where" questions. The answers to these questions can help uncover patterns of antecedents that predict that the problem behavior will occur.

Consequences. The third type of information to gather is about the consequences or what happens after the behavior occurs. Used in this sense, the term *consequences* refers not only to planned rewards or punishments that are being used but also to any event or circumstance that happens following the behavior (e.g., Do other people leave the student alone? Does a crowd of people gather? Does the student obtain some object that she or he had wanted? Do other students laugh? Is the student reprimanded by an adult?). Learning theory tells us that the student would not continue to use the behavior unless it was effective—at least some of the time—in helping to meet some need or purpose. Information about the consequences that follow the behavior indicates what the person is accomplishing by using the behavior or, in other words, how the environment is reinforcing and therefore maintaining the behavior.

When thinking about how consequences maintain a behavior, it is important to realize that our intentions do not necessarily match the way our actions affect another person's behavior. For example, we may think that reprimanding a student for acting out serves as a punishment and that the student will act out less in the future if our reprimands are consistent. If the purpose of the student's acting out is to gain attention, however, then our attention may be rewarding to the student, even if we believe that a reprimand is a negative consequence.

Hypothesis Statements. The three types of FBA data are used to generate hypothesis statement(s) about the antecedents that predict that the problem behavior will or will not occur and the way that consequences maintain the behavior. Recall from Chapter 1 that the most common purposes of problem behavior are obtaining social interaction or some activity or item, and avoiding social interaction or some activity or item. For example, an FBA for Alicia might indicate the following:

When Alicia is alone in the cafeteria or in the hallway during class transitions and she sees classmates engaged in socializing, she interrupts her peers' conversation, taunts them, and calls them names. The other students tell Alicia to "knock it off" and tease her in return. If we repeatedly observe this pattern in Alicia's behavior and also observe that when Alicia does not interact in these negative ways she has little interaction of any kind with her peers, we might hypothesize that the underlying purpose or function of Alicia's taunts is to gain her peers' attention.

The less common purposes of problem behavior are obtaining internal or sensory stimulation or avoiding internal stimulation. For example, an FBA for Daniel might indicate the following:

When there are no ongoing activities, Daniel rocks and bites his fingers. When Daniel rocks and bites his fingers, a teacher or aide goes to him and gives him one of his toys. Daniel then stops rocking and biting his fingers and plays with the object. If we find that Daniel's behavior repeatedly follows this pattern, regardless of whether he is receiving social attention at the time, the purpose of Daniel's problem behavior may be to obtain sensory input or internal stimulation when he is bored and has nothing to do.

FBA does not require formal testing of the hypothesis statement(s) about the triggering antecedents of the problem behavior and the consequences maintaining the behavior—although simpler verification methods may be used to test hunches. *Functional analysis* is the process of systematically manipulating the variables (i.e., antecedents and/or consequences) that are believed to be affecting the problem behavior in order to test the accuracy of initial hypotheses (O'Neill et al., 1997). Functional analysis is used primarily in experimental research about behavior problems, but it is seldom used by teachers in school settings for a number of reasons (Horner et al., 2002; Snell et al., 2005). Figure 4.1 provides further description of these differences and advice regarding the use of functional analysis. The FBA described in this book utilizes a process for verifying hypotheses that seeks a middle ground between formal functional analysis and simply going with a hunch or best guess.

When Is a Functional Behavioral Assessment Needed?

Schools should, of course, follow the Individuals with Disabilities Education Act (IDEA) requirements for conducting an FBA. It is important, however, to recognize that FBA was a standard of effective practice for addressing the challenging behavior of students with disabilities for a number of years before it was first required by IDEA.

Students whose behavior remains an impediment to their learning and/or that of their peers, their mental health, or their social relationships in spite of schoolwide and selected interventions are candidates for individualized FBA. FBA is best used proactively, however, and should not be reserved only for use in crisis situations. As a matter of good practice, an FBA should be done during the prereferral intervention process or during initial evaluations or reevaluations if a

student's behavior inhibits his or her learning or that of others. A simple, commonsense guideline to follow is this: If everyone who knows the student is concerned about his or her behavior, it is time to take a proactive, systematic, and analytical approach to addressing those problems. FBA is such a process.

The FBA approach—with its emphasis on being analytical and diagnostic rather than reactive punitive—is useful for all sorts of behavior problems. The complete, formal FBA, however, is used only on behalf of students in need of the tertiary level of intervention—those students with IEPs who have significant, persistent behavior problems.

The schoolwide behavior support system should include delineation of the processes and procedures for initiating and conducting an FBA and developing a PBS plan. These processes and procedures should include 1) the composition of a multidisciplinary assessment or support team; 2) the tools and strategies used to conduct an FBA; 3) guidelines for intervention planning; 4) guidelines for data collection to monitor and evaluate interventions; and 5) ways to involve, communicate with, and support families.

Conducting a Functional Behavioral Assessment

Figure 4.2 lists the four steps for creating a system of positive behavior supports and the forms and worksheets (blank copies of which are provided in Appendix A) to be used during the process. In addition to the forms accompanying each step, use the Team Meeting Agenda and Minutes form (a completed sample is provided in Figure 1.4; a blank copy is included in Appendix A) to plan each team meeting and maintain written records of all decisions made and actions taken. On the form, be sure to identify not only the planned actions but also who will carry

Functional Behavioral Assessment and Functional Analysis: What Is the Difference?

What is functional behavioral assessment (FBA)?

- FBA is a process for gathering and analyzing information to determine the antecedents that predict or set the stage for a behavior problem, the consequences that maintain the behavior, and the purpose the behavior serves for the student.

- FBA does not require testing the hypothesis about the triggering antecedents of the problem behavior and the purpose it serves for the student.

What is functional analysis?

- Functional analysis is a test to confirm or refute the accuracy of a hypothesis about the problem behavior's function and the triggering antecedents when these are not clear *even after a thorough FBA.*

- Functional analysis requires intentional and precise presentation of the conditions that provoke the problem behavior, while directly observing and recording the problem behavior.

- Functional analysis can vary in complexity and precision:

  - The most complex versions require experimental manipulation of the antecedent and/or consequent events believed to be responsible for the behavior; this experiment is usually conducted in controlled, often unnatural settings (e.g., Iwata, Dorsey, Silfer, Baumna, & Richman, 1994; Wacker, Cooper, Peck, Derby, & Berg, 1999).

  - Other versions involve testing the likely functions of problem behavior in natural settings by scheduling a purposeful manipulation of antecedents and/or consequences during typical routines (Carr et al., 1994). This verification process is less precise but tests whether the problematic variables (e.g., the difficulty of tasks, the availability of social interaction) are valid and relevant to what happens to the person on a day-to-day basis.

What cautions and considerations apply when using functional analysis?

- Functional analysis enables the assessor to learn what the purpose of the problem behavior is and to use that information to develop effective behavioral interventions. However, its benefits must be weighed against the risks involved: Functional analysis requires *creating* a situation in which the problem behavior occurs and purposefully providing reinforcement for the problem behavior; the risk to the student and/or others must be minimal.

- Formal, experimental functional analysis artificially isolates the antecedents right before the behavior and the reinforcement right after the behavior, and therefore is most often conducted in an isolated setting; the process cannot capture the influence of setting events and other variables that occur in the student's real life, such as the possible influence that peers may have on the behavior (Bambara & Kern, 2004; O'Neill et al., 1997).

When is functional analysis used in schools?

Only if …

- The behavior problem is a serious, destructive behavior

- Intervention methods are failing

- Other reliable sources of FBA information do not provide a clear set of validated hypothesis statements

- The school team has the needed support of a trained PBS consultant and/or PBS behavior analyst

- Parents and/or care providers have given permission (as well as human subjects committees or review boards, as required; Bambara & Kern, 2004; O'Neill et al., 1997).

What alternatives are there to functional analysis?

Conduct simple checks of your hunch by observing the student during typically occurring activities when you have made short-term, nonintrusive alterations to the antecedents (e.g., tasks that are easy or hard) and/or consequences (e.g., obtaining or not obtaining teacher attention) for the problem behavior. Base your support program on functions that can be verified informally.

Is functional analysis always needed in order to verify hypothesis statements and develop an effective PBS plan?

- No. Research has shown that hypotheses based on descriptive information (i.e., interviews, rating scales) from parents, teachers, and students themselves, and/or on direct observations in natural settings, can be highly consistent with those confirmed by functional analysis (Arndorfer, Miltenberger, Woster, Rortvedt, & Gaffaney, 1994; Newcomer & Lewis, 2004).

- Although careful functional analysis must be required for published research, teachers and other practitioners should use the most efficient functional behavioral assessment methods required to create an effective intervention plan (Scott, Bucalos, & Liaupsin, 2004).

Figure 4.1. Functional behavioral assessment and functional analysis: What is the difference?

Steps and Tools to Develop Individualized Positive Behavior Supports (PBS)		
Student Jason	**Date initiated** January 15, 2007	
School Lincoln Elementary	**Grade** fourth	

Members of PBS Team

Jared Simms/special education teacher   Rita Santos /fourth-grade teacher

Marianne Josephs/school district behavior specialist   Ashley Giles/instructional aide

Rob Moore & Carly Roberts/parents   Mara Kellam/school psychologist

Steps and Accompanying Functional Behavioral Assessment (FBA) Tools
(Check box when completed)

Step 1: Identify and Prioritize the Problem(s); Make a Safety Plan

    Step 1A: Identify the Problem(s) and Decide on Priorities

      ☑ Step 1A Worksheet: Problem Identification and Decisions About Priorities

      ☑ Team Meeting Agenda and Minutes form (use at each team meeting)

    Step 1B (if necessary): Make a Safety Plan

      ☑ Step 1B Worksheet: Safety Plan

      ☑ Incident Record

Step 2: Plan and Conduct the Functional Behavioral Assessment (FBA)

    Step 2A: Gather Descriptive Information

      ☑ Step 2A Worksheet: Student-Centered Functional Behavioral Assessment Profile

      ☑ Student Schedule Analysis

    Step 2B: Conduct Direct Observations

      ☑ Interval Recording or Scatter Plot

      ☑ Antecedent-Behavior-Consequence Observation

    Step 2C: Summarize Functional Behavioral Assessment and Build Hypothesis Statement(s)

      ☑ Step 2C Worksheet: Summary of Functional Behavioral Assessment and Hypothesis Statement(s)

    Step 2D (if necessary): Verify Hypotheses

      ☐ Team Meeting Agenda and Minutes with plan for verifying hypotheses

      ☑ Interval Recording or Scatter Plot and/or

      ☑ Antecedent-Behavior-Consequence Observation

      ☐ Revision of Step 2C Worksheet

Step 3: Design a Positive Behavior Support Plan

      ☑ Step 3 Worksheet: Positive Behavior Support Plan

Step 4: Implement, Monitor, and Evaluate the PBS Plan

      ☑ Step 4 Worksheet: Implementing, Monitoring, and Evaluating the PBS Plan (decisions recorded on Team Meeting Agenda and Minutes form)

Figure 4.2. Steps and tools to develop individualized positive behavior supports for Jason.

out these responsibilities and by when. Accountability is crucial to effective PBS teamwork. Other guidelines for making team meetings efficient and genuinely collaborative are described in Chapter 1.

As a general guideline, expect to complete the FBA over the course of two to three weeks, with team meetings held weekly or biweekly, and then to develop a PBS plan that is initially implemented for two weeks or so, and then reviewed and revised as necessary at follow-up meetings every two to four weeks.

Student Snapshot

Jason is a fourth grader who is classified as having mental retardation and displays some autism-like behaviors. He reads picture books, can write some words and phrases, and communicates through a combination of words and gestures. His IEP goals include both simplified academics in math, reading, language arts, and the content areas and functional goals for using communication and self-help skills (see Figure 4.3). Since he was a small child, Jason has dis-

played various behaviors that have concerned his parents and teachers. His problem
behaviors and the decisions that his teachers
and parents have made about how to support
improvements in his behavior are described in
the worksheets that accompany each step of
the four-step process.

The remainder of this chapter explains
the process of conducting an FBA for
Jason and other students with disabilities
and serious behavior problems. The
accompanying figures illustrate how
Jason's support team used the forms pro-

vided in this book to guide their information gathering, problem solving, and
decision making.

STEP 1

IDENTIFY AND PRIORITIZE THE PROBLEM(S); MAKE A SAFETY PLAN

Figure 4.4 summarizes the first step in the FBA process. In Step 1A, the team defines the behaviors of concern, categorizes their seriousness, and

Program-at-a-Glance	
Student Jason	**Date** January 2007
IEP Goals	**IEP Accommodations**
Social/communication • Use simple sentences to express needs, feelings, ask questions, make choices, respond yes/no • Greetings and good-byes: initiate and respond to peers and adults • Relate recent events in simple sentences (subject+verb+object or modifier; correct pronouns and verb tense) Functional skills • Follow classroom schedule with same cues provided to classmates • Independence in school arrival, departure, restroom, lunch routines • Independence in school/classroom jobs and management of belongings, materials Math • Addition and subtraction to 20 • # line for less than, more than • Time to minute (face, digit) • Count combinations of coins and bills to $10; use money in functional contexts Language arts • Literal comprehension questions, novels, and other literature selections • Read adapted novels/stories at first-grade level • Compose three-sentence paragraph with capitalization and punctuation (period and question mark) • Read/write/spell functional words, novel unit vocabulary, and content unit vocabulary; add to personal word bank Content areas • Key concepts for each unit	• Receive special education assistance/instruction with academics, daily routines, transitions, support for communication, peer interactions • Weekly curricular adaptations by special education and general education teachers (simplified and reduced content) • Assignments modified (e.g., simplified/reduced content, fewer items per page, word banks) • Designated location in school for breaks • Real coins and bills for counting money • Textbook read orally to him • Adapted quizzes/tests based on IEP goals and "nice-to-know" content
Academic/social management needs • Gestural prompts and visual organizers work well • Peer buddies assigned for recess, lunch	**Comments/special needs** • Anecdotal records for IEP progress • Core team meetings weekly; whole team monthly

Figure 4.3.   Program-at-a-Glance for Jason.

decides which behavior(s) are intervention priorities. If a student has seriously destructive or dangerous behaviors, the optional Step 1B, developing a safety management plan, also is completed. If a safety management plan is needed, it should be implemented immediately, even before the FBA is completed.

Step 1A: Identify the Problem(s) and Decide on Priorities

Using the Step 1A Worksheet: Problem Identification and Decisions About Priorities (Figure 4.5 gives an example), team members who know the student best describe the problem(s) as precisely as possible, in terms of the observable actions. Make your description as specific as possible so that every member of the team knows exactly which behavior is being considered. For example, instead of describing the behavior in vague terms (e.g., "Jeremy just won't do anything I tell him to"), describe exactly what Jeremy does when he is told to do something. Does Jeremy tear or throw papers when you hand them to him? Does he sit down on the floor and say "You can't make me" when it is time to go to music? Instead of defining the behavior as "Erin gets upset all the time," try to describe what Erin does that tells you she is upset. Does she cry, scream, and hide under the desk? Does she run out of the classroom?

Notice the difference between the two lists of descriptions in Figure 4.6. The general labels in the right-hand column do not actually describe what the student does. For example, *aggressive* could mean pushing, hitting, biting, yelling, or many other actions. These general labels tell us more about how we feel about the behavior than about what the behavior itself looks like. In contrast, the observable behaviors listed in the left-hand column are specific and state exactly what the student did or did not do.

Often, students have more than one problem behavior. Several behaviors may happen at once in the same situation, or one behavior may precede another as part of a sequence. (The technical term for a set or group of behaviors that occur together in the same context or serve the same purpose is *response class.*) If a particular set of behaviors accelerates or decelerates together, these behaviors should be addressed collectively within the PBS plan. For example, a student may put his head down on his desk, cry, and then scream and throw things during the same incident. These four behaviors should be described and worked on together. Some problem behaviors, however, may not be closely related. A student may cry when left alone but may put his head down on

---

Step 1
Identify and Prioritize the Problem(s); Make a Safety Plan

Ask: What, specifically, is the problem?
Define the problem behavior(s) in observable terms.

Ask: What behavior or behaviors have priority and warrant an FBA and PBS plan?
Determine the priority level for each behavior—destructive, disruptive, or distracting—and the rationale for intervention. If there are several problems, target the most serious for comprehensive PBS and focus on positive programming and improvements in the environment to address those of lesser concern.

Ask: Is a plan for safety management to protect and calm during destructive or seriously disruptive incidents needed immediately?
Develop a written Safety Plan that details when and how to respond to critical incidents, including a procedure for completing Incident Records.

Figure 4.4. Step 1: Identify and Prioritize the Problem(s); Make a Safety Plan.

Step 1A Worksheet: Problem Identification and Decisions About Priorities		

| **Student** Jason || **Date** January 15, 2007 |

As specifically as possible, describe each problem behavior—what it looks and sounds like, how intense it is, and how long each has been a problem. Estimate the frequency and duration of each behavior. Label the behaviors according to their level of priority.

Description of problem behaviors	Level of priority
1. Pushing adults or peers with one or both hands. Usually not hard enough to hurt, but enough to move peers out of his way. Has been a problem for at least 2 years. Occurs several times per day.	☐ Destructive ☑ Disruptive ☐ Distracting
2. Kicking adults or peers using foot or leg. Kicks others on their legs if he is standing or sitting at desk, on feet, on legs, or at times on back if students are sitting on the floor. Occasionally bruises a peer. Behavior started this year. Occurs 2 or 3 times a week, usually along with pushing.	☑ Destructive ☐ Disruptive ☐ Distracting
3. Refusing to do tasks/assignments. Leaves seat or assigned area; does not take out or put away needed materials; pushes materials around his desk, tears them, or drops them on the floor. Has been a problem for several years but has worsened the past year.	☐ Destructive ☑ Disruptive ☐ Distracting
4. Yelling and screaming, usually directed at adults (e.g., "You're not the boss," "No!," or "nonsense" noises). Has been somewhat of a problem since first grade but is worse this year. Occurs every day.	☐ Destructive ☑ Disruptive ☐ Distracting
5. Occasionally displays "tantrums" with all of the above behaviors plus destroying materials, lying on the floor, very loud yelling/screaming. Has escalated in past several months. Occurs about once a week but sometimes more.	☑ Destructive ☐ Disruptive ☐ Distracting

Decision and rationale: Which behaviors should be priorities for intervention and why?

Pushing and kicking are the most serious because they are very disruptive to learning (for Jason and his classmates) and other students are bruised occasionally. The two behaviors often occur together. However, all four behaviors—pushing and kicking as well as refusing and yelling—sometimes happen in a sort of chain reaction that leads up to a tantrum. All of these behaviors seem to be getting worse. Also, they are interfering with Jason's relationships with his classmates. Therefore, we think that a PBS plan for Jason should address all of these behavior concerns.

Is a Safety Plan needed immediately?   (Yes)   No

Figure 4.5. Step 1A Worksheet: Problem Identification and Decisions About Priorities for Jason.

his desk when asked to work on an assignment. These behaviors are probably not closely related. As you generate hypotheses about the functions of the problem behaviors, you may find that several behaviors are used to achieve the same purpose (e.g., escape difficult tasks). In that case, the support plan should address these behaviors as a set.

Although it is important to define all problem behaviors in observable terms, several behavior problems may be

Observable behaviors	General labels
Hitting adults and other students with a fist or open hand	Aggressive
Using profane words in school and on bus	Mean
Crying during instructional time	Self-stimulatory
Rocking upper body back and forth while sitting at desk or table	Frustrated
Throwing books, pencils, papers, and other instructional materials	Uncooperative
Banging head on the floor	Upset
	Angry
	Anxious
	Rude

Figure 4.6. Differences between observable behavior and general labels.

grouped into categories such as "physical aggression," "verbal aggression," "non-participation," "noncompliance," or "self-stimulation." In these cases, you would give the set of behaviors a general descriptor such as "aggression" but also list the observable actions that fit under that category, such as "hitting or kicking peers, throwing objects at peers, and making threatening gestures."

Also, record an estimate of the frequency and duration of each problem behavior. These estimates should later be verified more systematically (e.g., through direct observation), but this information may be relevant to the team's decisions about priority behaviors.

After defining the behaviors of concern (still using the Step 1A Worksheet: Problem Identification and Decisions About Priorities), the team should rate the seriousness of each problem behavior and decide which behaviors are of greatest concern at the time. To decide where to start, think of three priority levels for problem behaviors: *destructive, disruptive,* and *distracting* (Janney, Black, & Ferlo, 1989; see Evans & Meyer, 1985, for another way to categorize the seriousness of problem behavior).

Destructive behaviors are health- or life-threatening behaviors to the student or others and should always be top priority. Destructive behaviors include biting or hitting, eye poking, head banging, scratching, cutting, and refusing to eat.

These behaviors should be addressed immediately through a plan for safety management until an FBA is conducted and a comprehensive PBS plan developed.

Disruptive behaviors are next highest in priority. These behaviors prevent teaching and learning from taking place or prevent the student from participating in daily living activities at school, at home, or in the community. Disruptive behaviors include "acting out" behaviors as well as persistent withdrawal from social contact through not speaking, crying, or literally or figuratively pushing away other people to avoid interaction. Stereotypic behaviors (e.g., hand flapping, other repetitive movements) can be disruptive if they prevent the person from engaging in interaction and participation, but this judgment should be based on an FBA. Disruptive behaviors typically should be addressed through a behavior support plan unless the student has more serious destructive behaviors that should be given higher priority.

Distracting behaviors are given the third and lowest priority. Such behaviors may include echolalia, tics, rocking, hand flapping, fidgeting, and other behaviors that are bothersome but do not really cause harm. In general, such behaviors are not part of a formal FBA or intervention plan unless they are either a high priority to the family or in danger of becoming more serious if ignored. For example, persistent scratching may become self-injurious if it is serving to gain attention for the person, echolalia or hand flapping may interfere with social acceptance in public places, and rocking may become disruptive if it increases in intensity as a response to work that is too easy or too difficult. If distracting behaviors become targets for intervention, the focus often is primarily on teaching alternative behaviors if such goals are consistent with the student's other IEP goals.

The discussion of intervention priorities may lead the team to decide that lower priority disruptive and/or distracting behaviors need only to be addressed by improving the environment and preventing the problem behavior. For example, if it is clear that Jeremy displays disruptive behaviors such as throwing and tearing materials only when paper-and-pencil tasks that are not matched to his skill level are assigned to him, the task requirements could be adapted, or he could be assigned different tasks that are hands-on, reflective of his interests, and better matched to his skill level. In such situations, the formal FBA may be discontinued, although it is wise to monitor whether the desired changes in the student's behavior problems and/or academic work occur.

In the lower portion of the Step 1A Worksheet, write the team's decision about which behavior(s) should be targeted for intervention and give the rationale for the decision. Behavior change goals are, of course, part of a student's IEP, so decisions regarding priorities should be made in conjunction with the student's IEP team.

Step 1B: Make a Safety Plan (If Necessary)

If a student is known to display destructive, dangerous behaviors that can cause serious harm to the student or others, the support team should immediately develop a Safety Plan even before the FBA is conducted. The purpose of a Safety Plan is to protect the student and others and to deescalate the problem as quickly as possible.

Creating a Safety Plan requires team problem solving to tailor an individualized plan that will be effective for a particular student's pattern of escalation and recovery and that will have good contextual fit with the particular school and classroom. One way to organize a written Safety Plan is according to the phases of the crisis cycle of behavior, which is illustrated in Figure 4.7 (Colvin, 1993). The Step 1B Worksheet: Safety Plan (see Figure 4.8) assists staff by 1) clarifying who should intervene in a critical incident, 2) giving directions for how to intervene and support the student during the five phases of the crisis cycle, and 3) setting consistent guidelines for reporting on serious incidents and the use of the Safety Plan. The Safety Plan includes the following information:

1. The names of the people who will intervene in a serious behavioral episode. If only one adult is present, should someone else be called to assist? How will that other person be made aware of the situation? If there are several adults present, who is best at helping the student calm down and therefore should be the first person to intervene?

2. Directions for how to intervene and support the student during the five phases of the crisis cycle:

    a. *Trigger Phase:* What physical, verbal, or affective signals does the student send that he or she is feeling threatened and that a serious incident might occur? For example, does the student demonstrate loss of attention, physical agitation, heightened color, ex-

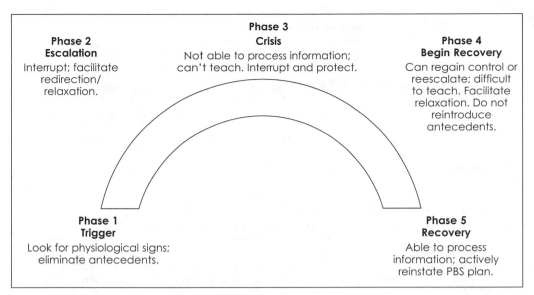

Figure 4.7. Phases of the crisis cycle and corresponding interventions. (*Source:* Colvin, 1993.)

cited speech, tears, or sweating? How can *antecedents* that may have triggered the problem (e.g., a difficult task, waiting for attention, repeated prompts/demands, corrections, teasing) be eliminated? How quickly does the student's behavior tend to accelerate during the trigger phase? (Bambara & Kern [2004] likened the concept of a crisis cycle to an "acting out cycle," and contended that some students have fast versus slow acceleration and slow versus fast deceleration. The student's rates of acceleration and deceleration influence how much time you have to respond and thus what strategies you might use in a critical incident.)

b. *Escalation Phase:* How will the behavior be *interrupted* and how will the student be redirected? Will humor, getting a drink of water, running an errand, or switching gears to move to another place or activity help interrupt the chain of behaviors? What are some strategies for engaging the student in the new

activity? Are there relaxation strategies that the student has been taught such as deep breathing, visualization, or positive thinking aloud? What posture and tone of voice should the adult maintain?

c. *Crisis Phase:* If the problem behavior is not interrupted, how will you protect the student and everyone present? Will you remove other students? Will you try to move the student to a quiet place? Will the student be momentarily restrained? Will aggressive actions be blocked? What position and proximity to the student should the person who is intervening maintain? Will music, deep breathing, taking a walk, or talking to the student about other things in a soothing voice help him or her regain control? (Make sure staff members understand that the student essentially is on "automatic pilot" and in a "fight or flight" mode at this point. He or she is unable to process complex verbal or rational information, so this is

Step 1B Worksheet: Safety Plan	
Student Jason	**Date** January 19, 2007

Behavior(s) that call for use of the Safety Plan

Yelling/screaming for over 2 minutes at a level that halts instruction and/or pushing or kicking any peer or adult a second time after being reminded of the rules and the need to stay in control

Who will intervene in a serious behavioral episode?

The special education teacher or instructional aide who is nearest to Jason at the time

---

How to intervene and support the student during phases of the crisis cycle

1. **Trigger Phase:** *Describe signals the student sends that indicate feeling threat/discomfort. Describe antecedents known to trigger problems and how to eliminate them.*
   a. Any of Jason's problem behaviors can be signals: yelling/screaming, refusing to work, dropping or destroying materials, pushing or kicking other people.
   b. Triggers include
      - Receiving a minus on his point card—especially the fifth one or higher. If this has happened, remind Jason that he can still have a good day and will have another chance tomorrow.
      - Facing a difficult writing task. Review the task with Jason, making sure he knows what to do. Remind him that teachers are here to help him if needed.

2. **Escalation Phase:** *Tell how to interrupt, redirect, and facilitate relaxation.*
   a. Position yourself on Jason's level physically; use eye contact. In a neutral but firm tone of voice, remind him of the rules and that he is able to stay in control.
   b. Say "Let's take two deep breaths," and model for him. Praise him for doing this.
   c. Provide structure for the task at hand: Tell him how much longer or how many more items he will be doing. Direct him to the schedule to show him what's next.
   d. Redirect him to the task/activity (e.g., "You did this one just right. Here's where the next one goes.").
   e. As soon as Jason makes any attempt to participate, give verbal encouragement and a visual signal such as a thumbs up or high five.
   f. Be assertive and calm. Do not beg, plead, cajole, or bargain with Jason for cooperation. Give visual cues and prompts.

3. **Crisis Phase:** *Describe how to interrupt and protect the student and others.*
   a. If the behavior does not stop, move Jason immediately to the conference room or the special education office. Use a route that keeps him as far from the other students as possible. Use your body position to guide him, touching him as little as possible.
   b. Remain calm and emotionally neutral while doing this. Do not talk about the behavior; just tell Jason that it is time to go to the conference room so that the class will not be disrupted, he can calm down, and everyone will be safe.
   c. Take along the work in progress if possible. There is a box of alternative work in the conference room to use when needed.
   d. Do not talk about the problem behavior yet. Remind Jason that the two of you will stay in the conference room until he is calm and has finished his work or the class period ends while he is working.
   e. Use the red pass to get help from someone on the crisis team if you feel yourself getting upset, if you need a break, or if it becomes necessary to physically stop Jason from leaving the room, destroying property, or hurting you (this seldom occurs). Send this pass to the office with any student or other person passing by, and the secretary will send help immediately.

Figure 4.8.   Step 1B Worksheet: Safety Plan for Jason.

---

4. Begin Recovery Phase: *Describe how to avoid reescalating the behavior and continue to reach full recovery.*

a. Use gestures, modeling, and other visual prompts to redirect Jason to his work. Give verbal and gestural praise as soon as Jason even attempts to participate. The goal is to enable Jason to calm down but not to allow him to escape from the task that triggered the problem. Give as much support and encouragement as needed, however, to engage him in the task. Make it fun and interactive.

b. Jason returns to the classroom either 1) as soon as he completes the task for the current class period, or 2) when the class period ends, if he is attempting to do the work. The goal is to move the schedule along so that Jason has an opportunity to try again. Jason returns to the class with a clean slate.

c. If the class period ends and Jason has not attempted any of his work and is not calm enough to return to the classroom, ask the secretary to call Mr. Simms (special education teacher), who will gather new materials for the next activity on the schedule.

---

5. Recovery Phase: *Describe any processing/reflecting that should be done with the student and how to reinstate the PBS plan.*

a. Remind him of the rules for expected behavior and tell him that you know he can be more successful next time.

b. At this point, we are not doing any processing with Jason about incidents; later, the PBS plan may include a strategy for Jason to reflect on his goals and better ways to reach them.

Directions for reporting and documentation: *Give instructions for reporting the incident and completing and filing Incident Records.*

a. Complete an Incident Record as soon as possible with as much detail as possible. Be objective in describing the incident, but then add your own ideas about why the incident happened and what might prevent it in the future. Give completed report to Simms, who will file the report in Jason's PBS notebook in the Student Services office.

b. We will have a quick emergency team meeting after any critical incident during which the red pass is used.

---

neither a good time to ask the student to process the experience nor an opportune time to try to rationally convince the student that his or her response is inappropriate. Trying to teach during this phase is not productive.)

d. *Begin Recovery Phase:* What antecedents should not be reintroduced because they might reescalate the behavior? What will help to further deescalate the problem? It is still difficult to teach at this point; instead, will music, deep breathing, walking, or talking about other things be used to further calm the student?

e. *Recovery Phase:* The student may be ready and able to discuss what happened and what can be learned from the incident. What sort of processing, if any, should be done with the student? Does the student complete a reflection or self-evaluation? How and where is the PBS plan reinstituted? Is the use of alternative behaviors prompted and rewarded? (Carr et al. [1994] urged teachers and caregivers to use the window of opportunity that follows the end of a crisis to reinstitute their teaching of alternative behaviors and not to pull back and bask in the return to peace and quiet.) How is the student assisted to reenter the original setting? What participation goal is set, and how is the student prompted to become engaged?

3. Directions for completing an Incident Record (see Figure 4.9). The adult who intervened in the situation should complete the report as soon as possible after the episode; the information should be as detailed and specific as possible. Ask the person completing the report to prob-

lem solve about ways the problem could have been prevented or can be handled more effectively in the future. Include instructions about who should be informed about the incident and where completed Incident Records are to be kept.

A written record of serious incidents and the use of a Safety Plan is required in most schools and can be helpful with regard to the information-gathering and problem-solving processes used in Step 2: Plan and Conduct the Functional Behavioral Assessment. An Incident Record such as that shown in Figure 4.9 serves both of these purposes. For example, the instructional aide who completed the sample Incident Record in Figure 4.9 noted that the transition from a preferred activity (journal writing on the computer) to a nonpreferred activity (language skills) may have helped trigger the incident and that Jason accomplished avoidance of the disliked task by engaging in the difficult behavior. Furthermore, the aide suggested that problems might be avoided in the future by better communication with Jason regarding the beginning and ending of activities and by having a way to distract him when his behavior begins to escalate.

It can be tempting to think that the way a serious behavioral incident is handled will be a primary factor in altering the student's behavior. It may be more fruitful, however, to view a crisis as an event that can be used for further problem solving by the support team. After a critical incident, the important question for teachers to ask is, "What did we learn that will help to avoid this situation in the future?" Jason's support team always organized a quick team meeting after any serious incident when the special education teacher had been summoned to intervene. The team realized that, aside from ensuring that the serious incident did not result in harm to the student or others, the most

important result would be using information about the incident to prevent future episodes.

STEP 2
PLAN AND CONDUCT THE FUNCTIONAL BEHAVIORAL ASSESSMENT (FBA)

 After defining the problem behaviors and making decisions about intervention targets (and addressing issues regarding safety management, if needed), the next step is to plan and conduct the FBA (Figure 4.10).

The time and effort required to conduct an FBA can vary greatly, depending on the seriousness, intensity, and resistance of the target behavior. As indicated previously, the process described in this book is designed for use by school teams who have some training in PBS, with outside expertise added as needed to conduct a valid FBA and to design and evaluate an effective PBS plan. When conducting an FBA, use the most *efficient* FBA methods required to create an *effective* PBS plan. The methods used must be adequate yet feasible given the context and the personnel available. A wise tactic is to gather information in stages, beginning with the simplest, most user-friendly methods available, and then proceeding, as necessary, to the use of more complex methods.

For some students, the FBA can rely primarily on indirect assessment methods completed by people who know the student well (and by the student, if possible). Discussions of pooled information from reviews of student records and the use of self-reports and interviews to complete FBA checklists and questionnaires may be adequate to enable the team to see the patterns of predictive antecedents and maintaining consequences and to build valid hypotheses. Direct observations methods would be required only to

Incident Record	
Student Jason	**Completed by** Ashley Giles (aide)

Day Friday	**Date** January 26, 2007	**Time** 1:00 P.M.–1:30 P.M.

Setting   Ms. Santos's fourth-grade classroom

Class or activity   Social studies, Activity Center rotation

Staff present   Ms. Santos, Ms. Giles

Students present   All 23 classmates, working in four groups at centers

1. **Describe what happened earlier in the day and/or just before the incident that may have led to the incident.**

   Jason had pushed a classmate at recess, so I had given him a minus on his point card. This meant that he would not have computer time this afternoon.

   Yesterday, the students started working at the solar system centers. They were split into four groups and were rotating through the four centers. The kids did two centers yesterday and would do the other two today. The centers were very hands-on and fun, so I thought Jason would enjoy them today like he did yesterday.

2. **Describe the student's behavior and others' responses during the *Trigger* and *Escalation* phases.**

   Ms. Santos gave instructions for the center activities and told the groups which centers to go to. Jason went with his group to the Planetary Bingo center. I saw his expression change when he realized that he would have to read the words on the bingo cards. I sat down behind him so that I could give him hints and read the words for him. But he still had a hard time keeping up with the game, and I could see him getting more frustrated. He stopped putting his markers on his card and hid them under the card instead. I reminded him that the bingo game was his assignment, handed him a marker, and pointed to the right space on the card. He said "Stupid game!" and started dropping his markers on the floor. I tried to ignore the behavior and just picked up the markers and put them back on the table. Jason kept yelling things like "Stupid bingo," and "I want a different game."

   Jamal was sitting beside Jason and said something like, "Come on, Jason, let's play the game. We're going to get in trouble." Jason pushed Jamal on the arm. I reminded Jason of the rule against pushing, and tried to block his arm, but he still managed to push Jamal on the arm a second time. Jason was yelling out nonsense noises at this point, and his group had stopped the game.

3. **Describe what the student and others did during the *Crisis* phase.**

   I told Jason that it was time for us to go to the conference room. I motioned for him to stand up and go to the door. I picked up his bingo card and some markers to take with me. Jason kept making loud noises but was not aggressive and went out the door ahead of me. He ducked into the restroom as we went by it, but came back out after about a minute. When we got to the conference room, he lay on the floor. I said, "Let's take some deep breaths; that will help us to calm down." He did the deep breathing. He was calm and quiet in about 3 minutes.

4. **Describe the *Begin Recovery* and *Recovery* phases. Describe how the PBS plan was reintroduced.**

   I put Jason's bingo card and markers on the table and said, "I bet I can say the names of all the planets in order from the sun." He started to say them with me. I reminded him of what would happen next—that we would finish playing the bingo game until he had five in a row, and then we would go back to the room. I started asking questions about the planets and giving him two choices for answers—he got most of the answers right. I put the markers on the card. Then he got up from the floor and started putting markers on the right spaces when I pointed to them. Then I got out a piece of paper and when he answered a question, I wrote down the answer for him so that he could find the right square on his bingo card. I said a lot of "good jobs" and gave him high-fives. We finished the game in about 7 minutes.

   Jason asked, "Do I get computer time now?" I said no, that it was time to go back to class to see Ms. Santos and the other boys and girls, and that it was almost time for recess. I reminded Jason to carry his materials back to class and put them away. He followed the direction and went to recess with the other students.

Figure 4.9.   Incident Record for Jason. *(continued)*

Figure 4.9. *(continued)*

5. **To what extent was the Safety Plan followed?**	(Fully) Somewhat Very little

6. **What is your hunch about the *setting events* and/or *triggers* of the behavior?**

Jason just hates the point system, even though he loves using the computer. He almost never gets the computer time. After he gets more than 5 minuses on his point card, he is so stressed and frustrated that he has a terrible time for the rest of the day. Also, when he saw that the Planetary Bingo game was going to be too hard for him, he just did not even try.

7. **What is your hunch about the *purpose of the behavior* or how it is "working" for the student?**

I think Jason knows full well that if he yells, pushes, and carries on, he will escape from a situation that is hard for him to cope with.

8. **What might *prevent* or *interrupt* the behavior more effectively in the future? What suggestions do you have to *improve the Safety Plan?***

- *The point system needs to be revised: Jason cannot get the reward very often, so he just gives up and does the behaviors that help him to escape situations that are hard for him (e.g., reading, writing).*
- *Jason's bingo card should have been adapted for him, or maybe the students could work in pairs so that Jason does not have to work alone.*

assess the baseline rate of the behavior and the effects of the PBS plan.

As the complexity of the student's behavior problem and other needs increases, indirect data-collection methods must be augmented by direct observations. In addition, a structured observational procedure to verify the team's hypotheses about the behavior may be required. This verification process, which is described later in this chapter, entails a very simple functional analysis procedure that is conducted in naturally occurring contexts.

In the most dangerous and complex cases, a combination of indirect methods, more extensive direct observations, and a formal functional analysis may be needed. This certainly may be the case for students with few conventional means of communication who have self-injurious behaviors that serve several purposes. Such procedures, however, should not be conducted without the guidance of a qualified specialist (Horner et al., 2000; Scott & Caron, 2005).

Because of these potential variations in the complexity of FBAs, Step 2 may require three or four substeps. Step 2A:

Gather Descriptive Information, Step 2B: Conduct Direct Observations, and Step 2C: Summarize Functional Behavioral Assessment and Build Hypothesis Statement(s) are always required; Step 2D: Verify Hypotheses may be required. Whether Step 2D is necessary depends on the amount and types of information gathering that are needed in order for the team to understand the behavior well enough to construct effective interventions.

Step 2A: Gather Descriptive Information

After defining the behavior(s) to be targeted for intervention, the team gathers descriptive information about the student and his or her behavior problems from people who know the student well and from the student, if possible. The tools for indirect data collection provided in this book are the Incident Record, the Student-Centered Functional Behavioral Assessment (FBA) Profile, and the Student Schedule Analysis. It should be noted that these specific data-collection tools have not been validated by research as ways to gather and analyze the informa-

---

Step 2
Plan and Conduct the Functional Behavioral Assessment (FBA)

Step 2A: Gather descriptive information from people who know the student well.

Ask: What do we know about the student's quality of life, needs, strengths, interests, and behavior history? Which classes and activities tend to be successful or unsuccessful?

Ask: How often and for how long do the behaviors targeted for intervention occur?

Ask: What information do we already have about the antecedents (both setting events and immediate triggers) that predict that the behavior will occur? What consequences may be maintaining the behavior? What hunches do we have about the purpose of the problem behavior?

Decide: Do we have full and accurate answers to these questions? If "yes," go to Step 2B; if "no," continue to gather descriptive information from key people in the student's life.

Step 2B: Conduct direct observations.

Ask: When, where, and how should direct observations be conducted so that we can gather the information we need to understand the behavior's antecedents, consequences, and purpose? Collect data for about 5 days.

Decide: Do we have adequate information to build solid hypotheses that will enable us to create an effective PBS plan? If "yes," go to Step 2C; if "no," conduct additional observations for about 5 days.

Step 2C: Summarize functional behavioral assessment and build hypothesis statement(s).

Ask: What have we learned about the setting events and triggers that predict the behavior, the consequences that are maintaining the behavior, and the purpose the behavior serves for the student? What alternative behaviors will serve the same purpose for the student that the problem behavior now serves?

Decide: Do we have adequate information to complete the Step 2C Worksheet, including valid hypothesis statements about the antecedents and consequences of the behavior and the purpose of the behavior? If "yes," continue to Step 3; if "no," go to Step 2D.

Step 2D: Verify hypotheses.

Ask: When, where, and how can we informally verify (or disprove) our hypothesis statement(s)? How can naturally occurring routines or activities be altered in nonintrusive ways to allow us to compare the student's behavior under the usual conditions and the altered conditions? How often should we conduct the verification test to be sure the results are accurate?

Decide: Now are we confident that we have built valid hypothesis statements based on the FBA? If "yes," continue to Step 3; if "no," continue verification process.

Figure 4.10. Step 2: Plan and Conduct the Functional Behavioral Assessment.

---

tion required to design an effective PBS plan. The format and content of these tools, however, are very similar to instruments that have been research-validated (e.g., the Functional Behavioral Assessment Interview [FBAI; Crone & Horner, 2003]). Furthermore, there is some evidence that the FBA data and hypotheses generated through indirect methods such as those provided in this book are substantially consistent with the results of

FBAs that employ direct observations and functional analysis (Newcomer & Lewis, 2004).

An important instrument that is not included in this book, but which the authors highly recommend, is the Student-Guided Functional Assessment Interview (SGFAI; O'Neill et al., 1997). This student-guided assessment was tested and found to have a high rate (over 75%) of agreement between students and their teachers on identifying the problem behaviors, their predictors, and the maintaining consequences of the behavior (Reed, Thomas, Sprague, & Horner, 1997). The FBAI, SGFAI, and several other interview and self-report instruments are in the resource list provided in Appendix B.

Student-Centered Functional Behavioral Assessment Profile

The Student-Centered Functional Behavioral Assessment Profile (see Figure 4.11) is used to gather information about relevant aspects of the student's social, personal, behavioral, physical, and academic history and current status. This assessment does not comprise a complete student-centered planning process. It is designed to focus the initial stage of the FBA on the student's quality of life and the extent to which the student's strengths, needs, and interests are reflected in his or her current educational programming. Kennedy and his colleagues (Kennedy et al., 2001) have demonstrated the effectiveness of incorporating this type of student-centered information into the design of PBS plans.

The importance of encouraging and valuing family involvement cannot be overstated. It is not enough simply to invite families to participate—their priorities and vision for the future should be the foundation for the PBS plan (Dunlap et al., 2001). Implementing a student-centered planning process that is more comprehensive than the one incorporated into the Student-Centered FBA Profile is one way to create a broader context for family participation. Such techniques include Making Action Plans (MAPs; Vandercook, York, & Forest, 1989), Planning Alternate Tomorrows with Hope (PATH; Pearpoint, O'Brien, & Forest, 1998), and Personal Futures Planning (Mount, 2000).

Before meeting as a team to complete the Student-Centered FBA Profile, team members should study the form so that they can come to the team meeting prepared to share their responses to the items on the profile. Then, at a team meeting, this information can be shared and discussed. If there are other people who know the student well (e.g., family members, previous teachers, paraprofessionals) but did not attend the team meeting at which the Student-Centered FBA Profile was originally filled out, arrange interviews with them as soon as possible. If first-hand interviews with key people are not possible, perhaps these people will be willing to respond through phone calls, e-mail messages, or by completing the form themselves.

The Student-Centered FBA Profile provides spaces to record relevant information about each of the following aspects of the student's quality of life, needs, and strengths:

1. *Quality of life.* How are quality-of-life indicators such as the presence of supportive people, access to objects and activities of interest, and opportunities to make choices and decisions in place for the student? How often is the student expected to participate in contexts that are known to be disliked by or challenging for the student? After recording this information, assign a baseline rating for each indicator: Is the presence of each indicator "good," "fair," or "poor" at this time? If there are shortcomings in the presence of these critical indicators, consider incorporating ideas for improvement into the student's PBS plan. Indeed, if any quality-of-life indicators are rated as "poor," making improvements in these areas should be a priority. Others who write and conduct research on positive behavior supports have expressed similar sentiments (Turnbull et al., 2004).

2. *Behavior.* Based on a review of IEP files and the knowledge of team

members, describe what has and has not helped the student's behavior in the past. If formal behavioral intervention plans have been implemented, you may want to summarize them and their results briefly and keep copies with the student's other PBS records.

3. *Academics.* Appraise the student's general academic strengths and liabilities. List as much information as you can about the teaching approaches

and strategies that have and have not worked for the student in the past. List what works (i.e., strategies that help learning and avoid behavior problems) and does not work (i.e., strategies that hinder learning and incite behavior problems) with the student.

4. *Communication.* Because communication is so essential to social and behavioral health and competence, catalog the student's ability to communicate

---

Step 2A Worksheet: Student-Centered Functional Behavioral Assessment (FBA) Profile

Student Jason	**Date** January 22, 2007
People providing initial information	**Other people who should be interviewed**
Jared Simms, special education teacher	Carly Roberts & Rob Moore, parents
Mara Kellam, school psychologist	Rita Santos, fourth-grade teacher
Marianne Josephs, school district consultant	

Directions: At a team meeting, summarize existing information about the student's problem behavior and begin to analyze the possible relationships among the behavior, the student's wants and needs, and the environment.

SECTION I: QUALITY OF LIFE

Ratings
Good = Indicator is in place satisfactorily.
Fair = The indicator is partially in place but improvement is needed.
Poor = The indicator is in place to an unacceptable degree or not at all.

Indicator	How is indicator in place?	Rating G F P
Supportive people		
a. Family	a. Lives with parents, older brother and sister; sees paternal grandparents often	a. Good
b. Adults at school	b. Has positive relationships with special education teacher and aide; fair relationship with classroom teacher; poor relationship with PE teacher	b. Fair

(continued)

Figure 4.11. Step 2A Worksheet: Student-Centered Functional Behavioral Assessment Profile for Jason.

Figure 4.11. *(continued)*

c. Peers at school	c. Several classmates have known Jason since first grade and are supportive friends, but some are just tolerant and a few are nervous or frustrated around him.	c. Fair to poor
d. Peers outside of school	d. Two classmates live in the neighborhood and are friends with Jason; also has a cousin who is a buddy.	d. Fair
Successful places and activities at school	Participates in activities in all areas and activities at school, but sometimes has to leave the library, computer lab, or playground because of behavior.	Fair
Successful places and activities at home and in the community	Successful at most family events/activities (picnics, hikes, church, shopping); movies and restaurants can be difficult at times. Parents would like Jason to be able to go to neighborhood park or YMCA with his older brother or friends and to play a team sport.	Fair
Interests and preferences	Picture books Computer games, certain DVDs, television Likes being outdoors Difficult to get him to try new things—places, activities, food, clothes, and so forth.	Fair
Opportunities to make choices appropriate for age	Chooses his clothes, lunch, free-time activities at home—but gets stuck on certain things. Does not ask to go places with friends as other boys his age do. At school, has difficulty choosing activities at recess, free time.	Fair

Based on the quality-of-life indicators, list shortcomings that might be addressed in a PBS plan.

Improvements in peer relationships at school and outside of school; Jason needs a broader circle of friends. He

needs social skills for initiating interactions, maintaining interactions, and managing frustration.

Difficulty with making choices, tolerating new places or activities, and having a wide range of interests.

SECTION II: ACADEMICS AND COMMUNICATION

Academic strengths	Academic liabilities
Numbers: counting, adding/subtracting, identifying	Weak at writing of any kind
Listening comprehension—loves to listen to others read	Difficulty staying on task
Very good general knowledge	Easily frustrated

Summarize the current fit between the student's educational programming and his or her academic strengths and liabilities.

Jason's learning goals are at a much lower level than his classmates', but many of the regular lessons and activities are adapted for him. The difficulties are the reading and writing demands in fourth grade. Jason's attention span is also put to the test, as most lessons are at least twice as long as he can tolerate.

Communication

What is the student's primary mode of communication (e.g., speech, signs, gestures, electronic devices) and how successful is the student in using it?

Jason uses speech and gestures; he seems to be able to get his basic wants and needs across to people. Does not express feelings in words. People who do not know him well can have difficulty understanding him.

How does the student accomplish these communicative purposes?

1. Gets attention/help/interaction: At times, asks appropriately; at other times, uses problem behaviors.

2. Gets preferred activities or tangible items: Gets it himself if possible; can usually tell you what he wants if it's food or something tangible. The problem is when he is not allowed to have it.

3. Avoids/escapes attention/interaction: Sometimes he just ignores you; sometimes pushes you away.

4. Avoids/escapes activity or item: "No," "I don't want to," pushes the item away, or leaves the area.

5. Calms self when agitated, upset, angry: Overstimulated: Will try to go outdoors if possible; not sure he has any other strategy.

6. Gets sensory stimulation: (e.g., when bored): Yells and screams? Not sure.

(continued)

Figure 4.11.   *(continued)*

SECTION III: MEDICAL, HEALTH, AND SENSORY CONCERNS

Describe any health concerns or medication that may be affecting the student's mood or behavior.
None at this time; has regular checkups

Describe any of the student's sensory difficulties or needs.
Parents thought that Jason might have a slight visual impairment, but he checked out ok.

Other important information about the student's medical and health history
None

SECTION IV: TARGET BEHAVIOR(S)

From the Step 1 Worksheet, which behavior or behaviors will be targeted for intervention? Define the behaviors as clearly and specifically as possible. These are the definitions that will be used to collect any additional information and to develop the PBS plan.

1. Pushing and kicking: Pushing an adult or peer with one or two hands on any part of the other person's body; kicking an adult or peer with a foot or part of the leg on any part of the other person's body.
2. Yelling/screaming: Very loud negative comments (e.g., "No, no!" "I won't!" "Stop it now!" or nonsense words) that can be heard by everyone in the room. Usually occurs in a burst of two or three phrases, so each burst will count as one yell.
3. Refusing to do tasks or assignments, as indicated by not being in assigned seat or location and tearing, dropping, or otherwise misusing materials.
4. Serious incidents that include an acceleration of pushing/kicking and yelling until Jason is out of control.

Describe any current interventions for the behavior(s) and summarize their effects. (Or attach any behavioral intervention plan that is currently in use.)

*   Jason starts the day with a blank point card. He gets a minus for each time he pushes or kicks someone and is told "Do not hit/kick. That hurts people." If he has four or fewer minuses per day, he gets to use the computer for the last 10 minutes of the day.
*   For yelling, pushing papers, and so forth, he is reminded of the class rules and is visually and verbally redirected to the task.

What works to prevent or interrupt the behavior(s)?	**What does not work to prevent or interrupt the behavior(s)?**
• Give him a break to look at a book or take a walk	• Time-out—he prefers it
• Find a hands-on activity instead of paper-and-pencil, or adapt the written task for him	• Too many paper-and-pencil tasks
• Let him know the schedule, what's coming up	• Getting into a tug-of-war, getting lots of corrections or threats

SECTION V: PRELIMINARY HUNCHES			
When these **Antecedents (Setting Events** and/or **Triggers)** occur	the student is likely to **(Target Behavior[s])**	and these **Consequences** tend to occur	Therefore, the **Function** of the behavior may be
1. Paper-and-pencil tasks	Will not get out his materials; plays with materials or drops them on the floor; leaves his seat or assigned area	Aide gets out Jason's materials and tries to focus him on the task; if materials are on the floor, Jason has to pick them up and then is redirected to the task.	To avoid or escape difficult or nonpreferred tasks
2. Tasks he does not understand (i.e., it's not very structured, it's unfamiliar, he doesn't know when it will end)	Will not get out his materials; pushes materials around his desk or onto the floor	Same as above	To avoid or escape difficult or frustrating tasks
3. At recess/free time, receives no attention from peers, is not asked to play a game, or is ignored when he tries to initiate an interaction	Pushing and/or kicking peers—mostly pushing	Some peers tell him to stop, some try to pacify him, some leave. An adult tells Jason to apologize; he receives a minus on his point card.	To get attention from peers
4. Lots of prompts and/or corrections, annoyed or authoritarian tone of voice or body language by an adult	Yells "no" or makes nonsense noises, tears or drops materials; sometimes pushes and/or kicks the adult.	Adult tells him to stop, uses gestures and verbal prompts to try to redirect him; if he does not stop, adult takes him into the hall to calm down.	To escape from adult interaction and from the difficult task

SECTION VI: DECISIONS AND NEXT STEPS

1. Should any other people be interviewed to ensure that the information on this profile is complete and accurate?   (Yes)   No

    If "yes," list others who should be interviewed:

    Ashley Giles, instructional aide; Ben Barrett, PE teacher
    _____

    _____

2. Does quantifiable baseline data on the targeted behaviors need to be collected?
    (Yes)   No

    If "yes," when, where, and how will data be collected? _____

    We will use the Interval Recording or Scatter Plot form to collect frequency data on both pushing/

    kicking and yelling/refusing for 5 days. Jared, Mara, and Marianne will develop a schedule among themselves.

(continued)

Figure 4.11.   *(continued)*

3. Is additional information needed to determine if the current "hunches" about the antecedents, consequences, and purposes of the behaviors are accurate?   (Yes)   No

    If "yes," when, where, and how will data be collected? _____

    The Interval Recording or Scatter Plot will give us information about the antecedents and consequences
    of the behaviors.
    Antecedent-Behavior-Consequence observations will be done during the four times of day that are usu-
    ally the most difficult: Morning Meeting, English/language skills, math, and PE. Each class or activity will
    be observed three times for about 20 minutes each time. Jared, Mara, and Ashley (instructional aide)
    will develop a schedule for conducting the observations.
    We also will keep Incident Records on use of the Safety Plan.

various wants and needs. Describe how the student requests attention, help, and tangible items and how the student protests or rejects a situation or activity. Many students with developmental disabilities experience shortcomings in their communication abilities—and in the ability of others in their environment to interpret and/or provide support for their communication. These shortcomings should be addressed in the PBS plan.

5. *Medical, health, and sensory.* Make note of any medical, health, and/or sensory difficulties that may be affecting the student's mood, concentration, physical comfort, or behavior.

6. *School records.* In this section of the worksheet, note relevant information from school records such as official disciplinary actions and attendance information.

7. *Preliminary hunches about the behavior.* The team may or may not choose at this time to brainstorm some preliminary hunches about the predictive antecedents and maintaining consequences for each target behavior identified in Step 1. These hunches also can be informed by the Student Schedule Analysis and any Incident Records that have been completed. Figure 4.12 provides a list of questions

to ask as you brainstorm about possible setting events and triggers and the purposes the problem behavior may be serving for the student.

The Student Schedule Analysis (see Figure 4.13 for an example) is a simple yet helpful way to start looking for patterns in the student's behavior. To complete the Student Schedule Analysis, the classroom teacher and other team members who are familiar with the student's performance on a typical day enter the student's daily schedule in the first column of the form and estimate the average success rate for each class or activity in the second column. The third, fourth, and fifth columns on the form provide spaces to describe the behavior, the grouping arrangement, the task type (i.e., whether the activity involves paper and pencil, oral communication, or hands-on learning), and the staff member or members who are with the student at that time. You may find that you want to use the columns on the Student Schedule Analysis for factors other than the ones included in Figure 4.13. For example, if you think there may be a relationship between the behavior and the type of seating arrangement or positioning, you could use one column to note whether the student is positioned, for example, at a desk, in a wheelchair, or on the floor for each activity.

The Student Schedule Analysis may help to detect predictive antecedents. It also provides a record of how successful the classroom teacher and other team members perceive each class or activity to be. The opinions of the teacher and other people about whether the problem behavior improves or worsens are one meaningful indicator of the success of a behavioral support plan. It is important to collect more objective data on the behavior, however, so that you can tell whether the behavior does in fact improve as a result of the intervention plan.

The Incident Record described earlier in this chapter and illustrated in Figure 4.9 serves as a way to keep track of the use of the Safety Plan that is necessary for some students. Completed Incident Records also yield information useful to the FBA because they include a report of the antecedents that led up to the critical behavior, what the student did throughout the incident, and the consequences that followed. Examining this information can assist in determining the predicting antecedents and maintaining functions of the behavior.

Completed Incident Records can be sorted into categories according to the types of antecedents that preceded each incident and the consequences that followed. If the majority of incidents were preceded by the same or similar triggers and followed by the same consequences (e.g., the student obtained something tangible that he or she wanted, a difficult task was terminated), a functional hypothesis may be revealed.

Questions to Ask About Antecedents and Consequences of Problem Behaviors

Teams can use this list of questions to prompt their thinking about 1) setting events, 2) specific triggers that may predict the problem behavior(s), and 3) consequences that may be maintaining the target behavior(s).

1. **Questions to ask about *triggers* (or close antecedents):**

   Who? *The answers to "who?" questions help you to see whether particular people or groups are related to the problem behavior.*

   Who is present when the problem behavior occurs?

   Who is present when the problem behavior seldom or never occurs?

       Are teachers, parents, staff, peers, older students, or strangers present?

       How many people?

       Is the student in a one-to-one, small-group, or large-group lesson?

       Is someone about to come in or about to leave?

       Is the student alone, with no interaction?

   What? *The answers to "what?" questions help you discover whether certain tasks or activities are related to the problem behavior.*

   What is going on when the problem behavior occurs?

   What is going on when the problem behavior seldom or never occurs?

       What kind of task is the student being asked to do? Is it hands-on, paper-and-pencil, reading a textbook, or playing a board game?

       What type of instruction is occurring? Is it individual seatwork, a cooperative group activity, or a lecture?

       What subject or class is taking place? Is it math, English, PE, or music class?

       Is the task structured or unstructured? Are the expectations clear or unclear?

       Is the student being asked to do something too easy/boring or too hard/frustrating?

       Is the student having to wait for help, attention, or a turn?

       What type of interaction is the student involved in? Is he or she alone, being prompted or corrected, or being spoken to in a particular tone of voice?

Figure 4.12. Questions to ask about antecedents and consequences of problem behaviors. *(continued)*

Figure 4.12.   *(continued)*

> **When?** *The answers to "when?" questions help you determine whether time of day, days of the week, and schedules are related to the problem behavior.*
> When does the problem behavior occur?
> When does the problem behavior almost never occur?
>   Before school?
>   During the morning? During the afternoon?
>   At the end of the day?
>   Before, during, or after lunch?
>   During transitions?
>
> **Where?** *The answers to "where?" questions help you understand whether places and spaces are related to the problem behavior.*
> Where does the problem behavior occur?
> Where does the problem behavior seldom or never occur?
>   On the playground?
>   In the classroom?
>   In the gym, library, or cafeteria?
>   In the restroom?
>   In the hallways?
>   On the bus or in the car?
> 2. **Questions to ask about *setting events* (or *distant antecedents*):**
>   What *physical factors* may be relevant? Noise? Crowds? High or low temperature? An uncomfortable body position?
>   What *social factors* may be relevant? The presence or absence of particular people? Being isolated when other peers are in groups? A conflict at home?
>   What *biological* factors may be relevant? A lack of sleep? Allergies? Hunger? Constipation? Menses? A sore throat, cold, or ear infection?
> 3. **Questions to ask about *consequences*:**
>   Does the student obtain attention? From peers? From adults? From parents?
>   Does the student obtain a desired object, activity, food?
>   Does the student escape or avoid an activity, task, or situation? Do demands stop? Is the student sent to the office or time-out?
>   Does the student escape or avoid adult or peer interaction? Do people back off?

Direct observations will be needed to assess the baseline rate and/or duration of the problem behavior before implementing a PBS plan. Even though school-based PBS teams are not conducting research, it is difficult to justify using a behavioral intervention plan without having a modicum of objective data to show that the target behavior is improving— and improving at an acceptable rate.

Step 2B: Conduct Direct Observations

The amount of time and effort that the behavioral team spends doing direct observations depends on many factors including how much the behavior varies from one situation or one day to another, the number of problem behaviors targeted for intervention, how often the behaviors occur, and so on. This section describes two ways to gather information through direct observation of the focus student in naturally occurring situations. The Interval Recording or Scatter Plot form (Figures 4.14 and 4.15) can be used to gather baseline data on the frequency with which the target behavior occurs and also is designed to provide information to aid in building and/ or confirming hypothesis statement(s). The Antecedent-Behavior-Consequence (A-B-C) Observation form (Figure 4.16)

Student Schedule Analysis

Student	Jason		Staff who work with the student on a regular basis		Specialty teachers:
Date	January 20, 2007				Barrett, PE; Jones, library;

Ashley Giles, aide (AG)
Rita Santos, fourth grade (RS)
Specialty teachers: Barrett, PE; Jones, library; Pena, art; Vanier, music

Jared Simms, special education teacher (JS)

Target behavior(s)

1. Refuse/yell: Refusing to do tasks or assignments; indicated by leaving seat or assigned area, not taking out or putting away materials, not moving to next location, and/or pushing or dropping materials; making very loud negative comments that can be heard by everyone in the room (e.g., "No," "I won't," "Stop it," nonsense noises).
2. Push/kick: Pushing adults or peers with one or both hands on any part of the other person's body; kicking adults or peers with foot or leg on any part of the other person's body.

Time	Class/activity	Rating & behavior + = mild/rare − = excessive/often v = variable	Grouping i = independent 1:1 = one-to-one sg = small group lg = large group	Task type Paper/pencil Oral/listening Hands-on Activity/routine Computer	Staff
9:00	Arrival: Walk from bus to classroom	+	i	Activity/routine	AG
9:10	A.M. routine: Unpack backpack, order lunch, turn in notes, classroom jobs	+	i	Activity/routine	AG
9:30	Morning Meeting	v (push/kick)	lg	Oral, hands-on	RS
9:45	English/language skills	− (refuse/yell)	lg	Oral, paper/pencil	RS
10:25	Snack/break	v (push/kick)	i	Activity/routine	RS
10:30	Reading: M/W/F, novel groups; T/Th, theme reading	+	sg	Oral, paper/pencil or computer	JS
11:00	Math	v (refuse/yell)	lg and sg or i	Paper/pencil, hands-on, or computer	RS & AG
11:45	Lunch	v (refuse/yell)	lg	Activity/routine	cafeteria aides
12:15	Specialties: M/W, physical education; T, art; Th, music; F, library	PE, − (push/kick) Art & library, + Music, v (push/kick)	lg	PE: activity Art: hands-on Music: hands-on Library: oral/listening	specialty teachers
12:45	Alternating days: social studies or science	v (refuse/yell)	lg and sg	Oral/paper/pencil, or hands-on	RS & AG
1:30	Recess	v (push/kick)	i	Activity/routine	RS
2:00	Theme activities for topical unit	+	sg	Hands-on	RS & JS
2:45	Pack up, departure; computer time if earned	+ if he has earned computer time; − if he has not (both behaviors)	1:1	Activity/routine and computer	AG

Figure 4.13. Student Schedule Analysis for Jason. (From Meyer, L., & Janney, R. [1989]. User-friendly measures of meaningful outcomes: Evaluating behavioral interventions. *Journal of The Association for Persons with Severe Handicaps, 14*[4], 267; adapted by permission.)

also gives a wealth of information about the antecedents and consequences influencing the behavior. Although using the data-collection methods described next requires some commitment of time and energy, they can be essential to creating an effective PBS plan. The support plan will be built from hypotheses that are based on answers to the following questions: What triggers and setting events predict the behavior? What consequences are maintaining the behavior? What purpose does the behavior serve for the student? There are no hard-and-fast rules about the time needed to gather baseline data that will help answer these questions, but five consecutive days are a reasonable start (McConnell, Cox, Thomas, & Hilvitz, 2001).

When Are Direct Observations Conducted and by Whom?

The more time-consuming direct observation methods do not necessarily need to be used across entire days. Observations can be scheduled for times when the information gathered for Step 2A indicates that the problem behavior is most and least likely to occur. For example, the Student Schedule Analysis might indicate that the student's behavior is predictably more of a problem in certain classes or situations than in others; additional data-collection can focus on gathering more specific, objective information about the student's behavior in those situations, rather than continuously.

If a behavioral consultant or school psychologist is assisting the team, she or he will be available to conduct at least some of the direct observations or teach other team members, teaching or administrative interns, other support personnel, or paraprofessionals how to do them. Although it may not be feasible for a teacher to do an A-B-C recording while teaching a lesson, it has been the authors' experience that many teachers are able to

maintain frequency counts using the Interval Recording or Scatter Plot form. If a special education teacher and a general education teacher are teaching collaboratively, using some co-teaching time for data collection can be a legitimate use of a teacher's time. If an instructional assistant, student teacher, or intern is available, he or she can be trained to assist in data collection.

As is suggested for all team decisions, use the Team Meeting Agenda and Minutes form (Figure 1.4) to record your decisions about which direct observation methods will be used, the names of the persons responsible for completing them, and the dates and times when they will be completed.

Measuring Frequency or Duration

In the following explanations of the use of these two direct observation methods, we use examples of problem behaviors that have a clear starting and stopping point, which enables the observer to count *how often* the behavior occurs. For example, if the problem behavior is hitting other people, the observer would count the frequency with which this happens. Note, however, that if the problem behavior is one that does not have a clear starting or stopping point or if it occurs for greatly varying periods of time, then the observer would need to measure *how long* each instance lasts. For example, if the student's crying episodes sometimes last just a few minutes and other times last 10 minutes or more, then simply counting the number of times that the student cries would not show whether the amount of time spent crying was decreasing over time. A student could cry five times in one day for a total of 5 minutes, or he or she could cry five times in one day for a total of 90 minutes. In this case, the duration of the crying is important information to have in addition to the number of times the student cries.

Interval Recording and the Scatter Plot

Use of the Interval Recording or Scatter Plot form (see Figure 4.14) involves counting (or estimating) the frequency with which a behavior occurs during predetermined intervals of time (e.g., 1 minute, 10 minutes, 30 minutes). The Interval Recording or Scatter Plot form can be used in several different ways. One way would be to conduct a *frequency count*. The observer tallies each time the behavior occurs during each time period. A second way would be to create a scatter plot (Touchette, MacDonald, & Langer, 1985). A scatter plot estimates the number of times a behavior occurred by doing *partial interval recording*: The observer uses a code to record the relative frequency of the behavior during each time interval. For example, in Figure 4.15, an open circle (○) was used to indicate that the behavior had occurred once during a 30-minute time period. The circle was filled in (●) to show more than one occurrence of the behavior. In other words, the first time the behavior occurred, the person recording the data drew an open circle. Then, if the behavior occurred a second time during that 30-minute interval, the open circle was filled in. Further instances of the behavior were not counted again until the next interval began.

When doing interval recording and/or creating a scatter plot, it is important to use intervals that are short enough to estimate the behavior's frequency as closely as possible. For instance, if the time intervals are 30 minutes and the behavior sometimes occurs up to 10 times per interval, then a closed circle will not tell whether the behavior occurred 2 times or 10 times during an interval. This means that the recording method could mask a great deal of change in the student's behavior. If the time intervals are 10 minutes long and the behavior typically occurs between one and three times per interval, a scatter plot will accurately reflect a change in the behavior. When using the Interval Recording or Scatter Plot, try to establish a time interval that will reliably show variations in the behavior, yet will still be feasible for data collection in a classroom situation.

Use of the Interval Recording or Scatter Plot form has a great advantage over simply keeping a running tally of the number of times the behavior occurs daily. Interval recording provides information about the relative frequency of the behavior during different time periods so that hypotheses about antecedents and consequences that may be influencing the behavior can be developed. By examining the intervals when the behavior is most and least likely to occur, you can begin to identify particular people, types of activities, amounts of attention, and types or intensity of demands that tend to trigger the problem behavior. For example, Figure 4.14 shows that Jason was more likely to scream and cry during oral reading and language skills lessons, lunch, physical education, and recess. His support team analyzed what those times of day had in common. They realized that lunch, physical education, and recess all involved large groups of students and lots of noise and physical activity. The problematic reading and language skills intervals involved large-group activities that required a lot of waiting and few opportunities to respond actively. In contrast, the shared reading and theme activities that were part of the morning language arts and reading block involved more individual or small-group activities, which provided many more opportunities for Jason to manipulate and respond to materials. This information gave the educational team a starting point for developing ways to alter the antecedents to make the periods when Jason was most likely to scream and cry more similar to the time periods when he was least likely to exhibit problem behaviors.

Interval Recording or Scatter Plot												

Student Jason **Dates** 1/22/07 through 1/26/07

Target behaviors

Behavior 1. Refuse/yell: Refusing to do tasks or assignments, indicated by very loud negative comments, leaving seat, not taking out or putting away materials, not moving to next location, and/or tearing or dropping materials.

Behavior 2. Push/kick: Pushing with one or both hands on any part of the other person's body; kicking with foot or leg on any part of the other person's body.

Used for ✓ Frequency count (tally each time behavior occurs within each interval)
_____ Scatter plot (Key: ○ = 1 occurrence; ● = more than 1 occurrence)
✓ Critical incident and use of Safety Plan (indicated by "X")

Time	Activity	Mon. 1/22 Refuse/yell	Push/kick	Tues. 1/23 Refuse/yell	Push/kick	Wed. 1/24 Refuse/yell	Push/kick	Thurs. 1/25 Refuse/yell	Push/kick	Fri. 1/26 Refuse/yell	Push/kick	Total Refuse/yell	Push/kick
9:00	Arrival/A.M. routine											0	0
9:15	↓	/								/	/	2	1
9:30	Morning Meeting				/		/				/	0	3
9:45	English/language skills					/				/		2	0
10:00	↓	/				/	/					2	2
10:15	↓ (Break at 10:25)	/	/	/		//	/	/		//	/	7	3
10:30	Reading					/				/		2	0
10:45	↓							/				1	0
11:00	Math (group lesson)									/		1	0
11:15	↓ (practice activity)			//						/		3	0
11:30	↓ (practice activity)	/				/		/		//	/	5	1
11:45	Lunch				/						/	0	2
12:00	↓				/		/		/		/	0	4
12:15	Specialties (M/W, PE; T, art; TH, music; F, lib)	/	/			/	/					2	2
12:30	↓			/	//				//	/	//	2	6
12:45	Social studies/science											0	0
1:00	↓					/				///	// X	4	2
1:15	↓	//				/					↓	3	1
1:30	Recess				/		/		/		/	0	4
1:45	↓Bathroom				/	/	/		/	/		2	3
2:00	Theme activities											0	0
2:15	↓											0	0
2:30	↓									//		2	0
2:45	Pack up; computer time if earned	/				//		//	/	//	//	7	3
Total target behaviors/day		9	7	3	5	12	8	5	5	18	12		

	Refuse/yell	Push/kick	Critical incidents/ use of Safety Plan
Total per week	47	37	1
Average per day	9	7	n/a
Average per hour	1.5	1	n/a

Figure 4.14. Interval Recording or Scatter Plot form used to gather frequency data on Jason's target behaviors.

Interval Recording or Scatter Plot							
Student Jason			**Dates** 1/22/07 through 1/26/07				
Target behavior(s) <u>Pushing and/or kicking: pushing with one or both hands on any part of</u> <u>the other person's body; kicking with foot or leg on any part of the other person's body</u>							

Used for   ____   Frequency count (tally each time behavior occurs within each interval)
     ✓   Scatter plot (Key: ○ = 1 occurrence; ● = more than 1 occurrence)
     ✓ Critical incident, use of Safety Plan (indicated by "X")							

Time	**Activity**	**Mon.** 1/22	**Tues.** 1/23	**Wed.** 1/24	**Thurs.** 1/25	**Fri.** 1/26	**Total**
9:00	Arrival/A.M. routine						0
9:15	↓	○				○	2
9:30	Morning Meeting	○		○		○	3
9:45	English/language skills						0
10:00	↓		○	○			2
10:15	↓ (Break at 10:25)	○		○		○	3
10:30	Reading						0
10:45	↓						0
11:00	Math (group lesson)						0
11:15	↓ (practice activity)						0
11:30	↓ (practice activity)					○	1
11:45	Lunch		○			○	2
12:00	↓		○	○	○		3
12:15	Specialties	○		○			2
		(PE)	(Art)	(PE)	(Music)	(Library)	
12:30	↓	●		●		●	3
12:45	Social studies/science					● X	1
1:00	↓				○		1
1:15	↓				○		1
1:30	Recess	○		○	○		3
1:45	↓ Bathroom	○	○		○		3
2:00	Theme activities						0
2:15	↓						0
2:30	↓					○	1
2:45	Pack up; computer time if earned				○	●	2
Total intervals per day in which behavior occurred		7	4	7	6	9	
Total intervals per week in which behavior occurred							33

Figure 4.15. Interval Recording or Scatter Plot form used to create a scatter plot for Jason's target behaviors.

Antecedent-Behavior-
Consequence (A-B-C) Observation

Using an A-B-C Observation form (see
Figure 4.16 for a completed form)
involves observing the student in a naturally occurring situation and immediately
recording 1) the antecedents to the student's problem behavior; 2) the student's
problem behavior; 3) the consequences,
or anything that happens after the student's problem behavior; and 4) the
observer's hypothesis about the purpose
or function of the problem behavior that
was observed. With respect to time and
effort, A-B-C observations are the most
difficult type of information-gathering
discussed in this chapter; however, these
observations can be extremely helpful for
problem solving. Furthermore, you can
use information from the Student Schedule Analysis and/or a completed Interval
Recording or Scatter Plot to find the specific periods of time that are the most
problematic and then conduct observations only during those times.

Figure 4.16 shows a sample A-B-C
observation of Jason, who is classified as
having mental retardation and autism-
like behaviors. Jason's teachers were
concerned about a number of related
behaviors that prevented him from participating in class activities. The specific
behaviors included crying, screaming,
and leaving his assigned area. A guidance
counselor conducted three half-hour
observations of Jason on three different
days. The A-B-C observations shown in
Figure 4.16 were recorded during language skills, which the Student Schedule
Analysis and Scatter Plot had shown to be
predictably problematic. When Jason's
teachers and other support team members examined the A-B-C observations,
they noticed immediately that when Jason
was participating appropriately in lessons
and activities (e.g., when he was sitting at
his desk and using materials in desired
ways), he received very little attention or

encouragement from the teacher or the
classroom assistant. When Jason exhibited the behaviors that were the focus of
concern, however, the consequences
were attention and support from the
adults. This example shows that A-B-C
recording can provide helpful information about how adult responses to a student's behavior can actually reinforce a
problem behavior by allowing it to work
better for a student than a positive behavior. Altering these consequences so that
positive behavior was reinforced and
problem behavior was not became a strategy in Jason's PBS plan.

Step 2C: Summarize Functional Behavioral Assessment and Build Hypothesis Statement(s)

Step 2C consists of summarizing all data
that have been gathered and developing
hypothesis statement(s) about the behavior (Figure 4.17). The Step 2C Worksheet:
Summary of Functional Behavioral Assessment and Hypothesis Statement(s) asks
for a report on the baseline frequency
and duration of target behavior(s) along
with a listing of the antecedents (i.e., who,
what, when, and where; which setting
events) predicting that the behavior will
or will not occur and the consequences
that are maintaining the behavior. Based
on these A-B-C chains, the student's PBS
team generates hypotheses about the
function that targeted problem behavior
serves for the student and describes alternative behaviors that may serve the same
purpose for the student. Once the team
reaches consensus that the Step 2C Worksheet is complete and accurate, it is time
to begin building a PBS plan.

Decision Point: Do Hypotheses Need Verification?

Generating a valid hypothesis about the
purpose of the problem behavior is one of

Antecedent-Behavior-Consequence (A-B-C) Observation				

Student Jason   **Day and date** Tuesday, January 30, 2007

Setting Ms. Santos's fourth-grade classroom   **Observer** Mara Kellam (school psychologist)

Class/subject or activity English/language skills: Writing book reports. Mr. Simms, special education teacher, is co-teaching with Ms. Santos.

Target behaviors(s) (see Student-Centered FBA Profile, Step 2A Worksheet, for observable definitions of behaviors)
1. Refusals/yelling
2. Pushing/kicking

Time	Antecedents — What was going on before the behavior? What was being said and done?	Behavior — What did the student do?	Consequences — What happened after the behavior? How did people react?	Hypothesis — About the function of the behavior
10:00	Ms. Santos finishes her explanation and demonstration of how to use a "book report organizer." She tells the students to use their own organizers to begin their book reports. They must work alone for 15 minutes and then will get into writer's workshop teams to give one another feedback. Most students begin right away; some ask questions ("Do we have to use pencil?" "Can your book be one you used last year?").	Jason sits quietly, appears to be listening. His pencil and book report organizer (adapted for him with larger print and fill-in-the-blank spaces) are on his desk. He looks around, watches other students as they start writing. He picks up his pencil, slowly writes his name and then puts the pencil down and looks around.	None	
10:10	Ms. Santos walks around the room, goes to students who have raised their hands, answers questions. She says to the class, "I appreciate the way so many students have quietly started their work. Nice job, Carrie and Bethany. Jonah, that pencil is sharp enough."	Jason picks up his pencil, starts to write the date on his paper. He looks up, scans the room, catches Mr. Simms's eye.	Mr. Simms walks by Jason, says to the student next to Jason, "Kate, would you please see if Jason needs help with the date? Thanks." Kate looks at Jason's paper, says, "He's got it," and smiles at Jason.	Get attention from Mr. Simms; not a very successful attempt.
10:15	Mr. Simms is helping a student a few desks away from Jason: "What was the setting of the book?"	Jason rolls his pencil across his desk several times, then drops it on the floor and picks it up.	Mr. Simms, from the other student's desk: "Jason, you were off to a good start, let's keep it up." Mr. Simms continues helping the other student.	Get attention from an adult to get help with a difficult task. Attempt was successful, but attention was not very positive.

Figure 4.16. Antecedent-Behavior-Consequence Observation form for Jason.

(continued)

Figure 4.16. *(continued)*

Time	Antecedents	Behavior	Consequences	Hypothesis
10:20	Mr. Simms assists individual students; he occasionally glances in Jason's direction. Ms. Santos gives instructions to a classroom volunteer.	Jason makes several random marks on his paper, and then raises his hand, but only for a few seconds. He makes more marks.	Neither Mr. Simms nor Ms. Santos sees Jason raise his hand.	Get attention from adult to get help with difficult task. Again, not successful in using appropriate behavior.
10:25	Mr. Simms and Ms. Santos stand at Ms. Santos's desk and confer for a few minutes.	Jason scribbles on the back of his paper, pushes it around the desk, and then pushes it off the desk so it drops to the floor. He stands up and leans over to pick up the paper.	Mr. Simms comes to Jason, picks up the paper from the floor and puts it on Jason's desk. He says, "Remember, no dropping things on the floor. Now, what was the name of your book?"	Get attention from Mr. Simms. Negative behavior was successful.

the most important steps in developing a plan for PBS. It also can be a very difficult step. Sometimes, the information that has been gathered through indirect methods and direct observations reveals clear patterns that suggest hypotheses about the behavior's purpose(s), as illustrated by the following Student Snapshots:

Student Snapshots

Sofie's problem behavior was throwing materials and sometimes hitting adults on the arm or hand. When the team used a scatter plot to analyze the antecedents of Sofie's throwing and hitting, they noticed that the behaviors tended to occur at about the same times each day, during one-to-one instructional sessions with the special education teacher or assistant. The behaviors did not occur during small-group or large-group lessons of any kind. Incident Records of the times Sofie hit other people showed that the consequence for hitting was to take Sofie to a time-out chair at the back of the classroom, where she had to sit for 10 minutes. Because Sofie's one-to-one instructional sessions were only about 10 minutes long, it usually was time for the next activity when Sofie had completed her time-out, so she never completed the tasks provided during her one-to-one instruction. Sofie's

hitting did not decrease during the 2 weeks that the team gathered information. The team hypothesized that the purpose of Sofie's throwing and hitting might be to escape from the intensive demands of one-to-one instruction. The time-out, which had been intended as a punishment for hitting, was actually negative reinforcement for Sofie, who was using the hitting to escape from a situation she found difficult.

In cases such as Sofie's, the patterns between antecedents and consequences were quite obvious and the function of the problem behavior was clear. In other cases, it is not so easy to identify the function of the behavior.

When Darin had to work independently on lengthy tasks— even tasks that were at an appropriate skill level—he would make no attempt to do the assignment and would instead tell jokes and talk to his classmates. When Darin engaged in these off-task behaviors, his classmates would laugh, and the classroom teacher would come to Darin's desk, remind him of the consequences of not completing his class work, and assist Darin with his assignment. When Darin was involved in small-group activities directed by the classroom teacher or the special education teacher, however, he did relatively well on his schoolwork. The team

Step 2C Worksheet: Summary of Functional Behavioral Assessment and Hypothesis Statement(s)

Directions: Summarize the FBA information that has been gathered from all sources to build hypothesis statement(s) about targeted problem behaviors. If the student has appropriate alternative behaviors that serve the same purpose as the problem behavior (alternative behaviors may be nonexistent or very weak), describe those behaviors. Then determine if any data are missing and/or team members disagree or are uncertain about their hypotheses. Make a plan for further data collection and verification of hypotheses if necessary.

Student Jason	**Date of initial summary** February 5, 2007	**Revision date (if necessary)** _____

Persons completing this form

Jared Simms, special education teacher	Carly Roberts & Rob Moore, parents	_____
Ashley Giles, aide	Mara Kellam, school psychologist	_____
Rita Santos, fourth-grade teacher		_____

FREQUENCY: On average, HOW OFTEN does the behavior occur?

Behavior 1:   Refusing/yelling   Per Hour?   _2_   Per day?   _12_   Per week?   _58_

Behavior 2:   Pushing/kicking   Per Hour?   _1_   Per day?   _7_   Per week?   _35_

DURATION: On average, HOW LONG does the behavior occur?

Behavior 1:   Refusing/yelling: Each incident is usually less than a minute, but incidents can occur intermittently for 10 minutes.

Behavior 2:   Pushing/kicking: Most incidents are fairly mild, with only one or two pushes at a time, mostly to the other person's upper arm. Kicking occurs very seldom.

1.   **Describe chains of antecedents (both setting events and triggers) that predict that the target behavior will occur, observable definitions of the target behaviors, and consequences that seem to be maintaining the behavior. Then hypothesize about the function or purpose of the target behavior(s).**

When these **Antecedents** (**setting events** and/or **triggers**) occur	the student is likely to (describe **Target Behavior[s]**)	and these **Consequences** maintain the behavior	Therefore, the **Function** of the behavior may be
Setting event: None **Trigger(s):** Paper-and-pencil tasks that require writing words. Writing is difficult for Jason because of weak fine motor skills, difficulties with letter formation and spelling, and weak vocabulary.	Refuse to get out his materials (e.g., paper, pencil, workbook), push and drop materials, scribble on his papers, leave his seat. These behaviors may be followed by yelling/screaming (e.g., "No, no, no!").	Adults assist him to do the task; if yelling persists, the adult removes Jason from the classroom.	To avoid/escape difficult and non-preferred tasks.
Setting event: Presence of Ms. Santos, fourth-grade teacher. **Trigger(s):** Ms. Santos is persistent in prompting Jason to complete a paper-and-pencil task or other non-preferred task, and corrects him for not completing his work and for his inappropriate behavior.	Yell "No" (etc.) to Ms. Santos and push her away.	Ms. Santos asks Ms. Giles or Mr. Simms to take Jason from the classroom to cool down; they take him for a brief walk. Jason gets a "minus" on his daily point card.	To escape from difficult or non-preferred task.

(continued)

Figure 4.17.   Step 2C Worksheet: Summary of Functional Behavioral Assessment and Hypothesis Statements for Jason.

Figure 4.17. *(continued)*

When these **Antecedents** (**setting events** and/or **triggers**) occur	the student is likely to (describe **Target Behavior[s]**)	and these **Consequences** maintain the behavior	Therefore, the **Function** of the behavior may be
Setting event: Jason has received four or more "minuses" on his point card. **Trigger(s):** Jason has an unsuccessful peer interaction (e.g., is left out of a game at recess, is not included in a conversation at lunch, attempts to interact with a peer and is not understood).	Jason pushes his peers and any adult who intervenes. About once a week, a "critical incident" follows.	Some peers tell Jason to stop it, some push back, some try to calm him down. Jason is sometimes removed from the situation or, if his behavior is escalating, the Safety Plan is instituted. Jason does not get computer time at the end of the day.	To obtain some peer interaction, even if it is negative.
Setting event: Jason has received four or more "minuses" on his point card. **Trigger(s):** Jason is working in a small group on a task that is new or difficult (e.g., requires writing), and he is not sure what to do.	Jason yells and makes non-sense noises, plays with and drops materials, sometimes pushes a peer.	Peers may tell Jason to stop, try to help him, or push him back. Jason is sometimes informally removed from the group or, if his behavior is escalating, the Safety Plan is instituted. Jason does not get computer time at the end of the day.	

2. **Describe alternative behaviors that the student has demonstrated (the behaviors may be very weak) that may serve the same function as the problem behavior(s).**
- Jason has been observed scanning the room and also raising his hand to get adult attention when faced with a difficult task, but he does not persist for long and teachers did not reinforce his alternative behaviors.
- Jason sometimes stands close to peers and observes them at recess or during breaks but does not have more effective ways to obtain peer attention.
- When instructional activities are adapted appropriately for Jason, he is quite willing to complete them. He does have the ability to stay focused and has completed paper-and-pencil tasks that were suited to his abilities.
- Several times, Jason has used self-calming strategies (e.g., deep breathing, taking a walk) to prevent or interrupt a serious behavior incident. These strategies could be strengthened and generalized.

3. **Are additional data needed to build hypothesis statement(s)?**   Yes   (No)
Is Step 2D, Verify Hypotheses, needed to confirm or refute hypotheses? Yes   (No)
If "yes," use the Team Meeting Agenda and Minutes form to plan how, when, and by whom further FBA data collection and/or verification tests will be conducted. Decide on a date for the next team meeting, at which this Step 2C worksheet will be revised.

was not sure whether the purpose of Darin's problem behaviors was to gain attention from his peers and the teacher or to escape from difficult tasks. They needed a strategy to determine which of these hypotheses could be verified.

Building hypotheses can be especially difficult when a student uses a particular problem behavior for more than one purpose. For example, a student with an intellectual disability and no speech may cry in order to say, "I want more juice," "This is too hard," or "I don't feel well." Some students may use several different problem behaviors for the same purpose. A student may express anger or frustration in several different ways (e.g., tantrums, self-injury, hitting others). At times, it can be tempting to conclude that a behavior happens for no reason or has no pattern at all. In actuality, this is seldom the case. If there truly is no discernable pattern to the behavior and it is equally likely to occur in every situation, it is possible that the behavior is related to a physiological problem. For example, a student with very limited communication skills might slap the side of his face with his hand to numb the pain of an unfilled cavity in a tooth.

This information is essential to the development of an individualized plan for PBS because the plan will include strategies for teaching the student new skills that will accomplish the purpose of the problem behavior in more positive, effective, and efficient ways. After summarizing the results of the FBA on the Step 2C Worksheet, the team must evaluate its findings. If the team is confident of the validity of its hypotheses, work on a PBS plan can begin. If there is a lack of consensus among team members and lingering uncertainty about the antecedents and/or the purpose of the problem behavior, however, tentative hypotheses may require conducting Step 2D: Verify Hypotheses.

Step 2D:
Verify Hypotheses

Verifying hypotheses requires observing the student during typical routines that vary in particular conditions (differing sets of antecedents and consequences). This procedure allows greater certainty about the triggers of the behavior, the maintaining consequences, and the function or purpose that it serves for the student. It is not recommended that the sort of extensive, precise functional analyses that are conducted in controlled research environments be conducted in classrooms. Educators can, however, make simple, short-term alterations to typically occurring activities that will enable them

to be more accurate in designing intervention plans that are related to the specific function of the target behavior. The brief functional analysis tests that educators conduct depend on their hunch about the purpose(s) of the problem behavior. Manipulating the factors that appear to affect problem behavior helps increase confidence that it is these factors, not others, that are responsible for the problems, which is extremely important, because *knowing the function is the key to successful behavior change or intervention.*

The steps of the verification process are the following:

1. The team identifies what hypothesis needs testing.

2. The team decides how to do this and schedules a desired manipulation in a routine in which it "fits." For example: If the hunch is that the student has tantrums in order to escape from difficult tasks, the teacher presents a difficult task demand several times during a regular instructional period or presents and removes the task (hard task, easy task, hard task, easy task). The hunch is confirmed if the student immediately stops the tantrum when the hard task is taken away. Everything else about the situation should stay the same—the seating arrangement, the teacher, the time of day, and so forth. The tasks should be familiar to the student, so that the teacher knows which is easy and which is hard for the student.

3. The team determines how often to do this test. This depends on the size of the effects and how quickly they occur: Large effects right away (e.g., the student stops crying immediately after a difficult task demand is removed) mean that the hypothesis is likely to be accurate. Small or no

effects mean that the hypothesis is not likely to be accurate.

During the manipulation, we give unconditionally what the person wants and then see if it eliminates the problem behavior. It is crucial, however, to understand that this *is not the solution to the behavior problem. This is a specific context that has been set up in order to demonstrate quickly the controlling factors for the behavior.* It usually is necessary to observe these situations several times to be certain that the variables being manipulated are, indeed, the ones influencing the behavior. It also can be helpful

to test more than one hunch about the possible function of a behavior (O'Neill et al., 1997).

Figure 4.18 gives several other hypotheses and possible verification tests that can be administered by teachers in classrooms and other naturally occurring school settings.

After conducting function tests and observing effects on the student's behavior that are convincing enough to verify hypotheses about the behavior's function(s), the student's PBS team meets again to revisit the Step 2C Worksheet: Summarize Functional Behavioral Assess-

Problem behavior and hypothesis	Function test and result that verifies hypothesis
Behavior: Candice runs from the cafeteria; a paraprofessional brings Candice's lunch to her classroom for her. **Hypothesis:** When Candice is in a very noisy place, she gets anxious and experiences sensory overload. She escapes from the situation as a way to self-regulate sensory input.	**Test:** Compare Candice's behavior in the cafeteria at lunch with places where others are present but the noise level is much lower, such as her class's library time or in the cafeteria during study hall. **Result that verifies hypothesis:** Candice runs from the cafeteria during lunch, but not from the library or the cafeteria during study hall.
Behavior: Jonah is off-task, talks out, and sometimes grabs other students when he has to wait for the teacher's attention (e.g., during a large-group lesson, during seatwork); the teacher angrily tells him to stop and then gives Jonah a turn or helps him with his work. **Hypothesis:** Jonah has found a way to obtain attention from the teacher.	**Test:** Compare Jonah's behavior under the typical condition with how he behaves when the teacher (or other adult) regularly provides attention before Jonah does the behavior (e.g., "I'll be with you in just a second," "How are you doing?" "You've got it!"). **Result that verifies hypothesis:** Jonah does the problem behaviors less frequently or not at all when the teacher regularly gives him attention and he does not have to tolerate as much waiting.
Behavior: Molly, when asked to write with paper and pencil, throws the materials and cries. Materials are then taken and she is given a break to calm down. **Hypothesis:** Molly is escaping from a task she dislikes because it is too hard.	**Test:** Compare Molly's behavior in the same situation but with a change in the materials (markers, crayons, adapted scissors with help) and alternate with the difficult paper and pencil. **Result that verifies hypothesis:** Molly throws things and cries only with paper and pencil tasks.
Behavior: Ashley screams and hits herself when she cannot have more juice at snack. Sometimes, the teacher will go to the cafeteria to get more juice; Ashley stops screaming. **Hypothesis:** Ashley is trying to obtain something she wants (juice).	**Test:** Compare Ashley's behavior when juice is and is not freely available. Also compare her reaction to the availability and unavailability of other beverages (milk, water) to see if it is juice in particular that she wants, or if it's any beverage. **Result that verifies hypothesis:** Ashley screams when juice is not readily available, not when it is available. She stops screaming when she is given juice. She also screams when beverages other than juice are available, so the screaming does not indicate that she is simply thirsty, but instead indicates that she prefers juice to other beverages.

Figure 4.18. Verifying hypotheses.

ment and Build Hypothesis Statement(s). Once the team reaches consensus that the Step 2C Worksheet is complete and accurate, it is time to begin building a PBS plan.

CONCLUSION

More research is needed to tell us the specific assessment strategies required to generate accurate FBAs in schools. Clearly, in schools and other natural settings, teachers and caregivers want to use assessments that are accurate as well as efficient. Another question that has not yet been answered is exactly how much and what kinds of training are required to enable school teams to conduct valid FBAs and implement behavioral support plans themselves (Snell, 2006). Practitioners must act now—they cannot wait until all the data are in. Therefore, the authors of this book take the position that school teams should use all available evidence and resources to make decisions that are consistent with the knowledge and values on which a positive behavior supports orientation is based:

- Problem behavior is learned behavior and can be replaced with other more

appropriate and effective learned behavior.

- Teachers and other adults control many aspects of the environment that have a powerful influence on behavior and behavior change.

- Positive behavior supports include multiple interventions that are based on data and logic—and on respect.

- The goals of PBS are long-term reduction in problem behavior, increases in appropriate behaviors, and improvements in quality of life.

The authors suggest that *all* teachers should be familiar with the essential theory of FBA, the crucial role it plays in designing PBS plans, and the variety of data-collection measures from which the team can select to complete the FBA. Only when we come to appreciate the purposes that problem behavior can serve for a student do we understand the significant role that the environment—which we play a large role in creating—serves in teaching, maintaining, and remediating behavior problems. The assistance of psychologists, counselors, researchers, and outside behavioral experts should be used to *supplement* but not *supplant* the efforts of teachers who support students with serious behavior problems.

Chapter 5

Designing, Using, and Evaluating Individualized Positive Behavior Supports

This chapter presents Steps 3 and 4 of the process of creating an individualized system for positive behavior support (PBS). Step 3: Design a Plan for Positive Behavior Support entails using assessment information to create a comprehensive support plan to improve the focal student's behavior and enhance his or her participation at school, at home, and in the community. Step 4: Implement, Monitor, and Evaluate the PBS Plan requires the support team to put the plan into action, to monitor its implementation, and to evaluate its effects.

A plan for PBS is not a plan to control behavior problems. A PBS plan is a comprehensive, integrated set of interventions and supports designed to promote improvements in behavior, academics, physical well-being, school and community participation, and social relationships. By definition, a PBS plan is based on assessment information. The intervention strategies selected reflect what has been learned about the antecedents that set the occasion for the behavior and the consequences that maintain the behavior. In addition to designing and implementing the elements of the plan, the support team also needs to put into place strategies to ensure that the plan is being implemented reliably and that the behaviors of concern are improving. If they are not, additional problem solving will be needed to generate improved alternatives.

For students with significant emotional/behavioral disorders, school-based PBS is most beneficial when incorporated into a *wraparound* planning process that includes not only teachers and family members but also representatives from the community agencies that can assist in creating an integrated, comprehensive system of care for the student and his or her family. The scope of this book does not include a full explanation of the wraparound process, but Figure 5.1 gives a more detailed definition of the process and references some of the key research on its outcomes.

What the Research Says

Wraparound Planning for Students with Emotional or Behavior Disorders

Although their numbers are relatively small, students with extreme emotional and/or behavior disorders can present significant challenges to their teachers and peers in the school setting, and are at the greatest risk for removal to more restrictive settings and for poor school and life outcomes such as dropping out, poverty, incarceration, and unemployment. The school-based PBS process can lead to some positive results for these students, but using PBS as a complement to a broader *wraparound* process for planning comprehensive, integrated systems of care can yield greater benefits for students, their families, and their communities.

The wraparound process is a tool for building constructive relationships and support networks among youth with emotional and behavior disorders (E/BD) and their families, teachers, and other caregivers. Careful and systematic application of the wraparound process can increase the likelihood that appropriate supports and interventions are adopted, implemented, and sustained . ... Wraparound is a philosophy of care with a defined planning process for creating a unique plan for a child and family. ... [It] incorporates family-centered and strength-based philosophy of care... [and] involves all services and strategies necessary to meet the individual needs of students and their families. (Eber, Sugai, Smith & Scott, 2002, pp. 1–2)

Like the PBS approach, wraparound is individualized, strength-based, and multidisciplinary team-based; however, wraparound incorporates more community-based agencies and interagency resources, and it places even greater emphasis on creating a full and active partnership with families.

Research on wraparound planning to create integrated, comprehensive systems of care shows promising results that include decreased out-of-home and restrictive school placements along with improved behavioral, academic, social, and postschool adjustment factors for students with emotional and behavioral disorders (Burns & Goldman,1999; Burns, Schoenwald, Burchard, Faw, & Santos, 2000; Eber & Nelson, 1997; Malloy, Cheney, & Cormier, 1998).

Figure 5.1.   Wraparound planning for students with emotional or behavior disorders.

STEP 3
DESIGN A POSITIVE BEHAVIOR SUPPORT PLAN

A PBS plan typically includes three general types of intervention strategies: 1) preventing, 2) teaching, and 3) responding (Figure 5.2). (As was discussed in Chapter 4, a Safety Plan also should be developed and implemented immediately if the student exhibits behaviors that are seriously disruptive or destructive.) Each type of information collected to conduct an FBA has a counterpart in the behavior change strategies that compose a PBS plan. *Prevention* strategies change the antecedents—both the setting events and the triggers—of the problem behavior to create an environment more likely to lead to success. *Teaching* strategies change the student's behavior by replacing problem behaviors with alternative behaviors serving the same purpose and building other desired social and academic skills. *Responding* strategies change the consequences of behavior by giving the student access to the desired function when using the replacement behavior but not when using the problem behavior. Most plans for significant behavior problems require

all three types of strategies. Horner and his colleagues (2000) argued that this combination of interventions and supports is meant to accomplish three outcomes that compete with the problem behavior:

- Making the problem behavior *irrelevant* by creating an environment in which it is not necessary to use the problem behavior.

- Making the behavior *ineffective* by removing the consequences that were maintaining the behavior.

- Making the behavior *inefficient* by ensuring that a replacement behavior works better and more easily than the old behavior.

Figure 5.3 illustrates Horner and colleagues' competing behavior model, which shows how each part of the summary hypothesis statement that was constructed from the FBA relates to the three types of intervention strategies (Horner et al., 2000). The purpose of an intervention plan based on the competing behavior model is to make the problem behavior irrelevant, ineffective, and inefficient in serving its function. At the same time, the environment is altered to avoid the need

---

STEP 3
Design a Positive Behavior Support Plan

A good plan for positive behavior support has three parts:

1. **Preventing** the problem behavior through 1) strategies to remove or reduce the impact of setting events; 2) strategies to avoid triggers or immediate antecedents that predict the problem behavior; and 3) strategies to increase the likelihood that alternative behaviors will occur. If the Student-Centered FBA Profile indicated the need for improvements in quality-of-life indicators or in the fit between the student's educational programming and academic strengths and needs, include those strategies here.

2. **Teaching** interventions for 1) specific replacement behaviors to serve the same purpose as the problem behaviors; 2) other positive alternative behaviors to meet long-term goals (e.g., social skills, self-management strategies, academic skills).

3. **Responding** to the problem behavior when it occurs in ways that do not maintain it and responding to the replacement behavior in ways ensuring that it works more efficiently and effectively than the problem behavior. If a Safety Plan also is in use to manage dangerous or destructive behaviors, maintain records of its use. Evaluate and revise the plan as needed.

Figure 5.2. Step 3: Design a Positive Behavior Support Plan.

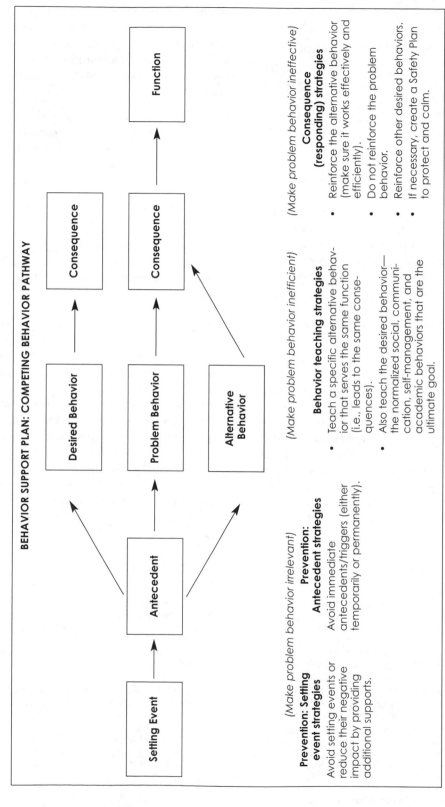

BEHAVIOR SUPPORT PLAN: COMPETING BEHAVIOR PATHWAY

(Make problem behavior irrelevant)

Prevention: Setting event strategies

Avoid setting events or reduce their negative impact by providing additional supports.

Prevention: Antecedent strategies

Avoid immediate antecedents/triggers (either temporarily or permanently).

(Make problem behavior inefficient)

Behavior teaching strategies

- Teach a specific alternative behavior that serves the same function (i.e., leads to the same consequences).
- Also teach the desired behavior—the normalized social, communication, self-management, and academic behaviors that are the ultimate goal.

(Make problem behavior ineffective)

Consequence (responding) strategies

- Reinforce the alternative behavior (make sure it works effectively and efficiently).
- Do not reinforce the problem behavior.
- Reinforce other desired behaviors.
- If necessary, create a Safety Plan to protect and calm.

Figure 5.3. Competing behavior model. (From Horner, R.H., Albin, R.A., Sprague, J.R., & Todd, A.W. [2000]. Positive behavior support. In M.E. Snell & F. Brown [Eds.], *Instruction of students with severe disabilities* [5th ed., pp. 207–243]. Upper Saddle River, NJ: Prentice Hall.)

Imagine what it would be like for a group of people to have a meeting to discuss you and your problems without your presence or input. Deciding how to involve the student in developing a behavioral support plan can be a difficult task, especially if the student does not talk or have another reliable way to communicate or does not have a trusting relationship with the support team.

"I have spent some time trying to figure out the etiquette of talking about people's difficult behavior. When I first started working, I was surprised by the unquestioned assumption that people would not be included in meetings about them. . . . I started insisting that people attend meetings about them in hopes that their presence would help. . . break the tradition of exclusion. . . . Generally, I found that inviting people to meetings is helpful. Sometimes people insist that if people cannot speak, they cannot contribute. My experience has been that ability has nothing to do with a person's contribution. Some people who do not speak with words can change the atmosphere of a meeting simply with their presence" (Lovett, 1996, p. 20).

Figure 5.4.   Learning to listen.

to use the problem behavior, and the new, alternative behavior becomes the most effective and efficient way to achieve the purpose that was served by the problem behavior.

In addition to the requirement that intervention strategies be based on an FBA, effective behavioral support plans need to include strategies chosen specifically to suit the student and family, the context, and the teachers and other personnel who will apply them. The criterion of contextual fit extends to all team members, particularly family members. If behavioral supports and interventions are to be optimally successful, student and family preferences and values must be taken into account, along with the social and structural context of family life.

Deciding how to involve the student in developing a behavioral support plan can be a difficult task, especially if the student does not talk or have another reliable way to communicate or does not have a trusting relationship with the support team. There are no rules for the best way to gain the student's involvement. Clearly, students who have a means to communicate with others can and should participate fully in setting goals, conducting self-assessments, and giving input for the ways they would like help in meeting their goals. For students with communication difficulties, teachers and staff members should offer choices that students can

understand and respond to, and they should observe carefully to understand the student's view (see Figure 5.4).

Prevention Strategies: Changing the Antecedents

The first type of behavioral support strategy is designed to prevent behavior problems from occurring. Prevention strategies address both specific triggers and setting events and may involve changing the physical environment, the daily schedule, the staff and peers who spend time with the student, or the activities in which the student engages. The changes made to antecedents are sometimes described as *stimulus-based interventions*, because they change the stimuli, or the "who-what-when-where" variables that set the stage for the behavior.

A prevention-oriented approach makes sense for several reasons. Removing the antecedents known to predict a problem behavior makes the behavior unnecessary or irrelevant. Therefore, the person is less likely to get more practice using the problem behavior. The more practice one has in using a behavior, the more the old behavior will compete with learning a new behavior. This rule applies both to the student with the problem behavior and to the adults and peers who interact regularly with that student. Teachers do not want to allow students to practice getting into fights, having tantrums, hurting themselves, destroying property, or exhibiting other disapproved behaviors. Teachers want to avoid a problem behavior while the student has a chance to learn new communication and coping skills, especially if the behavior is dangerous to the student or others or is seriously disruptive to the classroom.

Problem behaviors can be prevented in a range of ways. Setting events and triggering antecedents that have been detected through an FBA can be altered to prevent target behaviors from occurring. At a broader level, and less directly connected with immediate environmental antecedents, teachers can prevent behavior problems by providing students with choices and educational programming suited to the students' ages, abilities, and interests. The effects of choice making and effective instruction on behavior problems are discussed in the following section.

Prevention Through Choice Making and Appropriate Educational Programming

Increasing students' choice-making opportunities and making improvements to the students' educational programming can be viewed as broad interventions that improve the social and instructional context within which students are expected to function. The links between behavior problems and both choice making and curricular and instructional practices are clear.

Behavior problems can be prevented by ensuring that educational programming is well designed, that instruction is well matched with students' needs and abilities, and that the learning context capitalizes on students' interests and other motivations. All teachers have seen a student's attention and motivation vary along with his or her interest in the subject matter and his or her ability to successfully perform an activity. Students

may become disruptive when expected to complete assignments independently that are beyond their independent skill level—or when asked repeatedly to spend long periods of time practicing known skills. When the function of problem behavior is to escape from difficult tasks, teaching the student how to perform the skills required to complete the task alleviates the motivation for the behavior, and can even result in reductions in the off-task behavior or other problem behavior that was the original source of concern (Lee, Sugai, & Horner, 1999). When the function of problem behavior is to escape from boring or meaningless tasks, teachers need to reexamine the instructional focus so that new, relevant skills are being taught (Dunlap, Foster-Johnson, Clarke, Kern, & Childs, 1995). Figure 5.5 summarizes some of the other research on the positive relationship between appropriate behavior and appropriate educational programming.

Information gleaned from person-centered planning processes can assist in designing support plans that create a better fit between students' needs and abilities and their teachers' classroom practices. Kennedy and his colleagues (2001) found that when students were assigned classroom tasks that better reflected their strengths and interests, and teachers followed best practice guidelines such as providing predictable schedules, choices, and age-appropriate curriculum, students' behavior and general education participation improved. Students' behavior was convincingly linked with the implementation—or lack of implementation—of the behavioral support plan.

Choice making has been well documented as an effective support strategy for challenging behavior (Kern et al., 1998). Allowing and enabling students with disabilities to make choices can be both a broad, values-based element of positive educational programming and

What the Research Says

Appropriate Curriculum and Instruction as Positive Behavior Support

A number of research studies have shown that altering the curriculum—either its content or mode of delivery—can have a positive influence on problem behavior. Several studies have examined variations in students' academic performance and classroom behavior under two conditions: 1) "standard" instructional conditions (e.g., performing teacher-selected tasks, repetitive tasks designed for practicing isolated skills, mostly verbal tasks) and 2) instructional conditions that utilized assessment of student preferences and interests, functional activities, academic tasks broken into smaller segments, and/or shortened instructional sessions. In each case, the researchers found that students' task performance (e.g., productivity, on-task behavior, task completion) and behavior (e.g., leaving the instructional area, hitting materials on the desk, making loud noises) improved when the students were doing tasks that were designed to better match their instructional level, interests, and preferences and/or stamina or energy level (Clarke et al., 1995; Dunlap, Foster-Johnson, Clarke, Kern, & Childs, 1995; Dunlap, Kern-Dunlap, Clarke, & Robbins, 1991; Foster-Johnson, Ferro, & Dunlap, 1994; Moore, Anderson, & Kumar, 2005).

Kennedy and his colleagues (2001) integrated person-centered planning measures with the other typical direct and indirect methods used to conduct functional behavioral assessments for three elementary school students with behavior problems. After obtaining the support team's assessment of focal students' strengths, interests, and dislikes, the researchers assisted the team to construct a matrix showing the degree to which those individual strengths, interests, and dislikes were present in each class period across the day. In addition, they evaluated the quality of instruction in each class period based on the extent to which 14 distinct best practices were present. These sources of information were used to design support plans that created a better fit between the students' needs and abilities and their teachers' classroom practices. The tasks assigned to students better reflected their strengths and interests and best practice guidelines such as providing predictable schedules, choices, and age-appropriate curriculum. The improvements to students' behavior and general education participation were convincingly linked with the implementation—or lack of implementation—of the behavior support plan.

Figure 5.5.   Appropriate curriculum and instruction as positive behavior support.

an antecedent intervention for specific problem behaviors. Choice-making interventions have resulted in improved behavior in studies conducted with a wide range of participants (i.e., all ages from preschool students to senior citizens and participants with diverse intellectual and behavioral characteristics) and in studies of a wide array of academic, vocational, domestic, and recreational contexts (Bambara, Koger, Katzer, & Davenport, 1995; Dunlap et al., 1994; Kern et al., 1998).

Research on choice making has shown that students' problem behaviors decrease and task engagement increases when they are allowed to choose which assignment or activity they prefer to do (e.g., Dunlap, Kern-Dunlap, Clarke, & Robbins, 1991), or when they are offered choices about the order in which they want to do a list of required activities (Sey-

bert, Dunlap, & Ferro, 1996). Indeed, giving students opportunities to make choices is such a potent behavioral support strategy that rates of problem behavior have been shown to decrease when students are allowed to choose between two *lower preference* tasks rather than being assigned those lower preference tasks by their teacher (Vaughn & Horner, 1997). Even within a required activity, giving choices about how to complete an individual step of the activity can improve task success and reduce challenging behavior. For example, in a study by Cole and Levinson (2002), a student with developmental disabilities who exhibited high rates of disruptive behavior during his hand-washing routine was given choices such as whether to walk in front of or behind the instructional aide on the way to the bathroom and whether to rub his hands together quickly or slowly when washing his hands. The boy's behavior and task success improved dramatically.

The Student-Centered Functional Behavioral Assessment Profile (Figure 4.11) completed as part of an FBA includes information about the focal student's relationships with peers and adults, choice-making opportunities, preferences, interests, needs, strengths, and dislikes. If this information indicates shortcomings in the student's quality of life or educational programming, the PBS plan should incorporate prevention strategies to ameliorate the most dramatic of those shortcomings.

Prevention Through Alteration of Setting Events

Setting events involve two or more variables linked together that tend to lead to problem behaviors. For example, the absence of breakfast (setting event for Zack) can reduce Zack's tolerance for completing routine paper-and-pencil tasks, while allergies (setting event for Sarah) often mean that Sarah reacts negatively to teachers' requests. Setting events that occur prior to the presence of a specific antecedent stimulus (paper-and-pencil tasks or teachers' requests) can make it more likely that a problem behavior will follow, as illustrated in the following case study.

Student Snapshot

Jon, who has Asperger syndrome, would sometimes be verbally abusive and refuse to do any schoolwork. The FBA revealed that these behaviors could sometimes be predicted by disappointments or unanticipated changes at school, such as the absence of a bus driver, teacher, or one of his two best friends. While conducting the parent interview, the support team learned that Jon sometimes spent the weekend at a relative's home when both of his parents had to work on Saturday and Sunday. Jon did not sleep well at the relative's home and therefore was extremely tired on the Monday mornings following those visits. He also disliked the disruption in his schedule. After realizing that spending weekends with relatives was a setting event for Jon's being very frustrated and anxious with changes at school, several prevention strategies were incorporated in Jon's PBS plan. Home–school communication was improved: Jon's parents were careful to alert his teacher if he would be spending the weekend at the relative's home. Jon's teacher tried to inform Jon's parents before school on Monday if there would be a substitute teacher or bus driver, so that they could prepare Jon before his arrival at school. If the advanced alert was not possible, an instructional aide or peer mentor was asked to greet Jon at the door of the school to start his day off on a positive note.

Strong relationships between setting events and behavior problems have been documented in a number of research studies (Carr, Reeve, & Magito-McLaughlin, 1996; Horner, Day, & Day, 1997; Horner, Vaughn, Day, & Ard, 1996). For example, in one study, 13 of the 15 adolescents and young adults in the study with severe disabilities were twice as likely to display disruptive and self-injurious behaviors on days with targeted setting events than on days without targeted setting events. The setting events that influenced the participants' behavior included pain, fatigue, changes in staff or the schedule, and aversive events such as being denied a planned outing, losing a game, or being reprimanded (Horner et al., 1996). In another study that examined the influence of setting events, FBA and functional analysis of the severe problem behavior of four women with developmental disabilities revealed that menstrual discomfort was a setting event for problem behavior that was then triggered by task demands (Carr, Smith, Giacin, Whelan, & Pancari, 2003).

Setting events cannot always be avoided, but their negative influence can be mitigated if teachers, parents, and others who work with a student recognize these events, communicate about them, and include related strategies in a plan for PBS. If a teacher knows that a biological setting event is operative—that the student has not slept well, is ill, has an allergy—then extra care can be taken to make the student feel comfortable. If an environmental condition such as loud hallways, lots of people, or being in a small space acts as a setting event, that setting may be avoided for a period of time and then slowly reintroduced to the student as he or she gains needed self-regulation or communication skills. If particular adults or peers act as setting events for a student, then those people can work to establish rapport and interact with the focal student in more positive ways.

Prevention Through Altering Triggers

Another sort of prevention strategy involves changing the triggers uncovered by the FBA. Sometimes specific antecedents in the environment serve to trigger problem behaviors:

- When Jason's teacher told the class that it was time to put one activity away and begin another, Jason screamed and clung to whatever materials he was using.

- When Rick sat next to his friend Carlos for small-group lessons, Rick did not pay attention, refused to complete his work, and, if pressured, threw his books and papers on the floor.

- Sondra cried uncontrollably when she heard a loud noise such as the school bell, a lawnmower, or a siren.

Avoiding these triggers can be an effective prevention strategy. At times, the trigger may be avoided permanently; at other times, however, the changes that teachers make to help avoid problems will be temporary. If the antecedent context is one that is legitimate for the student to learn to cope with eventually, then teachers

might temporarily avoid that situation but eventually return the environment to "normal." For example, a student might have a disruptive response to virtually any paper-and-pencil academic task. These demands might be removed temporarily, but then slowly reintroduced using activities with a high likelihood of success and in a positive social context. The student could be provided with a visual schedule showing that the nonpreferred task will be brief and followed by a preferred activity. The teacher also could assign tasks to the student but allow the student to choose the order in which to do them. The temporary removal of the original task demands gives the student and the adults a clean slate and a chance to take small steps toward success.

Still, there are cases when an aversive environmental trigger should be changed permanently. For example, if a student is physically uncomfortable, it would only be appropriate to expect him or her to become accustomed to the discomfort if there is some future benefit to it. The following example involves a situation that was changed permanently as part of a behavioral support plan that was developed based on an FBA:

Kent, a kindergarten student classified as having autism, did not have a conventional way to communicate. Kent did not like to sit in a chair at the table to do his work and would often sit or lie down on the floor instead. The support team discovered that this "noncompliance" probably was because Kent, who was quite large for his age, was not comfortable sitting in a chair designed for a typical kindergarten student. The support team realized that providing Kent with a chair that fit him was a perfectly reasonable accommodation and that no student should be expected to be uncomfortable for significant periods of time.

Appropriate prevention strategies are one important part of a PBS plan and can help to reduce and even alleviate some problems. Avoidance of predictive antecedents, however, typically will not result in long-term behavior change unless students are also taught new ways to communicate and to manage themselves. The following are some examples of prevention strategies—both temporary and permanent—that have been used with students.

Student Snapshots

 Anthony hit and pushed the teacher or assistant as a way to avoid any activity that involved writing. The support team decided temporarily to reduce the amount of writing that Anthony was asked to do in each activity and to give him a choice of using a pen, pencil, crayon, or marker. The team members also arranged Anthony's schedule to alternate written activities with other types of activities that Anthony preferred, such as the teacher or assistant reading to him.

Lou, who was classified as having autism, often cried, screamed, and clung to her desk when it was time to make a class transition that required being in crowded and noisy hallways. Lou's teachers decided to allow Lou to change classes a few minutes ahead of the other students so that she did not have to be in the halls when they were crowded. This allowed Lou to become accustomed to being in the halls when they were quieter. Lou was gradually exposed to the halls when they were noisier, and she eventually was able to change classes with the other students.

Jim threw and tore materials at school. The support team noticed that Jim mostly threw items such as blocks and pegs and pegboards, items that involved sitting and assembling or sorting by color, and other materials that were used to practice preacademic skills. When Jim's teacher involved him in more functional activities such as preparing the snack, setting the table, running errands, and using the computer to write notes to friends, Jim did not throw and tear materials. These new activities made sense to Jim in a way that repetitive, nonfunctional activities did not; therefore, these activities were permanently incorporated into Jim's educational programming.

Eric, who had a learning disability in math, would swear and verbally threaten people when he was anxious about whether he could do his math assignments successfully. Eric's teacher decided to demonstrate the first math problem for Eric, to coach him through the steps of the second math problem, to watch him work on the third math problem, and then to ask Eric to raise his hand when he had finished the fourth math problem. After checking Eric's fourth problem, Eric's teacher would ask, "Are you ready to do the rest on your own?" Although Eric's teacher eventually phased out the use of this structured modeling and prompting sequence, he always made sure that Eric had an example of a completed math problem to use as a cue for doing independent math work.

There are many possible ways to alter triggering antecedents in order to avoid problem behaviors. Whereas the changes should be based on the FBA and not made willy-nilly, some changes in the social, physical, or academic context may be warranted based on standards for best practice, and some, such as providing a visual schedule, seem to be virtually always helpful. The following list summarizes some of the most typical ways antecedent stimuli are altered:

Who

- Change staffing (e.g., alternate staff, reduce the number of staff who work with a student).
- Change grouping (e.g., group with different peers, fewer peers, or more peers).

What

- Make instructional activities more functional.
- Change the level of difficulty (i.e., is the task too easy or too hard?).
- Provide a choice of activities or provide a choice of the order in which activities are completed.
- Prompt correct responses and positive behaviors before the student has a chance to make mistakes.

- Make activities structured and concrete (i.e., use hands-on materials and provide models, which are often especially important for students with intellectual disabilities or autism).

- Clearly define the beginning and the ending of an activity (e.g., "We'll do these five problems, and then we'll take a break").

- Use visual prompts and models (e.g., use First–Then pictures, do one math problem for the student, pick up a toy at clean-up time, use graphic organizers, provide a list of the steps for a science activity).

- Clearly communicate the rules, procedures, daily schedule, and how activities are structured.

- Provide more encouragement or a different type of encouragement (e.g., more/less proximity, more/less affect, more emphasis on self-evaluation).

When

- Communicate changes in the routine (e.g., verbally, through signs, pictures, symbols).

- Balance difficult and easy tasks; alternate preferred and nonpreferred tasks.

Where

- Alter the seating arrangement or the location of instruction.

- Prepare the student for entering problem environments (e.g., large, open spaces or crowded spaces) by showing the student the schedule, talking about what will happen, and reminding the student of calming strategies.

Teaching Strategies

A second type of intervention included in a comprehensive plan for PBS is to teach alternative behaviors. Indeed, the heart of a PBS plan is teaching effective, socially appropriate behaviors that help students meet their wants and needs. For most students with serious behavior problems, this means teaching specific replacement skills to achieve the same purpose as the target behavior and also teaching other interpersonal, self-management, and academic skills that will take longer to learn but will lead to the desired long-term outcomes.

In Step 2, your team answered the question "What is the purpose of the behavior?" The teaching strategies in a PBS plan involve helping the student learn and use alternative ways to accomplish that purpose. Teachers want to show students more positive ways to meet their needs. This means that first teachers have to accept the validity of what the student is trying to do or say. The unspoken message to the student should be: *"You do not have to go to this trouble to get what you want or need. If your wants or needs are legitimate, then we will help you to get them met. If they are not legitimate, then we will make an effort to explain why they are not, and we will help you find some suitable alternatives."*

Replacement Behaviors that Serve a Social-Communicative Function

Recall that the most common purposes of problem behavior are social-communicative: *obtaining attention*, nurturance, comfort, or help; *obtaining something tangible* or a preferred activity; *escaping or avoiding tasks or activities*; and *escaping or avoiding attention or other social interaction* (O'Neill et al., 1997). The problem behaviors serving these purposes can be viewed as a form of communication that takes an idiosyncratic or socially inappropriate form. Some students may use conventional forms of communication but be difficult to understand or communicate at an unacceptable rate. Other students may not have the communication skills needed to convey their messages in socially approved ways; they may have learned that problem behavior, such as hitting, throwing a tantrum, or destroying property, gets them the desired functions. There are even times when a problem behavior works better than a more appropriate behavior. Students need to be taught alternative skills that will serve the same social-communication functions but do so using a more desirable form of behavior (e.g., words, signs, pictures, an augmentative communication device).

In each example that follows, the student was taught a replacement behavior that communicated the same function as the problem behavior. In each case, the student at first was taught a new response that was very easy to do and was reinforced immediately, so that it was very efficient and effective. Later, the student learned more difficult responses that still achieved the same purpose but were more typical and age-appropriate in their form.

- Rob learned to point to a "break" card instead of running from the classroom to seek escape when he was tired of working. At first, he received a break immediately simply for pointing to the card; later, he learned to pick up the card and wait at the door until the teacher gave him permission to leave the room. (Function: Escape disliked tasks)

- Jade learned to tap a classmate's arm instead of grabbing the arm when she wanted to get the child's attention. Eventually, Jade also learned to use her classmates' names when initiating an interaction. (Function: Get peer attention)

- Kerry learned to ask her teacher for help by pointing to her "help" symbol in her communication wallet instead of scratching her arms to gain the teacher's attention when frustrated by

a difficult task. After she had learned that the new form of communication worked better and more easily than her old behavior, she was then able to learn to raise her hand for attention, as her peers did. (Function: Escape difficult tasks, get help)

- Mason learned to point to objects instead of crying and tugging on someone's arm when he wanted something that was out of his reach. Later in the school year, he was able to use a picture communication system to request items and activities. (Function: Get desired item)

Replacement Behaviors that Serve an Internal, Automatically Reinforcing Function

The other two purposes served by problem behaviors are quite different from the social-communicative purposes, although they still serve either to obtain something or avoid something. The internally controlled or automatically reinforcing functions of problem behavior are *obtaining internal stimulation* such as visual stimulation, endorphin release, or something fun to do; and e*scaping/avoiding internal stimulation* such as itching, sinus pain, noise, crowding, or hunger (O'Neill et al., 1997).

Problem behaviors that fit this category are not socially motivated but are internally motivated, making them more difficult to address in support plans. Behaviors that serve a self-regulatory purpose are not intended to communicate a message or to influence other people. Instead, the individual needs more or less internal stimulation and has found some way to accomplish that purpose. The person does not necessarily care how other people respond to the behavior. The internal stimulation that the behavior provides or alleviates is *automatically reinforcing*, or rewarding for its own sake.

Still, the same logic guides the choice of interventions for both social-communicative and self-regulatory behaviors: Students whose problem behaviors are maintained by the consequences of obtaining or avoiding internal stimulation need to learn a new way to achieve that purpose. For example, a student who covers her ears with her hands and screams to avoid loud noises that hurt her ears or frighten her could learn a different way to avoid this aversive sensory input (e.g., by using headphones to listen to music, going to a quiet place).

Self-regulatory behaviors often involve repetitive body movement—behaviors that may be described as *self-stimulatory* or *stereotypic*. It is important to understand that the topography of the behavior—the way the behavior looks—does not reveal its function. Flapping one's hands could be a way to relieve too much internal stimulation (e.g., sensory overload, anxiety), or it could be a way to get internal stimulation when one is bored or needs more physical movement. Teachers sometimes assume that all stereotypic behaviors interfere with the student's ability to listen or to focus on instruction. Instead, these behaviors may actually help a person to focus by regulating his or her internal state.

The teaching components of a PBS plan may include replacing certain existing self-regulatory behaviors with more normalized—and, in the case of self-destructive behaviors, safer—versions that provide the same sort of stimulation. In some cases, interventions are designed not to eliminate the behavior completely but to confine its use to particular times or places. For example, in a study involving a young student with autism, visual cue cards were used to signify the times when it was acceptable for him to engage in stereotypic behavior. At the beginning of instructional sessions, the student was reminded that it was not time for stereotypy; if he did the target behavior during the session, the teacher pointed to the "no" card and gave a verbal reminder. After the task was completed, the student was shown the "yes" card, and stereotypy was permitted (Conroy, Asmus, Sellers, & Ladwig, 2005). Another example is giving a student with autism a card or other symbol to use to request deep pressure or to ask for the weighted vest that provides the sensory input needed to feel comfortable. Most people would consider these alternatives to be more acceptable than running to the library to squeeze oneself between a bookshelf and the wall.

Replacement behaviors for self-injurious behaviors that serve a self-regulatory purpose have often been identified through a functional analysis, so that they not only serve the same general purpose of obtaining or escaping internal stimulation, they also provide the same sort of sensory stimulation as well (e.g., eye-poking to obtain visual stimulation should be replaced with looking at brightly colored computer images). But FBAs are also a powerful means for understanding if problem behaviors have a sensory function (obtaining or escaping internal stimulation), and informal checks can be made to verify the team's ideas for teaching replacement behaviors. For example, a student who rocks back and forth may need a different form of vestibular input, while a student who hums or moans incessantly may need to use headphones to listen to music. These replacement behaviors can be informally tested to see if giving the student access to the replacement behavior serves to reduce the problem behavior.

Other Desired Behaviors: Social Skills and Self-Control

In addition to learning specific replacement skills to accomplish their purposes, most students with serious behavior problems also benefit from general improvements in their social interaction and self-control skills. Although replacing a single problem behavior with a more appropriate way to communicate or regulate internal stimulation can decrease the incidence of problem behavior, students virtually always need to learn other social skills and self-control strategies in order to achieve the lasting behavior and lifestyle improvements that are the goal of positive behavior supports. To improve inadequate social skills, it is important to assess, target, and intentionally teach the necessary skills in natural contexts employing the same teaching principles and techniques used to teach academic skills. Using sound social skills training curricula (e.g., McGinnis & Goldstein, 1990, 1997a, 1997b), essential skills can be targeted for inclusion in a student's PBS plan. The student may participate in any universal social skill interventions occurring in the school, and also receive individualized or small-group instruction in targeted skills.

Self control and good problem solving are facets of the broader construct of self-management. Self-management methods involve teaching students to gain independence in the use of an academic, social, or behavioral skill (Cole & Bambara, 1992). Self-management entails using self-control to refrain from impulsive actions and problem-solving constructive alternatives, as well as using strategies to manage frustration, relax, and reduce anxiety. Self-management strategies have been used extensively within PBS plans for students with a wide range of ages and disabilities. Self-management systems can involve various combinations of self-cueing, self-monitoring, self-assessment, and self-reinforcement. For example, a third-grade boy and a fourth-grade boy with learning and/or physical disabilities who were included in general education classrooms learned to self-monitor their on-task behavior and to self-assess their task completion (Todd, Horner, & Sugai, 1999). The two boys also learned to use self-recruitment of teacher praise at regular intervals and

when they reached their daily objectives. The students' use of the self-management intervention was found to be functionally related to both increases in on-task behavior and task completion and decreases in problem behavior (Todd et al., 1999).

Other self-management methods have been demonstrated as effective in increasing rates of academic engagement, schoolwork completion, and hand-raising to request help and in decreasing disengaged and disruptive behavior for students with and without disabilities in a range of school contexts (Barry & Messer, 2003; Brooks, Todd, Tofflemoyer, & Horner, 2003; Callahan & Rademacher, 1999; Grandy & Peck, 1997; Koegel, Harrower, & Koegel, 1999; Rock, 2005). Not all of this research has used functional analysis to demonstrate a direct relationship between the self-management system and the behavioral improvement. It is clear, however, that self-management approaches, combined with other interventions such as instruction in replacement behaviors and reinforcement of approved behaviors, can yield meaningful benefits for students. Because they give students the ability to control their own behavior, self-management systems facilitate generalized, long-lasting results (Todd et al., 1999).

In addition to their effectiveness in improving self-control and academic behavior, self-management systems are quite efficient with respect to the amount of adult effort and involvement required to implement them. Teachers have reported high levels of satisfaction with the procedures and outcomes of self-management interventions (Koegel et al., 1999).

Methods for Teaching Alternative Skills and Other Desired Behaviors

Teaching alternative skills requires 1) identifying a replacement skill that will be easier for the student to perform than the problem behavior, 2) teaching the student how and when to use the skill, and 3) ensuring that teachers and others in the environment respond to the skill so that it works more effectively than the problem behavior. That is, the new, replacement behavior is meant to compete with the problem behavior and replace it because the new behavior works better. For the replacement skill to be truly functional for the student, performing the replacement skill needs to take less effort than the problem behavior (efficiency), and using the replacement skill needs to accomplish the desired purpose more often and more consistently than the problem behavior (effectiveness).

Student Snapshot

 Sidney, who typically did not talk and communicated using a few words and gestures, would grab teachers' or classmates' arms or clothing when he was left alone at his desk and wanted to gain their attention and interact with them. This was a behavior that was easy to do—he would grab whoever was nearby—and also was extremely effective in getting people to come close, talk with him, and touch him. At first, the support team provided Sidney with a photo album with pictures of his teachers and classmates as a device to assist his communication efforts. They tried to teach Sidney to find and point to a photograph of the person with whom he wanted to interact. Even when provided with adult assistance, however, it often took Sidney several minutes to retrieve the photo album and locate the picture of a particular person. Thus, this was not a very efficient replacement behavior. Also, the classmates or teachers that Sidney was pointing to in the photo album often were not in Sidney's immediate vicinity and did not notice that Sidney was pointing to their pictures. Therefore, the likelihood was not high that Sidney's attempt to gain the desired attention using the photo album would be successful; the effectiveness of the replacement behavior was not nearly as effective as Sidney's old behavior.

When Sidney was taught to hold out his hand to indicate "give me five" as a way to initiate an interaction, however, he had an easy-to-do replacement skill that was very likely to be reinforced immediately by gaining attention.

Teaching replacement skills requires developing an instructional plan ensuring that relevant adults and peers

- Know what the replacement skill is
- Know how, when, and by whom the skill will be taught
- Know how generalization and maintenance of the replacement skill will be ensured

Typically, a combination of methods is used, including 1) rearranging antecedents to prevent problem behaviors from occurring and to cue the use of the replacement skill; 2) incidental teaching to model, shape, prompt, and reinforce the use of the replacement skill in natural contexts; and, in some cases, 3) skill-based teaching approaches to provide direct instruction and practice of the replacement skill in instructional environments. If the replacement skill is to become more efficient and effective for the student than the problem behavior, instruction must take the student beyond the acquisition stage of performing the skill accurately in specific instructional contexts. The student also must learn when to use the skill and learn to use it fluently (i.e., fast enough for the skill to be effective in obtaining the desired results). A further consideration in teaching replacement skills is to ensure that the student's use of the skill generalizes to all of the people, places, and situations where the problem behavior is a concern, and that skill use is maintained over time.

Figure 5.6 outlines the instructional methods used to teach alternative skills, including both specific replacement skills and other desired social and self-management skills. The methods used will vary depending on the student's cognitive and communication abilities. For

---

Methods for Teaching Alternative Skills and Behaviors

- **Modeling:** When the student has an opportunity (contrived or naturally occurring) to use the new skill or behavior, an adult or peer demonstrates the skill. In some cases, salient features of the model may be verbally described to the student (i.e., the student may receive visual, verbal, or physical prompts as he or she performs the skill or behavior, and may later receive performance feedback).
- **Prompting and shaping:** When the student has an opportunity (contrived or naturally occurring) to use the new skill or behavior, a sequence of prompts is used to elicit the new skill, which then is reinforced by providing the requested object or activity. For example, the prompting sequence might be 1) a natural cue, 2) a gesture, and 3) a partial physical prompt. The new skill is shaped by reinforcing the student's current form of the skill (and/or the frequency with which it is used) and by slowly working toward the criterion form and frequency.
- **Behavior rehearsal:** The student practices role playing or rehearsing a target skill under controlled conditions (e.g., with the teacher in the classroom just before going to the lunchroom, where the problem often arises). The student also may verbalize what he or she will do or say when an opportunity to use the skill arises. Adapted approaches to this category of teaching method include social stories (Gray, 1998) and cognitive picture and script rehearsal strategies (Groden & LeVasseur, 1994). These two techniques, designed for students with Asperger syndrome, autism, or intellectual disabilities, provide the student with a social script, often accompanied by pictures or drawings, that leads him or her through the process of rehearsing for a difficult situation.
- **Coaching:** The student is given verbal directions on how and when to use the skill; skill use is followed by verbal feedback and discussion of the student's performance. Coaching is often used with modeling.
- **Incidental teaching:** Naturally occurring daily activities are used as opportunities for instruction. An adult or peer uses a combination of prompting, shaping, coaching, and modeling to improve skill use. Incidental teaching may make use of "teachable moments" when the student has missed an opportunity to use a skill, or activities may be arranged to provide teaching opportunities (e.g., a preferred item is purposefully left in sight but out of the student's reach).
- **Self-management strategies:** Students are provided with devices (e.g., a checklist, wrist counter, photo, picture series) that are used to cue the new skill and/or to self-evaluate their performance of the skill. This may be combined with self-reinforcement. Self-monitoring strategies (a type of self-management strategy) require teaching students to use a device (e.g., wrist counter, interval recording form, checklist) to count instances of their own behavior.
- **Social-cognitive processes:** Students are taught metacognitive processes that increase awareness of their own and others' behaviors and feelings. These processes, which are taught through direct instruction, include self-talk, problem-solving strategies, relaxation training, and behavior rehearsal. The processes are especially helpful when teaching the cognitive processes involved in using social and self-management skills such as anger control, problem solving, attribution training, and perspective taking.

Figure 5.6. Methods for teaching alternative skills and behaviors.

instance, cognitive strategies that involve self-talk may not always be the most appropriate intervention for students who have an intellectual disability. Many of the methods that require verbal mediation (e.g., role-playing, social-cognitive processes) can be adapted for students with cognitive disabilities, however, by using visual cues and by simplifying the steps in the process.

A specific approach to teaching alternative communication skills that deserves mention is *functional communication training* (Durand & Merges, 2001), or, more broadly, *communication-based intervention* (Carr, Levin, McConnachie, Carlson, Kemp, & Smith, 1994). Communication-based interventions, which are part of an overall PBS plan, are designed to teach persons with developmental disabilities (primarily those with intellectual disabilities and/or autism) and severe problem behavior to use positive forms of communication to achieve their goals (it does not address internal stimulation as a function of problem behavior). The approach is similar to the one described in this book, but it utilizes a more rigorous functional analysis and very intensive instructional programming to accelerate the acquisition of new communication skills, the generalization of new communication skills across people and stimulus conditions, and the maintenance of those skills across time. Functional communication training has been validated through extensive research in both clinical and community settings with people having developmental disabilities and severe behavior problems including aggression, self-injury, and property destruction (Carr et al., 1994; Durand & Merges, 2001).

Responding Strategies

Responding strategies (also known as *consequential strategies*) involve making changes to the consequences that follow the student's behavior with the intent of making the new, replacement behavior work better than the problem behavior. The PBS approach to behavior problems requires the adults in the student's life to change the ways they react to both positive and negative behaviors. The reinforcing consequences that were maintaining the problem behavior are now used to maintain the replacement behavior. When the problem behavior occurs, the response is nonreinforcement so that the problem behavior is eventually extinguished.

When a problem behavior occurs, some possible ways of responding that fit with this approach are 1) nonreinforcement followed by redirection to the acceptable behavior and 2) natural or logical and educational consequences. (When the behavior is seriously disruptive or destructive, a Safety Plan also is needed.) Conversely, adults and peers conscientiously provide reinforcement to the individual 1) when the alternative behavior is used and 2) when the problem behavior does not occur. The following is a brief description of each of these strategies and a discussion of some important decision rules to follow in deciding which strategies to use for a particular student:

Nonreinforcement and Redirection

Nonreinforcement means not responding to a behavior in a way that enables the behavior to achieve its purpose. It means not allowing the behavior to work for the student in the way it has worked in the past. Durand (1990) describes nonreinforcement as a *response-independent consequence* that makes the challenging behavior *nonfunctional.*

To be effective and educational, nonreinforcement must be used in conjunction with redirecting the student to an alternative behavior and then reinforcing the alternative behavior (or an attempt by the student to use an alternative behavior). In a sense, nonreinforcement means ignoring the problem behavior; it does not mean completely ignoring students and doing nothing to help them alter their behavior. For example, if Rose grabs a peer's shirt as a way to say "Hi, let's play," the teacher can prompt Rose to use the replacement behavior of tapping the peer on the shoulder and then praise Rose for using her new behavior. The peer also will then agree to play with Rose, which is where the real reinforcement occurs.

Nonreinforcement and redirection 1) show the student what to do as an alternative to a problem behavior and 2) provide the opportunity for reinforcement of the desired behavior. Teachers are not really *teaching* a student if their strategy is simply to ignore the student in the hope that she or he will eventually hit on the correct behavior.

Natural, Logical, and Educational Consequences

Certainly, one way that people learn to avoid making social and behavioral mistakes is by experiencing the consequences of their behavior. Sometimes there is a place for the use of negative consequences in a behavioral support plan but only if the consequences used meet several criteria. Negative consequences should not inflict pain, humiliation, or embarrassment on the student. They should not be chosen arbitrarily but should be in keeping with the hypotheses generated by the FBA.

When negative consequences are used, they should be naturally or logically related to the behavior. *Natural consequences* occur as a result of the behavior itself. For example, the natural consequence of breaking or losing a toy is that the item is no longer available. Some behaviors do not really have a natural consequence: There is no subsequent event that naturally is contingent on the behavior's occurrence. In such a case, *logical consequences* may be developed. Logical consequences are consequences that "fit" the behavior and are reasonably related to it. For example, a logical consequence for failing to finish work is not having free time.

It is extremely important to understand that negative consequences can be natural or logical but inconsistent with a positive behavior supports approach, if they are used in a manner that is cold, authoritarian, or uninformed by an understanding of the causes and functions of difficult behavior. Certainly, natural and logical consequences, by definition, can be punishing in that they are stimuli or events that are contingent on a behavior and decrease the future occurrence of the behavior. Exposure of students to natural or logical consequences, however, should never be done in a punitive or intemperate way. Theoretically, the natural consequence of running out into a street without looking is getting hit by a car. Yet this is not the way teachers would instruct students in street crossing. Therefore, it is not enough for consequences to be natural or logical; they also should be educational and respectful. Just as teachers should follow nonreinforcement with redirection to a more appropriate behavior, teachers also should follow natural or logical consequences with a response that is designed to strengthen the student's use of approved behavior.

The following are suggestions to consider when using four common negative consequences in ways that are not merely natural or logical but are also educational and respectful:

1. *Corrections and restitution.* Corrections, or having a student correct a behavioral "mistake," can be a logical, educational consequence. For example, prompting a student to hang her coat in her cubbyhole or locker after she had thrown it on the floor or having a student clean up milk that was spilled are corrections. Restitution is a particular type of correction that involves making things right with another person. Asking a student to apologize for hurting someone or to return a book that was stolen from a classmate are logical consequences that involve restitution and can be educational as well.

    There are several things, however, to watch out for when responding in this way. Forcing a correction or restitution may end up in a verbal or physical tug-of-war with the student. It can be difficult to conclude a tug-of-war in a way that is educational and respectful. Often, it is best to wait until the student is calm and has some perspective on the incident before discussing the correction. Otherwise, you even may lose sight of the original lesson you were hoping to convey, which has to do with being a good citizen and treating other people fairly and with respect.

2. *Verbal reprimands.* It is easy to fall into the habit of scolding students when they do things they should not do, but this often has a negative effect on students with problem behavior. Although at times scolding can be effective in halting a behavior, at other times it has no effect, or even the opposite effect, of what was intended. For instance, if a student has few positive ways to communicate and has learned that negative behavior is a more certain way to get attention than being quiet and compliant, verbal comments that teachers think of as being reprimands can actually be reinforcing to the student.

   When students understand words and rules and are "just testing" to see whether they can get away with a behavior without consequences, it makes sense to remind them of the rule that has been broken. For example, if a student runs down the hallway jostling other students but understands that this is not allowed and is doing it just to see whether he or she can get away with it, then it is appropriate to give a reminder: "Remember our hallway rule: Walk and stay in line." If a student who does not talk and does not understand rules is throwing art materials on the floor as a way to get attention, however, then talking about the behavior may teach that student that throwing is the way to say "Pay attention to me!" In that case, a better way to respond might be to interrupt the behavior by removing some of the materials and redirecting the student to the art project at hand.

3. *Response cost: Taking away privileges or things.* Taking away privileges as a consequence to problem behavior can be a logical and educational consequence. It needs to be accomplished, however, with the student's level of cognitive and social development in mind, and it needs to be followed by *teaching* so that the student learns what to do instead in the future. For example, a student hits a classmate while the science class is watching a nature movie that everyone has been looking forward to seeing. Simply not allowing the student to watch the movie for a few minutes can be just as effective, if not more so, than banishing him or her from the classroom until the movie is over or taking away movie-watching privileges for the semester. After the movie is over, the teacher could pull the student aside to discuss what happened and make a plan for success in the future.

   If a behavioral support plan includes taking away items or privileges, it should be done in a neutral way immediately after the problem has occurred, and whatever is taken away should be naturally or logically related to the problem behavior. For example, if a kindergarten student grabs a toy from a classmate, the toy might be taken away for a few minutes but not the child's dessert. To be educational, taking away items or privileges should be followed by an opportunity to practice an approved behavior. Thus, if a teacher has taken a toy away from a child for a few minutes, the teacher would let the child try playing with the toy again, spending a few minutes modeling and shaping an acceptable way to play in order to promote successful play.

4. *Taking a break. Taking a break* means simply having the student go to another part of the room, take a walk, or do something else to get away from

where the problem occurred for as long as it takes to interrupt the problem behavior and the student to calm down. This way of responding is theoretically similar to the idea of time-out, but the use of that term is avoided because there are many different ways to use time-out and most of them are punitive. The purpose of this strategy is to short-circuit the crisis cycle and prevent the student from losing control. It can also help students learn to control themselves. For example, the A-B-C information that Mike's team collected showed that Mike gets anxious and then disruptive when he does one lesson immediately after another with no time between to reorient himself. In addition to building more breaks into Mike's schedule and providing him with a picture schedule so that he would always know which activity was next, Mike was taught to perceive his own triggers and to ask, "May I take a short break?" when these signals arose. Eventually, Mike was taught internal self-calming strategies, which are more desirable self-management methods.

Reinforcement for the Absence of Problem Behavior

A plan for *differential reinforcement of other behavior* (DRO) allows you to provide a selected reinforcer to a student for each specified period of time in which the targeted problem behavior is *not* displayed. Used alone, this behavior-management strategy does nothing to teach an alternative behavior. DRO is consistent with a PBS approach, however, if used in conjunction with antecedent strategies and teaching replacement behaviors that match the functions of problem behaviors. A common DRO plan involves rewarding the student for not displaying any of several behaviors that

can be categorized as "off task" (e.g., talking to classmates, using materials inappropriately, staring out the window). Like other reward-based contingency programs, the reward must be easily attainable so that the student will actually receive the reward and not simply be frustrated by an enticement that is beyond reach. For example, if a student engages in some type of disruptive behavior (e.g., making loud noises, getting out of his or her seat, throwing materials) at an average rate of once every 2 minutes, and you devise a DRO plan in which the student must refrain from disruptive behavior for 1 hour to receive the reward, he or she will not be successful in obtaining the reward and may even stop trying.

Contingent reward programs such as DRO are more positive and proactive than contingent punishment programs such as *response cost*. The two interventions may at first seem to be similar, but there is a considerable difference between *taking away something valued* by the student as a consequence of demonstrating a negative behavior (as in response cost) and *bestowing something valued* by the student for demonstrating positive behavior (as in DRO). For example, as part of a response cost intervention, a student might have computer time scheduled after each academic period but have that time taken away if targeted problem behavior occurs during the academic session. A DRO intervention allows the student to earn computer time if the problem behavior does not occur during a specified period of time.

Although an environment that is rich in rewarding activities and interactions is one element of a plan for PBS, you should caution against making extrinsic rewards (e.g., grades, praise, edible treats) the centerpiece of a behavioral support plan. A more educational approach asks how the social context and the instructional activities can be altered to make learning and the social context more meaningful, rather than trying to find a treat that will induce short-term compliance in the student. Some students may not have learned that interacting with others and participating in daily activities can be rewarding. In that case, teaching the student the value of interaction and participation should be a top priority.

Suggestions for Comprehensive Positive Behavior Support Plans

Figure 5.7 provides a completed example of the Step 3 Worksheet: Positive Behavior Support Plan. This PBS plan, designed for Jason, a fourth-grade student with mental retardation, some autism-like characteristics, and a history of behavior difficulties, shows how preventing, teaching, and responding strategies fit together to create a comprehensive behavioral support plan. There are several important points to note about Jason's plan:

- Each strategy was based on specific information obtained through the FBA.

- The support plan was designed by a team that included general and special education teachers, an instructional assistant, a school psychologist, and Jason's parents. The speech-language therapist occasionally consulted with the team.

- The team included a special education teacher who had significant experience in the processes of conducting FBAs and developing behavior intervention plans. A behavior specialist who worked full-time for the school district, along with the special education teacher, taught the processes to the other team members, thus generating additional expertise that was then available for future PBS teams in the school.

- The plan provides a map or framework for supporting Jason at this point in time, but the plan will continue to be revised as its effects are evaluated by the support team. Employing the same A-B-C approach used during the FBA, the team continues to gather data on Jason's problem behavior and on the ways staff respond to it; this information helps them be objective in their evaluation of the effects of the support plan.

Naturally, the complexity of PBS plans varies widely depending on the complexity of the student's learning and behavioral needs and the support team's ability to implement interventions. No one knows exactly what the minimum requirements are for effective interventions for significant behavior problems; nor does anyone know exactly how much training a typical teacher or support team member needs to successfully implement a comprehensive PBS plan. Teachers should not be daunted, however, by the standards that researchers must follow for designing and implementing behavior interventions. More published research is being conducted in schools and other typical settings with researchers involved in developing procedures for hypothesis testing and data collection and school staff conducting the FBA and developing and implementing the interventions (e.g., Kern, Gallagher, Starosta, Hickman, & George, 2006). Researchers also are responding to the need to measure the contextual fit of the interventions, including the degree to which the implementers of the interventions are satisfied with the strategies and their results (Albin et al., 1996).

Many research studies conducted in schools show significant effects on students' behavior when relatively commonplace interventions and supports are implemented faithfully by teachers, student teachers, paraprofessionals, and par-

Step 3 Worksheet: Positive Behavior Support Plan

Student Jason   **Date** February 8, 2007

Team members designing this plan

Jared Simms, special education teacher   Rita Santos, fourth-grade teacher

Carly Roberts & Rob Moore, Jason's parents   Ashley Giles, instructional aide

Mara Kellam, school psychologist   Marianne Josephs, school district behavior consultant

Target behavior(s) and functions

1. Behaviors that serve to escape/avoid difficult and non-preferred tasks—especially paper-and-pencil tasks and loosely structured or unfamiliar tasks in English, social studies, and science (doing these tasks in small groups with peers is a strong predictor of any and all target behaviors):

   • Pushing/kicking (mostly pushing) an adult or peer

   • Yelling/screaming (e.g., "No, no!" "I won't!" "Stop it now!," nonsense words)

   • Refusals, as indicated by being out of assigned seat or location; tearing, dropping, or otherwise misusing materials

   • Serious incidents that include an acceleration of pushing/kicking, yelling/screaming, and refusals until Jason is out of control

2. Behaviors that serve to gain attention from peers: pushing (occasionally kicking)

Interventions and Support Strategies to Be Implemented

Preventing		Teaching replacement behaviors and other alternative skills	Responding
Setting events	**Triggers**		
• Ms. Santos develops a more positive relationship with Jason by spending time with him in low-demand situations (arrival, recess). Observes Mr. Simms and Ms. Giles as they teach Jason using unintrusive prompts and an upbeat tone.	• Modify paper-and-pencil tasks, (e.g., provide writing frames, fill-in-the-blank formats). • Give choices for independent practice activities, especially in English.	• Teach to request teacher assistance by raising his hand high while holding a small red card for "help" and seeking eye contact. Fade the card as he becomes proficient. • Teach independent time management through use of "to do" list and written schedule.	1. Respond to hand-raising as soon as possible. Ask Jason what he needs or if he has any questions. As Jason becomes more skillful, signal to him (e.g., hold up index finger) that you will be there in a few seconds.

Figure 5.7. Step 3 Worksheet: Positive Behavior Support Plan for Jason.

118

- Eliminate point system for earning computer time. Add computer time to choices for English assignments and free time. He does not need to "earn" these times; they are on his schedule.

- Consistent use of written schedule to check off completed tasks and signal transitions.
- For cooperative learning and other student-directed groups, assign Jason a specific role such as "materials manager." Provide unintrusive adaptations for his contributions to the group's work.
- Emphasize friendship-making skills and assertiveness skills in classwide social skills instruction.
- Seat Jason near Trey or Adam, friends from last year. Enlist them in supporting Jason socially. Teach them and other selected peers how to recognize and respond to Jason's appropriate initiation attempts.

- Provide structure and visual closure: "to do" work on desk; "finished" work in folder.
- Teach relaxation and self-calming strategies, first with direct training and then prompting use in natural situations when trigger events and signs of escalation occur.

- Teach Jason to use Hassel Log for processing critical incidents and his response to use of the Safety Plan. Help him to identify external triggers, feelings that escalate behavior; reality of what happened, and a plan for improving behavior next time.
- Teach replacement skill for pushing peers to gain attention: "Hi (name), how are you?" Or "Can I join you?"
- Rehearse for upcoming interaction opportunities (e.g., "Jason, remember what you learned about how to join in a conversation.").
- Provide booster and rehearsal sessions for classwide social skills training sessions; include a small group of peers with similar needs. Teach a self-monitoring system to check use of friendship-making skills.
- Teach skills for playing recess games—tag, kickball, ring toss (Jason's choices).

2. At first sign of escalation (begins with refusals), redirect with clear visual prompts and concrete directions for what to do (modeling is good here); give encouragement for any participation.
3. If redirection fails, interrupt by prompting use of self-calming strategy and reminder: "Teachers will help you."
4. If interruption fails, prompt Jason to ask for a break to take a walk. Attempt to reach a stopping point before going for a break (e.g., "I'll help you with that last word, and then you can take a break.").
5. If Jason is still not calm after the break, use the Safety Plan, including the Hassle Log. Note: This is not a punishment; it is for safety, to save Jason's reputation, and to prevent future problems.

- Peers' reinforcement of Jason's initiation and friendship-making skills are more important than adults', so teaching him the skills and teaching peers how to respond is essential. However, reinforce use of skills across the day, using thumbs-up, eye contact, smiles, and so forth.
- If pushing occurs, follow Safety Plan, which begins with one reminder of the rules and prompting use of alternative skill. If the interaction is already deteriorating, pull Jason aside and remind him of the rule: "Everyone deserves to feel safe at school."

Is Safety Plan still needed?   (Yes)   No
If so, attach Safety Plan that has been revised and updated as needed.

ents. Intervention plans in published research rely heavily on prevention of behavior problems through environmental or structural changes that are mostly low-effort (e.g., changing seating arrangements, reducing task length, interspersing easier and more difficult tasks, using proximity control, giving students choices in academic tasks), on instructional strategies that are almost universally effective (e.g., match task demands with learners' skill levels, use systematic instruction), and on consequence strategies that are based on accepted operant learning principles (e.g., give specific praise and attention for improved behavior, do not reinforce undesirable behavior).

Given these and other findings on effective behavioral support in schools, the following are some additional suggestions for making a successful plan for PBS that will be reliably implemented:

1. Start with strategies to improve the educational and social context, including building relationships between the staff and the student, creating peer support in the classroom and school, and ensuring that the educational programming is appropriate and meaningful. (The facilitation of positive relationships among students is examined in depth in the companion book *Teachers' Guides to Inclusive Practices: Social Relationships and Peer Support, Second Edition* [Janney & Snell, 2006].)

2. Target a particular time of day or a daily routine and implement supports during that time. A transition or any activity that occurs on a daily basis is often a good place to start.

3. It may be easier (and quite effective) to make structural changes (e.g., seating the student with a supportive peer or an adult, providing a visual schedule, providing tasks at the appropriate instructional level) first. Then focus on changing the teaching strategies and interactional components of the plan. Just as we cannot expect to change the student's problem behaviors all at once, we cannot expect the adults to change their behavior all at once either. Adults may need prompting, coaching, feedback, and reinforcement in order to give a student who challenges them more praise and positive attention.

4. Make a plan that fits the context. That is, devise a plan that is suitable for the culture of the school and the student, is regarded as doable by the implementers, and is likely to result in noticeable change in a short period of time.

5. Whenever possible, consult students themselves about their goals, interests, and feelings. Also consider consulting the student's peers and siblings; they may have insights about the student that adults do not.

6. Generalization and maintenance of positive behavior change is enhanced by implementing the PBS plan at school and at home (Carr et al., 1999), but remember that home is a very different context: It is mostly without professional or paraprofessional support or peer support or the structure that is provided by class schedules and bells. If multicomponent interventions cannot be implemented at home, aim for specific goals such as reinforcing replacement behaviors at home as well as at school. Some generalization can occur at home even when supports are implemented only at school; however, problems at school and at home may be further reduced when behavioral supports are implemented in both places (Harvey, Lewis-Palmer, Horner, & Sugai, 2003).

STEP 4

IMPLEMENT, MONITOR, AND EVALUATE THE PBS PLAN

After the behavioral support strategies have been developed, the support team must discuss the specifics of putting the plan into action (see Figure 5.8). Materials may need to be gathered, other individuals who work with the student but who have not been part of the planning team may need to be contacted, and responsibilities for monitoring the plan's implementation and effectiveness should be determined. At a team meeting, complete the Step 4 Worksheet: Implementing, Monitoring, and Evaluating the PBS Plan (see Appendix A) and record decisions made and actions to be taken on a Team Meeting Agenda and Minutes form (see Figure 1.4). The first section of the Step 4 Worksheet lists issues that need immediate

consideration in order to put the plan into place; the second section lists issues related to ongoing monitoring, evaluation, and revision of the PBS plan.

Evaluation typically requires a variety of formal and informal strategies; it is crucial that the strategies selected be user-friendly and efficient or else they will not be carried out. Support team members should not ignore their subjective evaluation of the results of the plan; after all, if those who directly support the student and have implemented the plan are satisfied with the results, then the behavior change has been noticeable, and the plan has been doable. The authors urge you, however, to conduct some formal, ongoing data collection and analysis as part of any behavioral support plan. One reason this is important is that behavior change and skill-acquisition goals associated with the PBS plan also are goals on the student's IEP, which must be moni-

---

STEP 4

Implement, Monitor, and Evaluate the PBS Plan

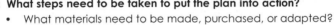

Ask: What steps need to be taken to put the plan into action?

- What materials need to be made, purchased, or adapted?
- Who else needs to be informed about the plan?
- What in-service training, modeling, and/or coaching do team members and other staff members need?
- Who will develop teaching plans for replacement skills and other alternative academic or social-communication skills, and how will the plans be shared with others?
- When, how, and by whom will behavior-change and skill-acquisition data be collected?
- When will we put the various intervention strategies of the plan into place?

Ask: How and when will the use and effects of the PBS plan be evaluated and the plan be revised as necessary?

- What rate of improvement in targeted behaviors and the use of alternative skills is acceptable?
- What is the system for monitoring whether the plan is being used as designed?
- How will we solicit and consider team members' and other relevant peoples' judgments about the plan's effectiveness, efficiency, appropriateness for the student and the context, and comfort level in implementing the plan?
- How will the student's feedback about the acceptability of the interventions and progress toward his or her goals be solicited?
- Are there temporary antecedent strategies that can be faded?
- Is there new information to suggest that the hypothesis about the predictive antecedents, maintaining consequences, or function of the behavior was not accurate?

Figure 5.8.　Step 4: Implement, Monitor, and Evaluate the PBS Plan.

tored at regular intervals. A second reason is that teachers and staff members can be tempted at times to stop using a support strategy too quickly because they are not able to see the small steps that could add up to important progress, or because they are not aware that the strategy has not been consistently implemented. (Teachers and staff members may believe that a strategy is working because it helps them feel like they are doing something to improve the situation, but the strategy may have few actual effects on the problem behavior.)

The system for monitoring and evaluating the PBS plan should address three questions:

1. What improvements have we perceived and documented in a) the target behavior, b) use of the replacement skill, and c) learning other alternative skills? Are improvements being made at an acceptable rate?

2. Have we followed through on using the plan as it was designed?

3. How and when will the PBS plan, its use, and its effects be evaluated and any needed revisions made to the plan?

Evaluating Progress

Progress data, often a continuation of the same data gathered during the functional behavioral assessment, should be examined at each team meeting and formally evaluated at regular intervals. The FBA tools presented in this book can be used on a periodic basis to evaluate the student's PBS plan. A method to evaluate the use of alternative behaviors and skills also should be devised.

Student Schedule Analysis

The Student Schedule Analysis, which was used to gather information in Step 2A (see Figure 4.13), can be useful for keep-

ing a record of the changes that are made to the student's schedule to create a more positive day and for assessing changes in staff perceptions of the student's degree of success throughout the day. Each time the student's daily schedule is revised to alter the antecedent conditions, complete a new Student Schedule Analysis. After the behavioral support plan has been in place for 2 weeks, and periodically from then on, you can calculate the percentage of the classes or activities on the student's daily schedule that the team has rated as successful or unsuccessful. If the rate of successful activities is not increasing, then you may need to look again at the antecedents of the successful and unsuccessful times of day or at your hypothesis about the function of the problem behavior.

Interval Recording or Scatter Plot

The Interval Recording or Scatter Plot (Figures 4.14 and 4.15) should be used almost daily during the initial implementation of the support plan, but as time passes, it can be used less frequently (e.g., once or twice a week, during the times of day that are the most problematic). Data on the problem behavior's rate of occurrence can be summarized daily or weekly and graphed to give a visual representation of progress (see Figure 5.9). Be sure to record comments that may be relevant to the student's performance on a particular day or week (e.g., Was a new support strategy implemented? Was there a substitute teacher?).

Incident Record

If Incident Records (Figure 4.9) continue to be needed, maintain a frequency count of the number of times the Safety Plan is used. Examine the Incident Records for problems with the Safety Plan or indications of antecedents that triggered the incident. If use of the Safety Plan does not decrease, there is a

Student: Jason   **Behavior: Pushing or kicking peers**
Dates: 2/15/07 – 2/27/07

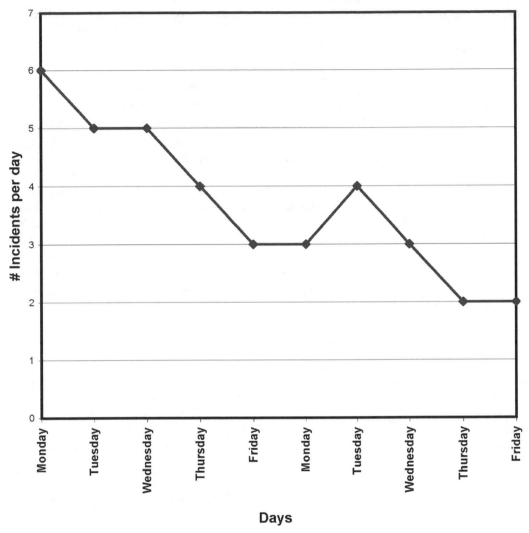

Figure 5.9. Behavior change graph for Jason.

definite need for more information gathering and analysis.

Progress on the Use of New Skills

Data on the use of new social-communication or self-regulation skills are important for evaluating IEP goals and for documenting the student's use of replacement behaviors. Figure 5.10 shows

how Jason's teacher collected data on Jason's use of a replacement skill to initiate interactions with peers. One of Jason's problem behaviors was that he would stand near peers when he wanted to gain their attention and to play with them. This was a positive behavior but it was not often successful. Therefore, Jason would sometimes push or kick to initiate an interaction. Jason's behavioral support plan called for teaching Jason to approach a peer, say "Hi," and initiate a topic of conversation or suggest an activity. Selected peers were taught to provide social cues for Jason during four targeted times each day: 1) arrival, 2) morning break, 3) after lunch, and 4) recess. The special education teacher or assistant used a partial interval recording system to observe and record Jason's peer interactions during those four intervals at least 2 days each week. Data were recorded by marking a + on a data-collection note card the first time Jason attempted an appropriate peer initiation during each time period and changing the plus to an asterisk (*) if the initiation was successful (see Figure 5.10). Jason's teacher graphed the data weekly on a simple line graph to create a visual representation of Jason's progress. She graphed the rate of Jason's peer initiations (i.e., the percentage of the four targeted intervals during which Jason initiated an interaction) so that if the number of targeted intervals was later expanded, the data still could be compared across time.

Lifestyle Improvements: Quality-of-Life Indicators

The quality-of-life indicators that were evaluated and recorded on the Student-Centered FBA Profile (Figure 4.11) can be updated periodically to show changes in the student's relationships, autonomy, and participation patterns. The number of new opportunities for participation in school and community activities, relationships, and choice making can be recorded as a way to check support team accountability for putting the planned supports into place.

Observations of Alternative Skills						
Student Jason			**Observer**	Simms		
Dates 2/12/07 – 2/30/07			**Observation schedule**	2 days per week		
Behavior Peer initiation: Approach available peer, tap peer on shoulder, say "Hi, (name), how are you?" or "Hi, (name), may I join you?" (or phrase with similar purpose)						
Coding + = attempt peer initiation ✱ = successful initiation − = no initiation Code the first initiation that occurs during each activity.						
	Mon.	Wed.	Tues.	Thurs.	Mon.	Fri.
Activity	2/12	2/14	2/20	2/22	2/26	2/30
Arrival/A.M. routine	+	+	✱	✱	+	✱
Morning break	−	−	✱	−	✱	✱
Lunch	✱	✱	✱	✱	✱	✱
Recess	−	✱	✱	✱	✱	✱
Totals (successes/attempts)	1/2	2/3	4/4	3/3	3/4	4/4

Figure 5.10. Observations of alternative skills for Jason.

Monitoring and Revising the Plan

Although behavior change takes time, a lack of noticeable progress after 2 weeks or so should alert the support team to the possible need to reconsider the FBA and to revise the PBS plan. After 2 to 3 weeks of using the initial plan, the support team should meet to 1) examine the student's progress data and 2) discuss implementation of the plan. These two topics should be discussed at each team meeting.

If some element of the plan is clearly aversive or anxiety producing for the student, impossible to implement, or otherwise disastrous, you would certainly consider dropping it right away. Do remember, however, that old habits die hard and the initial stages of a change are the most difficult for everyone involved. Be careful not to drop a promising support strategy too quickly because it has not performed miracles. Supporting a student with difficult behavior requires continuous problem solving and adjustments to the strategies being implemented. If a part of the plan you have implemented is not resulting in improvements after about 2 weeks, however, the support team may need to brainstorm again or talk to other people (parents or professionals) who may have ideas you have not thought of. It is also important to ensure that potentially effective strategies are being implemented as intended.

If the student's progress is generally consistent with the goals of the plan, you can soon begin slowly and methodically to remove some of the temporary prevention strategies. For instance, if the student's schedule had been adjusted so that short intervals of work time were alternated with short intervals of break time, those intervals can slowly become more typical, with the goal of eventually enabling the student to function on a schedule expected of a student his or her age. As the student experiences greater success and learns alternative skills, the need for safety-management procedures should be decreasing and the student's behavior change may be sustained through more typical rates of reinforcement. A key assumption behind the positive behavior support approach is that an effective plan is one that can be gradually phased out over time because the student has gained social-communication and self-management skills and the environment has become more supportive of positive behavior. Although some individuals with disabilities require lifelong accommodations and supports, the teacher's goal is always to help people lead a life that is as typical of their peers as possible.

CONCLUSION

There still is much to learn about supporting and teaching children and youth with seriously difficult behavior. Evidence of the effectiveness of comprehensive positive behavior supports based on FBA (and, in especially complex cases, functional analysis), however, is clear and convincing. One of the greatest PBS implementation difficulties occurs when the adults implementing the plan are accustomed to using reactive rather than proactive behavior interventions and are not skilled in the use of collaborative teaming (Scott, McIntyre, et al., 2005). Due to a variety of factors (e.g., previous instruction in behavior management that emphasized manipulating consequences over more educative approaches, lack of a school vision of the goal of behavioral support, inexperience that makes one fearful or insecure about teaching students with behavior difficulties, burnout and discouragement), team members can tend to conceive of behavior problems as needing *management* and to continue to use punishment-oriented, exclusionary, and other reactive approaches rather than the proactive approaches that define a PBS orientation (Scott, Nelson, & Zabala, 2003).

Although behavioral intervention plans for the students with the most dangerous or destructive behavior problems may require school-based teams to seek the assistance of expert consultants, teams that have been through relatively modest amounts of in-service training in the assessment, planning, and intervention processes—and who have a commitment to the education and well-being of the student—can create and implement supports that efficiently and effectively enable the student to make meaningful improvements. The satisfaction of students, family members, and teachers with the results is what will determine the ultimate outcomes for the student, which, we all hope, will be a supportive environment in which the student can thrive.

References

Aber, J.L., Brown, J.L., & Henrich, C.C. (1999). *Teaching conflict resolution: An effective school-based approach to violence prevention.* New York: National Center for Children in Poverty.

Aber, J.L., Jones, S.M., Brown, J.L., Chaudry, N., & Samples, F. (1998). Resolving conflict creatively: Evaluating the developmental effects of a school-based violence prevention program in neighborhood and classroom context. *Development and Psychopathology, 10,* 187–213.

Albin, R.A., Lucyshyn, J.M., Horner, R.H., & Flannery, B. (1996). Contextual fit for behavior support plans: A model for "goodness of fit." In L.K. Koegel, R.L. Koegel, & G. Dunlap (Eds.), *Positive behavioral support: Including people with difficult behavior in the community* (pp. 81–98). Baltimore: Paul H. Brookes Publishing Co.

Arndorfer, R., Miltenberger, R., Woster, S., Rortvedt, A., & Gaffaney, T. (1994). Home-based descriptive and experimental analysis of problem behaviors in children. *Topics in Early Childhood Special Education, 14,* 64–87.

Baker, B.L., Blacher, J., Crnic, K.A., & Edelbrock, C. (2002). Behavior problems and parenting stress in families of three-year-old children with and without developmental delays. *American Journal on Mental Retardation, 107,* 433–444.

Bambara, L., & Kern, L. (Eds.). (2004). *Individualized supports for students with problem behaviors: Designing positive behavior plans.* New York: Guilford Press.

Bambara, L.M., Koger, F., Katzer, T., & Davenport, T.A. (1995). Embedding choice in the context of daily routines: An experimental case study. *Journal of The Association for Persons with Severe Handicaps, 20,* 185–195.

Barry, L.M., & Messer, J.J. (2003). A practical application of self-management for students diagnosed with attention-deficit/hyperactivity disorder. *Journal of Positive Behavior Interventions, 5*(4), 238–248.

Berliner, D.C. (1986). In pursuit of the expert pedagogue. *Educational Researcher, 15*(7), 5–13.

Brooks, A., Todd, A.W., Tofflemoyer, S., & Horner, R.H. (2003) Use of functional assessment and a self-management system to increase academic engagement and work completion. *Journal of Positive Behavior Interventions, 5*(3), 144–153.

Brophy, J., & Good, T. (1986). Teacher behavior and student achievement. In M. Wittrock (Ed.), *Handbook of research on teaching* (3rd ed., pp. 328–375). New York: Macmillan.

Burns, B.J., & Goldman, S.K. (Eds.). (1999). *Promising practices in wraparound for children with serious emotional disturbance and their families* (1998 Series, Vol. 4). Washington, DC: Center for Effective Collaboration and Practice, American Institute for Research.

Burns, B.J., Schoenwald, S.K., Burchard, J.D., Faw, L., & Santos, A.B. (2000). Comprehensive community-based interventions for youth with severe emotional disorders: Multisystemic therapy and the wraparound process. *Journal of Child and Family Studies, 9,* 283–314.

Callahan, K., & Rademacher, J.A. (1999). Using self-management strategies to increase the on-task behavior of a student with autism. *Journal of Positive Behavior Intervention, 1*(2), 117–122.

Carr, E.G., Dunlap, G., Horner, R.H., Koegel, R.L., Turnbull, A., Sailor, W., et al. (2002). Positive behavior support: Evolution of an applied science. *Journal of Positive Behavior Interventions, 4,* 4–16.

Carr, E.G., Horner, R.H., Turnbull, A.P., Marquis, J. G., McLaughlin, D.M., McAtee, M. L., et al. (Eds.). (1999). *Positive behavior support for people with developmental disabilities: A research synthesis.* Washington, DC: American Association on Mental Retardation.

Carr, E.G., Levin, L., McConnachie, G., Carlson, J.I., Kemp, D.C., & Smith, C.E. (1994). *Communication-based intervention for problem behavior: A user's guide for producing positive change.* Baltimore: Paul H. Brookes Publishing Co.

Carr, E.G., Reeve, C.E., & Magito-McLaughlin, D. (1996) Contextual influences on problem behavior in people with developmental disabilities. In L.K. Koegel, R.L. Koegel, & G. Dunlap (Eds.), *Positive behavioral support: Including people with difficult behavior in the community* (pp. 403–423). Baltimore: Paul H. Brookes Publishing Co.

Carr, E.G., Smith, C.E., Giacin, T.A., Whelan, B.M., & Pancari, J. (2003). Menstrual discomfort as a biological setting event for severe problem behavior: Assessment and intervention. *American Journal on Mental Retardation, 108*, 117–133.

Clarke, S., Dunlap, G., Foster-Johnson, L., Childs, K.E., Wilson, D., White, R., et al. (1995). Improving the conduct of students with behavioral disorders by incorporating student interests into curricular activities. *Behavioral Disorders, 20*, 221–237.

Cole, C.L., & Bambara, L.M. (1992). Issues surrounding the use of self-management interventions in schools. *School Psychology Review, 21*, 193–201.

Cole, C.L., & Levinson, T.R. (2002). Effects of within-activity choices on the challenging behavior of children with severe developmental disabilities. *Journal of Positive Behavior Interventions, 4*(1), 29–37.

Collaborative for Academic, Social, and Emotional Learning. (2003). *Safe and sound: An education leader's guide to evidence-based social and emotional learning (SEL) programs.* Chicago: Author.

Colvin, B. (1993). *Managing acting-out behavior.* Eugene, OR: Behavior Associates.

Colvin, G., Sugai, G., Good, R.H., & Lee, Y. (1997). Using active supervision and precorrection to improve transition behaviors in an elementary school. *School Psychology Quarterly, 12*(4), 344–363.

Conroy, M.A., Asmus, J.M., Sellers, J.A., & Ladwig, C.N. (2005). The use of antecedent-based intervention to decrease stereotypic behavior in a general education classroom: A case study. *Focus on Autism and Other Developmental Disabilities, 20*(4), 223–230.

Crone, D.A., & Horner, R.H. (2003). *Building positive behavior support systems in schools: Functional behavioral assessment.* New York: Guilford Press.

Daunic, A.P., Smith, S.W., Robinson, T.R., Miller, M.D., & Landry, K.L. (2000). Implementing schoolwide conflict resolution and peer mediation programs: Experiences in three middle schools. *Intervention in School & Clinic, 36*(2), 94–100.

Didden, R., Korzilius, H., van Oorsouw, W., & Sturmey, P. (2006). Behavioral treatment of challenging behaviors in individuals with mild mental retardation: Meta-analysis of single-subject research. *American Journal on Mental Retardation, 111*, 290–298.

Donnellan, A.M., LaVigna, G.W., Negri-Shoultz, N., & Fassbender, L.L. (1988). *Progress without punishment: Effective approaches for learners with severe behavior problems.* New York: Teachers College Press.

Drummond, T. (1993). *The Student Risk Screening Scale SRSS.* Grants Pass, OR: Josephine County Mental Health Program.

Dunlap, G., dePerczel, M., Clarke, S., Wilson, D., Wright, S., White, R., et al. (1994). Choice making and proactive behavioral support for students with emotional and behavioral challenges. *Journal of Applied Behavior Analysis, 27*, 505–518.

Dunlap, G., Foster-Johnson, L., Clarke, S., Kern, L., & Childs, K.E. (1995). Modifying activities to produce functional outcomes: Effects on the problem behaviors of students with disabilities. *Journal of The Association for Persons with Severe Handicaps, 20*(4), 248–258.

Dunlap, G., Kern-Dunlap, L., Clarke, S., & Robbins, F.R. (1991). Functional assessment, curricular revision, and severe behavior problems. *Journal of Applied Behavior Analysis, 24*, 387–397.

Dunlap, G., Newton, J.S., Fox, L., Benito, N., & Vaughn, B. (2001). Family involvement in functional assessment and positive behavior support. *Focus on Autism and Other Developmental Disabilities, 16*(4), 215–221.

Durand, V.M. (1988). *Motivational assessment scale.* In M. Hersen & A.S. Belleck (Eds.), *Dictionary of behavioral assessment techniques* (pp. 309–310). New York: Pergamon Press.

Durand, V.M. (1990). *Severe behavior problems: A functional communication training approach.* New York: Guilford Press.

Durand, V.M., & Merges, E. (2001). Functional Communication Training: A contemporary behavior analytic intervention for problem behaviors. *Focus on Autism and Other Developmental Disabilities, 16*(2), 110.

Dwyer, K., & Osher, D. (2000). *Safeguarding our children: An action guide.* Washington, DC: U.S. Departments of Education and Justice, American Institutes for Research.

Eber, L., & Nelson, C.M. (1997). Integrating services for students with emotional and behavioral needs through school-based wraparound planning. *American Journal of Orthopsychiatry, 67*, 385–395.

Eber, L., Sugai, G., Smith, C.R., & Scott, T.M. (2002). Wraparound and positive behavioral interventions and supports in schools. *Journal of Emotional and Behavioral Disorders, 10*(3), 171–180.

Educators for Social Responsibility. (2006). *Elementary school: Resolving Conflict Creatively Program.* Retrieved January 13, 2007, from http://www.esrnational.org/es/rccp.htm

Elias, M.J., Zins, J.E., Weissberg, R.P., Frey, K.S., Greenberg, M.T., Haynes, N.M., et al. (1997). *Promoting social and emotional learning: Guidelines for educators.* Alexandria, VA: Association for Supervision and Curriculum Development.

Elliott, S.N. (1995, June). *Final evaluation report. The responsive classroom approach: Its effectiveness and acceptability.* Madison: University of Wisconsin.

Evans, I.M., & Meyer, L.H. (1985). *An educative approach to behavior problems: A practical decision model for interventions with severely handicapped learners.* Baltimore: Paul H. Brookes Publishing Co.

Fitzgerald, P.D., & Edstrom, L.V.S. (2006). Second Step: A violence prevention curriculum. In S.R. Jimmerson & M. Furlong (Eds.), *Handbook of school violence and school safety: From research to practice* (pp. 383–394). Mahwah, NJ: Lawrence Erlbaum Associates.

Flannery, D., Vazsonyi, A., Liau, A., Guo, S., Powell, K., Atha, H., et al. (2003). Initial behavior outcomes for the PeaceBuilders universal school-based violence prevention program. *Developmental Psychology, 39*(2), 292–308.

Forness, S. (1990). Early detection and prevention of emotional and behavioral disorders: Developmental aspects of systems of care. *Behavioral Disorders, 21*, 226–240.

Foster-Johnson, L., Ferro, J., & Dunlap, G. (1994). Preferred curricular activities and reduced problem behaviors in students with intellectual disabilities. *Journal of Applied Behavior Analysis, 27*, 493–504.

Freeman, R., Eber, L., Anderson, C., Irvin, L., Horner, R.H., Bounds, M., et al. (2006). Building inclusive school cultures using school-wide positive behavior support: Designing effective individual support systems for students with significant disabilities. *Research and Practice for Persons with Severe Disabilities, 31*(1), 4–17.

Golly, A., Stiller, B., & Walker, H.M. (1998). First Step to Success: Replication and social validation of an early intervention program for achieving secondary prevention goals. *Journal of Emotional and Behavioral Disorders, 6*(4), 243–250.

Gottfredson, D.C. (1997). School-based crime prevention. In L. Sherman, D. Gottfredson, D. Mackenie, J. Eck, P. Reuter, & S. Bushway (Eds.), *Preventing crime: What works, what doesn't, what's promising.* College Park: University of Maryland, Department of Criminology and Criminal Justice.

Grandy, S., & Peck, S.M. (1997). The use of functional assessment and self-management with a first grader. *Child and Family Behavior Therapy, 19*(2), 29–43.

Gray, C.A. (1998). Social stories and comic strip conversations with students with Asperger syndrome and high-functioning autism. In E. Schopler & G.B. Mesibov (Eds.), *Asperger syndrome or high-functioning autism? Current issues in autism* (pp. 167–198). New York: Kluwer Academic/ Plenum Publishers.

Greenberg, M.T., Kusche, C., & Mihalic, S.F. (1998). *Promoting Alternative Thinking Strategies (PATHS). Book Ten, Blueprints for Violence Prevention Series* (D.S. Elliott, Series Editor). Boulder: University of Colorado, Institute of Behavioral Science, Center for the Study and Prevention of Violence.

Greenwood, C.R., Delquandri, J., & Carta, J. (1997). *Together we can! Classwide peer tutoring to improve basic academic skills.* Longmont, CO: Sopris West Educational Services.

Gresham, F., & Elliot, S.N. (1990). *Social skills rating system.* Circle Pines, MN: American Guidance Service.

Groden, J., & LeVassuer, P. (1994). Cognitive picture rehearsal: A system to teach self-control. In K.A. Quill (Ed.), *Teaching children with autism: Strategies to enhance communication and socialization* (pp. 287–306). Albany, NY: Delmar Publishers.

Grossman, D.C., Neckerman, H.J., Koepsell, T.D., Liu, P., Asher, K.N., Beland, K., et al. (1997). Effectiveness of a violence prevention curriculum among children in elementary school: A randomized control trial. *Journal of the American Medical Association, 277*, 1605–1611.

Harvey, M.T., Lewis-Palmer, T., Horner, R.H., & Sugai, G. (2003). Trans-situational interventions: Generalization of behavior support across school and home environments. *Behavioral Disorders, 28*(3), 299–312.

Heaviside, S., Rowand, C., Williams, C., & Farris, E. (1998). *Violence and discipline problems in U.S. Public Schools: 1996–1997.* (NCES 98–030). Washington, DC: U.S. Department of Education, National Center for Education Statistics.

Henley, M. (2006). *Classroom management: A proactive approach.* Upper Saddle River, NJ: Pearson Education.

Horner, R.H., Albin, R.A., Sprague, J.R., & Todd, A.W. (2000). Positive behavior support. In M.E. Snell & F. Brown (Eds.), *Instruction of students with severe disabilities*

(5th ed., pp. 207–243). Upper Saddle River, NJ: Prentice Hall.

Horner, R.H., & Carr, E.G. (1997). Behavioral support for students with severe disabilities: Functional assessment and comprehensive intervention. *Journal of Special Education, 31*, 84–104.

Horner, R.H., Carr, E.G., Strain, P.S., Todd, A.W., & Reed, H.K. (2002). Problem behavior interventions for young children with autism: A research synthesis. *Journal of Autism and Developmental Disorders, 32*(5), 423–446.

Horner, R.H., Day, H.M., & Day, I. (1997). Using neutralizing routines to reduce problem behaviors. *Journal of Applied Behavior Analysis, 39*, 601–614.

Horner, R.H., Dunlap, G., Koegel, R.L., Carr, E.G., Sailor, W., & Anderson, J. (1990). Toward a technology of "nonaversive" behavioral support. *Journal of the Association for Persons with Severe Handicaps, 15*, 125–132.

Horner, R.H., Todd, A.W., Lewis-Palmer, T., Irvin, L.K., Sugai, G., & Boland, J.B. (2004). The school-wide evaluation tool (SET): A research instrument for assessing school-wide positive behavior support. *Journal of Positive Behavior Interventions, 6*(1), 3–12.

Horner, R.H., Vaughn, B.J., Day, H.M., & Ard, W.R., Jr. (1996). The relationship between setting events and problem behavior: Expanding our understanding of behavioral support. In L.K. Koegel, R.L. Koegel, & G. Dunlap (Eds.), *Positive behavioral support: Including people with difficult behavior in the community* (pp. 381–402). Baltimore: Paul H. Brookes Publishing Co.

Huggins, P. (1995). *The ASSIST Program-Affective/Social Skills: Instructional strategies and techniques.* Seattle: Washington State Innovative Education Program.

Hunt, P., Staub, D., Alwell, M., & Goetz, L. (1994). Achievement by all students within the context of cooperative learning groups. *Journal of The Association for Persons with Severe Handicaps, 19*, 290–301.

Individuals with Disabilities Education Act Amendments of 2004, PL 108-446; 20 U.S.C. §§ 1400 *et seq.*

Ingram, K., Lewis-Palmer, T., & Sugai, G. (2005). Function-based intervention planning: Comparing the effectiveness of FBA function-based and non-function-based intervention plans. *Journal of Positive Behavior Interventions, 7*(4), 224–236.

Irwin, L.K., Tobin, T.J., Sprague, J.R., Sugai, G., & Vincent, C.G. (2004). Validity of office discipline referral measures as indices of school-wide behavioral status and effects of school-wide behavioral interventions. *Journal of Positive Behavioral Interventions, 6*(3), 131–147.

Iwata, B.A., Dorsey, M.F., Silfer, K.J., Baumna, K.E., & Richman, G.S. (1994). Toward a functional analysis of self-injury. *Journal of Applied Behavior Analysis, 27,* 197–209.

Janney, R., Black, J., & Ferlo, M. (1989). *A problem-solving approach to challenging behaviors: Strategies for parents and educators of people with developmental disabilities and challenging behaviors.* Syracuse, NY: Syracuse University and Syracuse City School District.

Janney, R., & Snell, M.E. (2006). *Teachers' guides to inclusive practices: Social relationships and peer support* (2nd ed.). Baltimore: Paul H. Brookes Publishing Co.

Johnson, D.W., & Johnson, R.T. (1989). *Cooperation and competition: Theory and research.* Edina, MN: Interaction Book Co.

Johnson, D.W., & Johnson, R.T. (1995). *Teaching students to be peacemakers.* Edina, MN: Interaction Book Co.

Johnson, D.W., & Johnson, R.T. (1996). Conflict resolution and peer mediation programs in elementary and secondary school: A review of the research. *Review of Educational Research, 66*(4), 459–506.

Johnson, D.W., Johnson, R.T., & Dudley, B. (1992). Effects of peer mediation training on elementary school students. *Mediation Quarterly, 10,* 89–99.

Joseph, G.E., & Strain, P.S. (2003). Comprehensive evidence-based social-emotional curricula for young children: An analysis of efficacious adoption potential. *Topics in Early Childhood Special Education, 23*(2), 65–76.

Kamps, D., Kravits, T., Stoize, J., & Swaggart, B. (1999). Prevention strategies for at-risk students and students with EBD in urban elementary schools. *Journal of Emotional and Behavioral Disorders, 7*(3), 178–188.

Kennedy, C.H., Long, T., Jolivette, K., Cox, J., Tang, J., & Thompson, T. (2001). Facilitating general education participation for students with behavior problems by linking positive behavior supports and person-centered planning. *Journal of Emotional and Behavioral Disorders, 9*(3), 161–172.

Kern, L., Gallagher, P., Starosta, K., Hickman, W., & George, M. (2006). Longitudinal outcomes of functional behavior assessment-based intervention. *Journal of Positive Behavior Interventions, 8*(2), 67–78.

Kern, L., Vorndran, C.M., Hilt, A., Ringdahl, J.E., Adelman, B.E., & Dunlap, G. (1998). Choice as an intervention to improve behavior: A review of the literature. *Journal of Behavioral Education, 8*(2), 151–169.

Knoff, H.M., & Batsche, G.M. (1995). Project ACHIEVE: Analyzing a school process for at-risk and underachieving students. *School Psychology Review, 24,* 579–603.

Koegel, L.K., Harrower, J.K., & Koegel, R.L. (1999). Support for children with developmental disabilities in full inclusion classrooms through self-management. *Journal of Positive Behavior Interventions, 1*(1), 26–34.

Kounin, J.S. (1970). *Discipline and group management in classrooms.* Austin, TX: Holt, Rinehart & Winston.

Langdon, C.A. (1997). The fourth Phi Delta Kappa poll of teachers' attitudes toward public schools. *Phi Delta Kappan, 79,* 212–220.

Learning First Alliance. (2001). *Every child learning: Safe and supportive schools—A summary.* Washington, DC: Author.

Lee, Y., Sugai, G., & Horner, R.H. (1999). Using an instructional intervention to reduce problem and off-task behavior. *Journal of Positive Behavior Interventions, 1*(4), 195–204.

Lewis, T.J., Sugai, G., & Colvin, G. (1998). Reducing problem behavior through a schoolwide system of effective behavior support: Investigation of a schoolwide social skills training program and contextual interventions. *School Psychology Review, 27*(3), 446–460.

Loeber, R. (1991). Antisocial behavior: More enduring than changeable? *Journal of the American Academy of Child and Adolescent Psychiatry, 30,* 393–397.

Loeber, R., Green, S.M., Lahey, B.B., Frick, P.J., & McBurnett, K. (2000). Findings on disruptive behavior disorders from the first decade of the developmental trends study. *Clinical Child and Family Psychology Review, 3,* 37–60.

Long, N.J., & Newman, R.G. (1996). The four choices of managing surface behavior of students. In N.J. Long & W.C. Morse (Eds.), *Conflict in the classroom: The education of at-risk and troubled students* (5th ed., pp. 266–273). Austin, TX: PRO-ED.

Lovett, H. (1985). *Cognitive counseling and persons with special needs.* New York: Praeger.

Lovett, H. (1996). *Learning to listen: Positive approaches and people with difficult behavior.* Baltimore: Paul H. Brookes Publishing Co.

Luiselli, J.K., Putnam, R.F., & Sunderland, M. (2002). Longitudinal evaluation of behavior support intervention in a public middle school. *Journal of Positive Behavior Interventions, 4*(3), 182–188.

Malloy, J., Cheney, D., & Cormier, G. (1998). Interagency collaboration and the transition to adulthood for students with emotional and behavioral disabilities. *Education and Treatment of Children, 1,* 303–320.

March, R.E., & Horner, R.H. (2002). Feasibility and contributions of functional behavioral assessment in schools. *Journal of Emotional and Behavioral Disorders, 10*(3), 158–171.

Marquis, J.G., Horner, R.H., Carr, E.G., Turnbull, A.P., Thompson, M., Behrens, G.A., et al. (2000). A meta-analysis of positive behavior support. In R. Gersten, E.P. Schiller, & S. Vaughn (Eds.), *Contemporary special education research: Synthesis of the knowledge base on critical instructional issues* (pp. 137–178). Mahwah, NJ: Lawrence Erlbaum Associates.

Marzano, R.J., Marzano, J.S., & Pickering, D.J. (2003). *Classroom management that works: Research-based strategies for every teacher.* Alexandria, VA: Association for Supervision and Curriculum Development.

Marzano, R.J., Pickering, D.J., & Pollock, J.E. (2001). *Classroom instruction that works: Research-based strategies for increasing student achievement.* Alexandria, VA: Association for Supervision and Curriculum Development.

May, S., Ard, W., III, Todd, A.W., Horner, R.H., Glagow, A., Sugai, G., et al. (2002). *Schoolwide information system.* Eugene: University of Oregon, Educational and Community Supports.

Mayer, G. (1995). Preventing antisocial behavior in the schools. *Journal of Applied Behavior Analysis, 28,* 467–478.

Mayer, G.R., Butterworth, T., Nafpaktitis, M., & Sulzer-Azaroff, B. (1983). Preventing school vandalism and improving discipline: A three-year study. *Journal of Applied Behavior Analysis, 16*(4), 355–369.

Mayer, G.R., & Sulzer-Azaroff, B. (2002). Interventions for vandalism and aggression. In M. Shinn, H. Walker, & G. Stoner (Eds.), *Interventions for academic and behavior problems, II: Preventive and remedial approaches* (pp. 853–884). Bethesda, MD: National Association of School Psychologists.

McConnell, M.E., Cox, C.J., Thomas, D.D., & Hilvitz, P.B. (2001). *Functional behavioral assessment: A systematic process for assessment and intervention in general and special education classrooms.* Denver, CO: Love Publishing Co.

McGinnis, E., & Goldstein, A. (1990). *Skillstreaming in early childhood: Teaching prosocial skills to the preschool and kindergarten child.* Champaign, IL: Research Press.

McGinnis, E., & Goldstein, A. (1997a). *Skill-streaming the adolescent: New strategies and perspectives for teaching prosocial skills.* Champaign, IL: Research Press.

McGinnis, E., & Goldstein, A. (1997b). *Skill-streaming the elementary school child: New strategies and perspectives for teaching prosocial skills.* Champaign, IL: Research Press.

McKinney, J., Montague, M., & Hocutt, A. (1998). A two-year follow-up study of children at risk for developing SED: Initial results from a prevention project. In C. Liberton, K. Kutash, & R. Friedman (Eds.), *A system of care for children's mental health: Expanding the research base,* Tenth annual proceedings (pp. 271–277). Tampa: University of South Florida, Research and Training Center for Children's Mental Health.

Meyer, L., & Janney, R. (1989). User-friendly measures of meaningful outcomes: Evaluating behavioral interventions. *Journal of the Association for Persons with Severe Handicaps, 14*(4), 263–270.

Meyer, L.H., & Evans, I.M. (1989). *Nonaversive intervention for behavior problems: A manual for home and community.* Baltimore: Paul H. Brookes Publishing Co.

Mihalic, S., Fagan, A., Irwin, K., Ballard, D., & Elliott, D. (2004). *Blueprints for violence prevention.* Boulder: University of Colorado: Institute of Behavioral Science, Center for the Study and Prevention of Violence. (Available from http://www.colorado.edu/cspv/blueprints/)

Moore, D.W., Anderson, A., & Kumar, K. (2005). Instructional adaptation in the management of escape-maintained behavior in a classroom. *Journal of Positive Behavior Interventions, 7*(4), 216–223.

Mount, B. (2000). *Person-centered planning: Finding directions for change using personal futures planning.* New York: Graphic Futures.

Mount, B., & Zwernik, K. [1989]. *It's never too early, it's never too late: A booklet about Personal Futures Planning* [Report No. 421-88-109]. St. Paul: Minnesota Governor's Planning Council on Developmental Disabilities.

Nakasato, J. (2000). Data-based decision making in Hawaii's behavior support effort. *Journal of Positive Behavior Interventions, 2*(3), 247–251.

National Center for Education Statistics. (2006). *The condition of education 2006.* Washington, DC: Author. Retrieved February, 2007, from http://nces.ed.gov/pubsearch/pubsinfo.asp?pubid=2006071

Nelson, J.R., & Carr, B.A. (1999). *The Think Time Strategy.* Longmont, CO: Sopris West Educational Services.

Nelson, J.R., Gonzalez, J.E., Epstein, M.H., & Benner, G.J., (2003). Administrative discipline contacts: A review of the literature. *Behavioral Disorders, 28*(3), 249–281.

Nelson, J.R., Martella, R., & Galand, B. (1998). The effects of teaching school expectations and establishing a consistent consequence on formal office disciplinary actions. *Journal of Emotional and Behavioral Disorders, 6,* 153–161.

Nelson, J.R., Martella, R.M., & Marchand-Martella, N. (2002). Maximizing student learning: The effects of a comprehensive school-based program for preventing problem behaviors. *Journal of Emotional and Behavioral Disorders, 10,* 136–148.

Newcomer, L.L., & Lewis, T.J. (2004). Functional behavioral assessment: An investigation of assessment reliability and effectiveness of function-based interventions. *Journal of Emotional and Behavioral Disorders, 12*(3), 168–181.

Oakes, J. (1985). *Keeping track: How schools structure inequality.* New Haven, CT: Yale University Press.

Olweus, D., Limber, S., & Mihalic, S. (2002). Blueprints for violence prevention, book nine: Bullying prevention program. Boulder: University of Colorado, Center for the Study and Prevention of Violence.

O'Neill, R.E., Horner, R.H., Albin, R.W., Sprague, J.R., Storey, K., & Newton, J.S. (1997). *Functional assessment and program development for problem behavior: A practical handbook* (2nd ed.). Pacific Grove, CA: Brookes/Cole.

O'Shaughnessy, T.E., Lane, K.L., Gresham, F.M., & Beebe-Frankenberger, M.E. (2003). Children placed at risk for learning and behavioral difficulties: Implementing a school-wide system of early identification and intervention. *Remedial and Special Education, 24*(1), 27–35.

Osher, D., Dwyer, K., & Jackson, S. (2004). *Safe, supportive, and successful schools step by step.* Longmont, CO: Sopris West Educational Services.

Oswald, K., Safran, S., & Johanson, G. (2005). Preventing trouble: Making schools safer places using positive behavior supports. *Education and Treatment of Children, 28*(3), 265–278.

Pearpoint, J., O'Brien, J., & Forest, M. (1998). *PATH, a workbook for planning possible futures: Planning alternative tomorrows with hope for* schools, organizations, businesses, families. Toronto: Inclusion Press.

Reed, H., Thomas, E., Sprague, J.R., & Horner, R.H. (1997). The Student Guided Functional Assessment Interview: An analysis of student and teacher agreement. *Journal of Behavioral Education, 7*(1), 33–49.

Rimm-Kaufman, S.E. (2006). *Social and academic learning study on the contribution of the Responsive Classroom approach.* Greenfield, MA: Northeast Foundation for Children.

Rock, M.L. (2005). Use of strategic self-monitoring to enhance academic engagement, productivity, and accuracy of students with and without exceptionalities. *Journal of Positive Behavior Interventions, 7*(1), 3–18.

Rose, L.C., & Gallup, A.M. (2006). *The 38th annual Phi Delta Kappa/Gallup Poll of the public's attitudes toward public schools.* Bloomington, IN: Phi Delta Kappa.

Rosenshine, B. (1983). Teaching functions in instructional programs. *Elementary School Journal, 83*(4), 335–351.

Schrumpf, F., Crawford, D., & Usadel, C. (1991). *Peer mediation: Conflict resolution in schools.* Champaign, IL: Research Press.

Scott, T.M., Bucalos, A., & Liaupsin, C. (2004). Using functional assessment in general education settings: Making a case for effectiveness and efficiency. *Behavioral Disorders, 29*(2), 189–201.

Scott, T.M., & Caron, D.B. (2005). Conceptualizing functional behavior assessment as prevention practice within positive behavior support systems. *Preventing School Failure, 50*(1), 13–21.

Scott, T.M., & Eber, L. (2003). Functional assessment and wraparound as systemic school processes: Primary, secondary, and tertiary systems examples. *Journal of Positive Behavior Supports, 5*, 131–143.

Scott, T.M., & Hunter, J. (2001). Effective behavior support: Initiating school-wide support systems: An administrator's guide to the process. *Beyond Behavior, 11*, 13–15.

Scott, T.M., & Martinek, G. (2006). Coaching positive behavior support in school settings: Tactics and data-based decision making. *Journal of Positive Behavior Intervention, 8*(3), 165–173.

Scott, T.M., McIntyre, J.L., Liaupsin, C., Nelson, C.M., Conroy, M., & Payne, L.D. (2005). An examination of the relation between functional behavior assessment and selected intervention strategies with school-based teams. *Journal of Positive Behavior Interventions, 7*(4), 205–215.

Scott, T. M., Nelson, C. M., & Zabala, J. (2003). Functional behavior assessment training in public schools: Facilitating systemic change. *Journal of Positive Behavior Interventions, 5*, 216–224.

Scotti, J.R., Evans, I.M., Meyer, L.H., & Walker, P. (1991). A meta-analysis of intervention research with problem behavior: Treatment validity and standards of practice. *American Journal on Mental Retardation, 96*, 233–256.

Schrumpf, F., Crawford, D., & Usadel, C. (1991). *Peer mediation: Conflict resolution in schools.* Champaign, IL: Research Press.

Seybert, S., Dunlap, G., & Ferro, J. (1996). The effects of choice-making on the problem behaviors of high school students with intellectual disabilities. *Journal of Behavioral Education, 6*, 49–65.

Shores, R.E., Gunter, P.L., & Jack, S.L. (1993). Classroom management strategies: Are they setting events for coercion? *Behavioral Disorders, 18*, 92–102.

Shure, M.B. (1992). *I can problem solve (ICPS): An interpersonal cognitive problem-solving program* [3 volumes: Preschool; kindergarten/ primary grades; intermediate elementary grades]. Champaign, IL: Research Press.

Simmons, D.C., Kuykendall, K., King, K., Cornachione, C., & Kame'enui, E.J. (2000). Implementation of a schoolwide reading improvement model: "No one ever told us it would be this hard." *Learning Disabilities Research & Practice, 15*, 92–100.

Skiba, R.J. (2000). *Zero tolerance: Zero evidence: An analysis of school disciplinary practice.* (Policy Research Report #SRS2). Bloomington, IN: Indiana Education Policy Center.

Slavin, R.E. (1991, February). Synthesis of research on cooperative learning. *Educational Leadership, 48*(5), 71–82.

Slavin, R.E., Madden, N.A., & Leavey, M.B. (1984). Effects of team assisted individualization on the mathematical achievement of academically handicapped and nonhandicapped students. *Journal of Educational Psychology, 76*, 813–819.

Smith-Bird, E., & Turnbull, A.P. (2005). Linking positive behavior support to family quality-of-life outcomes. *Journal of Positive Behavior Interventions, 7*(3), 174–180.

Snell, M.E. (2006). What's the verdict: Are students with severe disabilities included in school-wide positive behavior support? *Research and Practice for Persons with Severe Disabilities, 31*(1), 62–65.

Snell, M.E., & Janney, R. (2005). *Teachers' guides to inclusive practices: Collaborative teaming* (2nd ed.). Baltimore: Paul H. Brookes Publishing Co.

Snell, M.E., Voorhees, M.D., & Chen, L. (2005). Team involvement in assessment-based interventions with problem behavior. *Journal of Positive Behavior Interventions, 7*, 233–235.

Solomon, D., Battistich, V., Watson, M., Schaps, E., & Lewis, C. (2000). A six-district study of educational change: Direct and mediated effects of the Child Development Project. *Social Psychology of Education, 4*, 3–51.

Strauss, M.A. (1994). *Beating the devil out of them: Corporal punishment in American families and its effects of children.* Lexington, MA: Lexington Books.

Sugai, G., & Horner, R.H. (2002). The evolution of discipline practices: Schoolwide positive behavior supports. *Behavior Psychology in the Schools, 24*(1, 2), 23–50.

Sugai, G., Sprague, J., Horner, R.H., & Walker, H. (2000). Preventing school violence: The use of office referral to assess and monitor school-wide discipline interventions. *Journal of Emotional and Behavioral Disorders, 8*, 94–101.

Sulzer-Azaroff, B., & Mayer, G.R. (1991). *Achieving educational excellence: Behavior analysis for achieving classroom and schoolwide behavior change.* San Marcos, CA: Western Image.

Taylor-Greene, S.J. (2002, Spring). The High Five Program: Support for all students—a middle school transformed. *Paradigm.* (Available from http://www.onlineparadigm.com)

Taylor-Greene, S.J., & Kartub, D.T. (2000). Durable implementation of schoolwide behavior support: The High Five Program. *Journal of Positive Behavior Interventions, 2*, 233–235.

Thorson, S. (1996). The missing link: Students discuss school discipline. *Focus on Exceptional Children, 29*(3), 1–12.

Todd, A.W., Horner, R.H., & Sugai, G. (1999). Self-monitoring and self-recruited praise: Effects on problem behavior, academic engagement, and work completion in a typical classroom. *Journal of Positive Behavior Interventions, 1*, 66–76.

Touchette, P.E., MacDonald, R.F., & Langer, S.N. (1985). A scatter plot for identifying stimulus control of problem behavior. *Journal of Applied Behavior Analysis, 18*, 343–351.

Turnbull, A., Edmonson, H., Griggs, P., Wickham, D., Sailor, W., Freeman, R., et al. (2002). A blueprint for schoolwide positive behavior support: Implementation of three components. *Exceptional Children, 68*, 377–402.

Turnbull, A.P., Turnbull, R.R., III, Poston, D., Beegle, G., Blue-Banning, M., & Diehl, K., et al. (2004). Enhancing quality of life of families of children and youth with disabilities in the United States. In A.P. Turnbull, I. Brown., & H.R. Turnbull, III (Eds.), *Families and people with mental retardation and quality of life: International perspectives.* Washington, DC: American Association on Mental Retardation.

U.S. Department of Education Safe, Disciplined, and Drug-Free School Expert Panel. (2001). *Exemplary and Promising Safe, Disciplined and Drug-Free School Programs.* Jessup, MD: U.S. Department of Education Publications Center. (Available from http://www.ed.gov/print/admins/lead/safety/exemplary01/panel.html)

Vandercook, T., York, J., & Forest, M. (1989). *MAPS: A strategy for building the vision.* Minneapolis: University of Minnesota, Institute on Community Integration.

Vaughn, B.J., & Horner, R.H. (1997). Identifying instructional tasks that occasion problem behaviors and assessing the effects of student versus teacher choice among these tasks. *Journal of Applied Behavior Analysis, 30*, 299–312.

Wacker, D.P., Cooper, L.J., Peck, S.M., Derby, K.M., & Berg, W.K. (1999). Community-based functional assessment. In A.C. Repp & R.H. Horner (Eds.), *Functional analysis of problem behavior: From effective assessment to effective support* (pp. 32–56). Belmont, CA: Wadsworth.

Walker, B., Cheney, D., Stage, S., & Blum, C. (2005). School-wide screening and positive behavior supports: Identifying and supporting students at risk for school failure. *Journal of Positive Behavior Interventions, 7*(4), 194–204.

Walker, H.M., Golly, A., McLane, J.Z., & Kimmich, M. (2005). The Oregon First Step to Success Replication Initiative: Statewide results of an evaluation of the program's impact. *Journal of Emotional and Behavioral Disorders, 13*(3), 163–172.

Walker, H., Hops, H., & Greenwood, C. (1993). *RECESS: A program for reducing negative aggressive behavior.* Seattle: Educational Achievement Systems.

Walker, H.M., Kavanaugh, K., Stiller, B., Golly, A., Severson, H.H., & Feil, E.G. (1997). *First Step to Success: An early intervention program for antisocial kindergarteners.* Longmont, CO: Sopris West Educational Services.

Walker, H.M., Kavanaugh, K., Stiller, B., Golly, A., Severson, H.H., & Feil, E.G. (1998). First Step to Success: An early intervention approach for preventing school antisocial behavior. *Journal of Emotional and Behavioral Disorders, 6*(2), 66–80.

Walker, H.M., Ramsey, E., & Gresham, F.M. (2004). *Antisocial behavior in school: Evidence-based practices.* Belmont, CA: Wadsworth/Thomson Learning.

Walker, H., & Severson, H. (1990). *Systematic Screening for Behavior Disorders: User's guide and technical manual.* Longmont, CO: Sopris West Educational Services.

Walker, H., Severson, H., & Feil, E. (1995). *Early screening project: A proven child-find process.* Longmont, CO: Sopris West Educational Services.

Walker, H., Stiller, B., Golly, A., Kavanaugh, K., Severson, H.H., & Feil, E. (1997). *First Step to Success: An early intervention program for antisocial kindergartners.* Longmont, CO: Sopris West Educational Services.

Zins, J.E., Weissberg, R.P., Walberg, H.J., & Wang, C. (Eds.). (2004). *Building academic success on social and emotional learning.* New York: Teachers College Press.

Appendix A

Blank Forms

Team Meeting Agenda and Minutes		
Student/team	**Date**	
People present	**Role for today**	**Absentees**
_____	_____	_____
_____	_____	_____
_____	_____	_____
_____	_____	_____
_____	_____	_____

Purpose of meeting

Agenda items	Decision or action to be taken	Who and when?

Agenda items for next meeting	Date:	Time:
1.		
2.		
3.		
4.		

Steps and Tools to Develop Individualized Positive Behavior Supports (PBS)	
Student	Date initiated
School	Grade
Members of PBS team	

Steps and Accompanying Functional Behavioral Assessment (FBA) Tools
(Check box when completed)

Step 1: Identify and Prioritize the Problem(s); Make a Safety Plan

    Step 1A: Identify the Problem(s) and Decide on Priorities

        ☐ Step 1A Worksheet: Problem Identification and Decisions About Priorities

        ☐ Team Meeting Agenda and Minutes form (use at each team meeting)

    Step 1B (if necessary): Make a Safety Plan

        ☐ Step 1B Worksheet: Safety Plan

        ☐ Incident Record

Step 2: Plan and Conduct the Functional Behavioral Assessment (FBA)

    Step 2A: Gather Descriptive Information

        ☐ Step 2A Worksheet: Student-Centered Functional Behavioral Assessment Profile

        ☐ Student Schedule Analysis

    Step 2B: Conduct Direct Observations

        ☐ Interval Recording or Scatter Plot

        ☐ Antecedent-Behavior-Consequence Observation

    Step 2C: Summarize Functional Behavioral Assessment and Build Hypothesis Statement(s)

        ☐ Step 2C Worksheet: Summary of Functional Behavioral Assessment and Hypothesis Statement(s)

    Step 2D (if necessary): Verify Hypotheses

        ☐ Team Meeting Agenda and Minutes with plan for verifying hypotheses

        ☐ Interval Recording or Scatter Plot and/or

        ☐ Antecedent-Behavior-Consequence Observation

        ☐ Revision of Step 2C Worksheet

Step 3: Design a Positive Behavior Support Plan

        ☐ Step 3 Worksheet: Positive Behavior Support Plan

Step 4: Implement, Monitor, and Evaluate the PBS Plan

        ☐ Step 4 Worksheet: Implementing, Monitoring, and Evaluating the PBS Plan (decisions recorded on Team Meeting Agenda and Minutes form)

139

Program-at-a-Glance	
Student	**Date**
IEP goals	**IEP accommodations**
Academic/social management needs	**Comments/special needs**

Step 1A Worksheet: Problem Identification and Decisions About Priorities

Student	Date

As specifically as possible, describe each problem behavior—what it looks and sounds like, how intense it is, and how long each has been a problem. Estimate the frequency and duration of each behavior. Label the behaviors according to their level of priority.

Description of problem behaviors	Level of priority
1. _____ _____ _____ _____	☐ Destructive ☐ Disruptive ☐ Distracting
2. _____ _____ _____ _____	☐ Destructive ☐ Disruptive ☐ Distracting
3. _____ _____ _____ _____	☐ Destructive ☐ Disruptive ☐ Distracting
4. _____ _____ _____ _____	☐ Destructive ☐ Disruptive ☐ Distracting

Decision and rationale: Which behaviors should be priorities for intervention and why?

_____

_____

_____

_____

_____

_____

Is a Safety Plan needed immediately?   Yes   No

141

Step 1B Worksheet: Safety Plan	
Student	Date

Behavior(s) that call for use of the Safety Plan

_____

_____

Who will intervene in a serious behavioral episode?

_____

How to intervene and support the student during phases of the crisis cycle

1. **Trigger Phase:** _Describe signals the student sends that indicate feeling threat/discomfort. Describe antecedents known to trigger problems and how to eliminate them._

2. **Escalation Phase:** _Tell how to interrupt, redirect, and facilitate relaxation._

142

3. **Crisis Phase:** *Describe how to interrupt and protect the student and others.*

4. **Begin Recovery Phase:** *Describe how to avoid reescalating the behavior and continue to reach full recovery.*

5. **Recovery Phase:** *Describe any processing/reflecting that should be done with the student and how to reinstate the PBS plan.*

Directions for reporting and documentation: *Give instructions for reporting the incident and completing and filing Incident Records.*

143

Incident Record	
Student	**Completed by**
Day	**Date**	**Time**
Setting	
Class or activity	
Staff present	
Students present	

1. Describe what happened earlier in the day and/or just before the incident that may have led to the incident.

2. Describe the student's behavior and others' responses during the *Trigger* and *Escalation* phases.

3. Describe what the student and others did during the *Crisis* phase.

4. Describe the *Begin Recovery* and *Recovery* phases. Describe how the PBS plan was reintroduced.

5. To what extent was the Safety Plan followed?   Fully   Somewhat   Very little

6. What is your hunch about the *setting events* and/or *triggers* of the behavior?

7. What is your hunch about the *purpose of the behavior* or how it is "working" for the student?

8. What might *prevent* or *interrupt* the behavior more effectively in the future? What suggestions do you have to *improve the Safety Plan*?

145

Step 2A Worksheet: Student-Centered Functional Behavioral Assessment (FBA) Profile

Student	Date

People providing initial information	Other people who should be interviewed
_____	_____
_____	_____
_____	_____
_____	_____
_____	_____
_____	_____

Directions: At a team meeting, summarize existing information about the student's problem behavior and begin to analyze the possible relationships among the behavior, the student's wants and needs, and the environment.

SECTION I: QUALITY OF LIFE

Ratings

Good = Indicator is in place satisfactorily.

Fair = Indicator is partially in place but improvement is needed.

Poor = Indicator is in place to an unacceptable degree or not at all.

Indicator	How is indicator in place?	Rating G F P
Supportive people a. Family	a.	a.
b. Adults at school	b.	b.

c. Peers at school	c.	c.
d. Peers outside of school	d.	d.
Successful places and activities at school		
Successful places and activities at home and in the community		
Interests and preferences		
Opportunities to make choices appropriate for age		

Based on the quality-of-life indicators, list shortcomings that might be addressed in a PBS plan.

_____

_____

_____

_____

(continued)

147

(continued)

SECTION II: ACADEMICS AND COMMUNICATION

Academic strengths

_____

_____

_____

Academic liabilities

_____

_____

_____

Summarize the current fit between the student's educational programming and his or her academic strengths and liabilities.

_____

_____

_____

Communication

What is the student's primary mode of communication (e.g., speech, signs, gestures, electronic devices) and how successful is the student in using it?

_____

_____

How does the student accomplish these communicative purposes?

1. Gets attention/help/interaction _____

2. Gets preferred activities or tangible items _____

   _____

3. Avoids/escapes attention/interaction _____

   _____

4. Avoids/escapes activity or item _____

5. Calms self when agitated, upset, angry _____

6. Gets sensory stimulation _____

SECTION III: MEDICAL, HEALTH, AND SENSORY CONCERNS
Describe any health concerns or medication that may be affecting the student's mood or behavior.
Describe any of the student's sensory difficulties or needs.
Other important information about the student's medical and health history

SECTION IV: TARGET BEHAVIOR(S)
From the Step 1 Worksheet, which behavior or behaviors will be targeted for intervention? Define the behaviors as clearly and specifically as possible. These are the definitions that will be used to collect any additional information and to develop the PBS plan.
Describe any current interventions for the behavior(s) and summarize their effects. (Or attach any behavioral intervention plan that is currently in use.)

What works to prevent or interrupt the behavior(s)?	What does not work to prevent or interrupt the behavior(s)?

(continued)

149

(continued)

SECTION V: PRELIMINARY HUNCHES			
When these **Antecedents** (**Setting Events** and/or **Triggers**) occur	the student is likely to (**Target Behavior[s]**)	and these **Consequences** tend to occur	Therefore, the **Function** of the behavior may be
1.			
2.			
3.			
4.			

150

SECTION VI: DECISIONS AND NEXT STEPS

1. **Should any other people be interviewed to ensure that the information on this Profile is complete and accurate?**   Yes   No

   If "yes," list others who should be interviewed.

   _____

   _____

   _____

2. **Does quantifiable baseline data on the targeted behaviors need to be collected?**   Yes   No

   If "yes," when, where, and how will data be collected? _____

   _____

   _____

   _____

3. **Is additional information needed to determine if the current "hunches" about the antecedents, consequences, and purposes of the behaviors are accurate?**   Yes   No

   If "yes," when, where, and how will data be collected? _____

   _____

   _____

   _____

   _____

   _____

   _____

151

Student Schedule Analysis

Student _____

Date _____

Staff who work with the student on a regular basis

_____

_____

_____

Target behavior(s)

_____

_____

Time	Class/activity	Rating & behavior + = mild/rare – = excessive/often v = variable	Grouping I = independent 1:1 = one-to-one sg = small group lg = large group	Task type Paper/pencil Oral/listening Hands-on activity/routine Computer	Staff

(From Meyer, L., & Janney, R. [1989]. User-friendly measures of meaningful outcomes: Evaluating behavioral interventions. *Journal of The Association for Persons with Severe Handicaps, 14*[4], 267; adapted by permission.)

In *Behavioral Support, Second Edition,* by Rachel Janney and Martha E. Snell. 2008 (Paul H. Brookes Publishing Co., Inc.) All rights reserved.

Interval Recording or Scatter Plot							
Student			**Dates**				
Target behavior(s) _____							
_____							
Used for _____ Frequency count (tally each time behavior occurs within each interval)							
_____ Scatter plot (Key: ○ = 1 occurrence; ● = more than 1 occurrence)							
_____ Critical incident and use of Safety Plan (indicated by "X")							
Time	**Activity**	**Mon.** _____ (date)	**Tues.** _____ (date)	**Wed.** _____ (date)	**Thurs.** _____ (date)	**Fri.** _____ (date)	**Total**
Total target behaviors/day							

153

Antecedent-Behavior-Consequence (A-B-C) Observation

Student _____   Day and date _____

Setting _____   Observer _____

Class/subject or activity _____

Target behavior(s) _____

_____

Time	Antecedents	Behavior	Consequences	Hypothesis
	What was going on before the behavior? What was being said and done?	What did the student do?	What happened after the behavior? How did people react?	About the function of the behavior

154

Step 2C Worksheet: Summary of Functional Behavioral Assessment and Hypothesis Statement(s)

Directions: Summarize the FBA information that has been gathered from all sources to build hypothesis statement(s) about targeted problem behaviors. If the student has appropriate alternative behaviors that serve the same purpose as the problem behavior (alternative behaviors may be nonexistent or very weak), describe those behaviors. Then determine if any data are missing and/or team members disagree or are uncertain about their hypotheses. Make a plan for further data collection and verification of hypotheses if necessary.

Student	Date of initial summary	Revision date (if necessary)

Persons completing this form

_____   _____   _____

_____   _____   _____

_____   _____   _____

_____   _____   _____

FREQUENCY: On average, HOW OFTEN does the behavior occur?

Behavior 1: _____   Per hour? _____   Per day? _____   Per week? _____

Behavior 2: _____   Per hour? _____   Per day? _____   Per week? _____

DURATION: On average, HOW LONG does the behavior occur?

Behavior 1: _____

Behavior 2: _____

1. Describe chains of antecedents (both setting events and triggers) that predict that the target behavior will occur, observable definitions of the target behaviors, and consequences that seem to be maintaining the behavior. Then hypothesize about the function or purpose of the target behavior(s).

When these **Antecedents** (**setting events** and/or **triggers**) occur	the student is likely to (describe **Target Behavior[s]**)	and these **Consequences** maintain the behavior	Therefore, the **Function** of the behavior may be
Setting event			
Trigger(s)			
Setting event			
Trigger(s)			

(continued)

155

(continued)

When these **Antecedents** (**setting events** and/or **triggers**) occur	the student is likely to (describe **Target Behavior[s]**)	and these **Consequences** maintain the behavior	Therefore, the **Function** of the behavior may be
Setting event Trigger(s)			
Setting event Trigger(s)			

2. **Describe alternative behaviors that the student has demonstrated (the behaviors may be very weak) that may serve the same function as the problem behavior(s).**

3. **Are additional data needed to build hypothesis statement(s)?**   Yes   No
Is Step 2D, Verify Hypotheses, needed to confirm or refute hypotheses? Yes   No
If "yes," use the Team Meeting Agenda and Minutes form to plan how, when, and by whom further FBA data collection and/or verification tests will be conducted. Decide on a date for the next team meeting, at which this Step 2C worksheet will be revised.

156

Step 3 Worksheet: Positive Behavior Support Plan

Student _____ Date _____

Team members designing this plan

_____

_____

_____

Target behavior(s) and functions

_____

_____

_____

_____

_____

_____

_____

Interventions and Support Strategies to Be Implemented

Preventing		Teaching replacement behaviors and other alternative skills	Responding
Setting events	Triggers		

(continued)

(continued)

Interventions and Support Strategies to Be Implemented

Preventing		Teaching replacement behaviors and other alternative skills	Responding
Setting events	**Triggers**		

Is Safety Plan still needed?   Yes   No

If so, attach Safety Plan that has been revised and updated as needed.

Step 4 Worksheet: Implementing, Monitoring, and Evaluating the PBS Plan

Student	**Date**

Directions: Use the Team Meeting Agenda and Minutes form to list issues and decisions made and actions to be taken in order to put the PBS plan into place, monitor its use, evaluate its effects, and make needed revisions. The first set of issues listed below relates to putting the plan into place and requires immediate consideration. The second set of issues relates to monitoring and evaluating the plan and will require ongoing consideration at future team meetings.

Issues for immediate consideration (check boxes as issues are addressed)

☐ Materials to be made, purchased, or adapted

☐ Communicating with others who need to know about the plan

☐ Developing and sharing teaching plans for replacement skills and other alternative academic or social-communication skills

☐ Developing a schedule for putting various intervention strategies of the plan into place

☐ Developing the in-service training, coaching, and/or modeling needed for team members and other staff

☐ Developing a system for monitoring whether the plan is being used as designed. Are prevention, teaching, responding, and safety management strategies being used consistently?

☐ Developing a team meeting schedule

Issues for ongoing consideration as the plan is implemented

☐ How often the use and effects of the PBS plan will be evaluated and the plan revised as necessary

☐ The rate of improvement in targeted behaviors and the use of alternative skills that are acceptable

☐ Parents, teachers, and other relevant peoples' judgments about the plan's effectiveness, efficiency, and appropriateness for the student and the context, as well as their comfort level in implementing the plan

☐ The student's feedback about the acceptability of the interventions and progress toward his or her goals

159

Appendix B

Resources on Behavioral Support

SCHOOLWIDE POSITIVE BEHAVIOR SUPPORT AND SYSTEMS-CHANGE STRATEGIES

Boynton, M., & Boynton, C. (2005). *The educator's guide to preventing and solving discipline problems.* Alexandria, VA: Association for Supervision and Curriculum Development.

Crone, D.A., & Horner, R.H. (Eds.). (2003). *Building positive behavior support systems in schools: Functional behavioral assessment.* New York: Guilford Press.

Dwyer, K., & Osher, D. (2000). *Safeguarding our children: An action guide.* Washington, DC: U.S. Departments of Education and Justice, American Institutes for Research.

Osher, D., Dwyer, K., & Jackson, S. (2004). *Safe, supportive, and successful schools step by step.* Longmont, CO: Sopris West Educational Services.

Scott, T.M., & Hunter, J. (2001). Initiating school-wide support systems: An administrator's guide to the process. *Beyond Behavior, 11,* 13–15.

Scott, T.M., & Nelson, C.M. (1999). Using functional assessment with challenging behaviors: Practical school applications. *Journal of Positive Behavior Interventions, 1,* 242–251.

Scott, T.M., Nelson, C.M., & Zabala, J. (2003). Functional behavior assessment training in public schools: Facilitating systemic change. *Journal of Positive Behavior Interventions, 5,* 216–224.

Taylor-Greene, S., Brown, D., Nelson, L., Longton, J., Gassman, T., Cohen, J., et al. (1997). School-wide behavioral support: Starting the year off right. *Journal of Behavioral Education, 7,* 99–112.

University of Vermont. (1999). *Prevention strategies that work: What administrators can do to promote positive student behavior.* Burlington: Author.

Walker, H.M., Ramsey, E., & Gresham, F.M. (2004). *Antisocial behavior in school: Evidence-based practices.* Belmont, CA: Wadsworth/Thomson Learning.

INDIVIDUALIZED POSITIVE BEHAVIOR SUPPORT PLANNING AND IMPLEMENTATION

Bambara, L., & Kern, L. (Eds.). (2004). *Individualized supports for students with problem behaviors: Designing positive behavior plans.* New York: Guilford Press.

Beach Center on Families and Disability. (1998). *What research says: Understanding challenging behavior.* University of Kansas, Lawrence: Author.

Carr, E.G., Levin, L., McConnachie, G., Carlson, J.I., Kemp, D.C., & Smith, C.E. (1994). *Communication-based intervention for problem behavior: A user's guide for producing positive change.* Baltimore: Paul H. Brookes Publishing Co.

Horner, R.H., Albin, R.A. Sprague, J.R., & Todd, A.W. (2000). Positive behavior support. In M.E. Snell & F. Brown (Eds.), *Instruction of students with severe disabilities* (5th ed., pp. 207–243). Upper Saddle River, NJ: Prentice Hall.

Koegel, L.K., Koegel, R.L., & Dunlap, G. (Eds.). (1996). *Positive behavioral support: Including people with difficult behavior in the community.* Baltimore: Paul H. Brookes Publishing Co.

O'Neill, R.E., Horner, R.H., Albin, R.W., Sprague, J.R., Storey, K., & Newton, J.S. (1997). *Functional assessment and program development for problem behavior: A practical handbook* (2nd ed.). Pacific Grove, CA: Brooks/Cole.

Scott, T.M., Liaupsin, C., & Nelson, C. M. (2001). *Behavior intervention planning: Using the outcomes of functional behavioral assessment.* Longmont, CO: Sopris West Educational Services.

Sprague, J.R., & Golly, A. (2004). *Best behavior: Building positive behavior in school.* Longmont, CO: Sopris West Educational Services.

Sprague, J.R., & Walker H.M. (2005). *Safe and healthy schools: Practical strategies.* New York: Guilford Press.

TOOLS AND HANDBOOKS FOR FUNCTIONAL BEHAVIORAL ASSESSMENT

Crone, D.A., & Horner, R.H. (2003). *Building positive behavior support systems in schools: Functional behavioral assessment.* New York: Guilford Press. (Includes the Functional Behavioral Assessment Interview [FBAI], the Functional Assessment Checklist for Teachers and Staff [FACTS], and the Functional Assessment Observation Form).

Durand, V.M., & Crimmins, D.B. (1988). *The Motivation Assessment Scale (MAS) administration guide.* Topeka, KS: Monaco & Associates.

O'Neill, R.E., Horner, R.H., Albin, R.W., Sprague, J.R., Storey, K., & Newton, J.S. (1997). *Functional assessment and program development for problem behavior: A practical handbook* (2nd ed.). Pacific Grove, CA: Brookes/Cole Thomson Learning. (Includes the Functional Assessment Interview [FAI] and the Student-Directed FA Interview [SFAI]).

CONFLICT MANAGEMENT, PROBLEM SOLVING, AND PEER MEDIATION

The Collaborative for Academic, Social, and Emotional Learning (CASEL). (2003). *Safe and sound: An education leader's guide to evidence-based social and emotional learning (SEL) programs.* Chicago, IL: Author. (Available at http://www.casel.org)

Flaxman, E. (Ed.). (2001). *Evaluating school violence programs.* Urban Diversity Series No. 113. ERIC Clearinghouse on Urban Education. New York: Teachers College Press.

Johnson, D.W., & Johnson, R.T. (1995). *Teaching students to be peacemakers.* Edina, MN: Interaction Book Company.

Johnson, D.W., & Johnson, R.T. (1996). Conflict resolution and peer mediation programs in elementary and secondary schools: A review of research. *Review of Educational Research, 66,* 459–506.

Mihalic, S., Irwin, K., Elliott, D., Fagan, A., & Hansen, D. (2001, July). *Blueprints for violence prevention (OJJDP Juvenile Justice Bulletin).* Washington, DC: U.S. Department of Justice, Office of Juvenile Justice and Delinquency Prevention. (Available at: http://www.ncjrs. gov/html/ojjdp/jjbul2001_7_3/ contents.html)

Schrumpf, F., Crawford, D., & Usadel, C. (1991). *Peer mediation: Conflict resolution in schools.* Champaign, IL: Research Press.

RESOURCES FOR RESEARCH-BASED INFORMATION, PLANNING, TRAINING, AND TECHNICAL ASSISTANCE IN POSITIVE BEHAVIOR SUPPORT

Center for Effective Collaboration and Practice (CECP) at American Institutes for Research: http://cecp.air.org

Center for the Study and Prevention of Violence (CSPV): http://www.colorado. edu/cspv/

Collaborative for Effective Academic, Social, and Emotional Learning (CASEL): http://www.casel.org

Educators for Social Responsibility (ESR): http://www.esrnational.org

National Association of School Psychologists (NASP): http://www.nasponline. org

National Information Center for Children and Youth with Disabilities (NICHCY): http://www.nichcy.org

National Technical Assistance Center on Positive Behavioral Interventions and Supports (CPBIS) at the University of Oregon: http://www.pbis.org

Rehabilitation Research and Training Center on Positive Behavioral Support: http://www.rrtcpbs.org

Index

Page numbers followed by "f" indicate figures; those followed by "t" indicate tables.